Multimedia Programming with Pure Data

A comprehensive guide for digital artists for creating rich interactive multimedia applications using Pure Data

Bryan WC Chung

BIRMINGHAM - MUMBAI

Multimedia Programming with Pure Data

First published: July 2013

Production Reference: 1020713

Published by Packt Publishing Ltd.
Livery Place
35 Livery Street
Birmingham B3 2PB, UK..

ISBN 978-1-78216-464-7

www.packtpub.com

Cover Image by Suresh Mogre (suresh.mogre.99@gmail.com)

Credits

Author

Bryan WC Chung

Reviewers

Buron Cédric

Guy John

Antonio Roberts

Greg Surges

Acquisition Editor

Vinay Argekar

Lead Technical Editor

Ankita Shashi

Technical Editors

Sampreshita Maheshwari

Kaustubh S. Mayekar

Zafeer Rais

Project Coordinator

Anurag Banerjee

Proofreaders

Amy Guest

Elinor Perry-Smith

Indexer

Rekha Nair

Production Coordinator

Prachali Bhiwandkar

Cover Work

Prachali Bhiwandkar

About the Author

Bryan WC Chung is an interactive media artist and design consultant based in Hong Kong. His interactive media artworks have been exhibited at the *World Wide Video Festival, Multimedia Art Asia Pacific, Stuttgart Film Winter Festival, Microwave International New Media Arts Festival*, and the *China Media Art Festival*. In the former *Shanghai Expo 2010*, he provided interactive media design consultancy to industry leaders in Hong Kong and China. Chung received a computer science bachelor degree in Hong Kong, an interactive multimedia master degree in London, and a fine art doctoral degree in Melbourne. He has been developing software libraries for the open source programming language—Processing. Currently, he is Assistant Professor in the Academy of Visual Arts, Hong Kong Baptist University, where he teaches subjects on interactive arts, computer graphics and multimedia design. His personal website is: http://www.magicandlove.com.

I would like to thank all my students and colleagues, especially Dr. Kam Wong, who had developed the syllabus of the course— Interactivity, which adopted Pure Data as the main teaching tool. I am also grateful to my wife, Dr. Kimburley Choi for her continuous support.

About the Reviewers

Cédric Buron, also known as Human Koala and Hektor Kafka is a Electronic Music Performer and Producer, GFX Developer, Web Developer, Technical Consultant for artists, and Pure Data Teacher. Since his first Computer, an 8-bit one, Computers was for HK a music instrument, a highly adaptable tool for graphic or musical creation. After following a Pure Data Formation. he has started to teach Pure Data, Processing at CRAS (Centre de Ressource d'Art Sensitif: `http://www.mainsdoeuvres.org/rubrique90.html`) at St Ouen. He is also admin for the Pure Data part of the `http://www.codelab.fr` Forum (a French forum about creative programming). Passionate about the interface between Technology & Art, he is occasionally Technical Consultant for Artists or Company to help building Tools for performance, or installation (Emilie Pitoiset, Radio Marais, SFR).

Music Producer and Performer as Human Koala/Hektor Kafka, he has played live in several place and several Digital Art and Performance Events in Paris:

- At Batofar (Radio Broadcast: Chambre à air 2011)
- At Palais de Tokyo (Radio Broadcast: Chambre à Air 2012)
- At 104 (Digital Art Event: Open your Web)
- At Point Ephémere(radio broadcast: Chambre à Air)
- At Divan du Monde (Performance Event: Dimanche Rouge)
- At Petit Bain (Performances Event: Dimanche Rouge)

One of his trax was aired by Ryuichi Sakamoto for his radio broadcast "Radio Sakamoto" (where am i-Dr Riot and Miss Velvet (Human Koala & Miho) Shinohara) His personal website is `http://www.humankoala.com`.

I would like to thank Agnès Le Foulgoc from CRAS to give me the opportunity to teach this wonderful language and Benoîte my wife.

Guy John is a professional software engineer, with a heavy interest in the meeting point of music, art and technology. Originally coming from a hardware and electronics background, he moved over to using more software upon discovering the sheer range of audio programming languages available, and has continued to use a number of them in his projects. Despite always finding new tools to learn, he still finds himself regularly coming back to PureData because of its power and flexibility.

I'd like to thank everybody at Packt publishing for letting me be involved with this book, and the Pure Data community for creating such an excellent piece of software.

Antonio Roberts is a new-media artist and curator based in Birmingham, UK, whose work focuses on the errors and glitches generated by digital technology.

Since 2007 he has curated a number of exhibitions and projects including *fizzPOP* (2009 - 2010), *GLI.TC/H Birmingham* (2011), the *Birmingham edition of Bring Your Own Beamer* (2012), and *Dirty New Media* (2013).

As a performer and visual artist his work has been featured at galleries and festivals around the world including *Databit.me* in Arles, France, *Laptops Meet Musicians* Festival in Venice, Italy, *Notacon* in Cleavland, Ohio, US, *Leeds International Film Festival* in the UK, and the *Barber Institute of Fine Arts* in Birmingham, UK.

In 2013 he contributed the foreword to AlphabeNt: Experiments from A-Z, which is an exploration of glitch art and typography by Australian authors Daniel Purvis and Drew Taylor (ISBN 978-0-98740-070-3).

I would like to thank the Pure Data community of developers and users for their unwavering devotion to developing the software.

www.PacktPub.com

Support files, eBooks, discount offers and more

You might want to visit www.PacktPub.com for support files and downloads related to your book.

Did you know that Packt offers eBook versions of every book published, with PDF and ePub files available? You can upgrade to the eBook version at www.PacktPub.com and as a print book customer, you are entitled to a discount on the eBook copy. Get in touch with us at service@packtpub.com for more details.

At www.PacktPub.com, you can also read a collection of free technical articles, sign up for a range of free newsletters and receive exclusive discounts and offers on Packt books and eBooks.

http://PacktLib.PacktPub.com

Do you need instant solutions to your IT questions? PacktLib is Packt's online digital book library. Here, you can access, read and search across Packt's entire library of books.

Why Subscribe?

- Fully searchable across every book published by Packt
- Copy and paste, print and bookmark content
- On demand and accessible via web browser

Free Access for Packt account holders

If you have an account with Packt at www.PacktPub.com, you can use this to access PacktLib today and view nine entirely free books. Simply use your login credentials for immediate access.

Table of Contents

Preface

This book will introduce the Pure Data software to visual artists, media designers, and programmers to develop multimedia applications graphically without the need to write codes. Creating interactive multimedia projects is a demanding task. The authoring process requires programming skills in addition to the techniques to prepare and edit digital media content. Proprietary software packages, such as Adobe Director and Adobe Flash are available for designers to author multimedia projects. For the web standard platform, designers can also use the HTML5, CSS, and JavaScript to author web-based multimedia content. Both cases demand the mastery of text-based programming skills such as JavaScript and ActionScript.

Pure Data is a free graphical programming environment where users can write programs by drawing visual objects on the screen and connect them together to form a program. This book will provide the step-by-step details to prepare interactive multimedia content by using Pure Data.

Miller Puckette is the main designer of Pure Data. When he worked at the IRCAM (Institut de Recherche et Coordination Acoustique/Musique) in France, he developed the software Max for interactive computer music applications. The Max/MSP software from Cycling'74 (`http://cycling74.com`) is the commercial derivative of the original Max. Pure Data (Pd) is the free version supported by the open source community.

Pure Data was originally written for electronic music applications. Over the years, developers contributed a lot of additional features, called externals in Pure Data terms. This book will use a major external Graphics Environment for Multimedia (GEM) for the demonstration. Towards the end of the book, it also explains how readers can add other external libraries to their own system.

What this book covers

Chapter 1, Getting Started with Pure Data, prepares the readers with the graphical programming environment and introduces various types of windows, menu items, messages, and operation modes of Pure Data.

Chapter 2, Computer Graphics with the GEM Library, starts creating 2D and 3D graphics and simple animation by using the objects in the GEM external library.

Chapter 3, Image Processing, illustrates the pixel operations in the GEM library. It includes commands to obtain external images from the still photos, digital videos, and live webcam, and also a number of imaging filters and effects that can be commonly found in an image-processing software, such as Photoshop.

Chapter 4, Interactivity, integrates the use of mouse and keyboard controls as interaction devices and introduces the mechanism to build graphical user interface with the GEM library.

Chapter 5, Motion Detection, applies a more advanced approach for interaction design. It shows the readers how to detect motion in front of a webcam and uses the information to create interactive applications.

Chapter 6, Animation with Particle System, explains the basics of particles system in the GEM library and combines the particles system to create an artwork that responds to the readers' body movement.

Chapter 7, Audio Programming, describes the use of audio in Pure Data and helps readers to integrate audio content in their multimedia production. It also uses sound input (microphone) as an interaction device.

Chapter 8, Interface with the Outside World, enables readers to connect Pure Data programs to other systems, such as computer network, mobile phone, and external hardware through microcontroller.

Chapter 9, Extending Pure Data, provides a conclusion of learning Pure Data for multimedia production, and points to the resources that readers can seek further reference. It also demonstrates how readers can install other external libraries, such as OpenCV, and Kinect libraries.

Appendix, Communities and References, provides more information on Pure Data.

What you need for this book

The main Pure Data website is http://puredata.info. Pure Data comes with two distributions: Pure Data and Pd-extended. Pure Data (vanilla) is the original version by Miller Puckette. Pd-extended contains Pure Data itself and a number of commonly used external libraries. This book will use the Pd-extended version as it already includes the GEM library. The website for GEM is http://gem.iem.at.

Download Pd-extended for your operating system from http://puredata.info/downloads/pd-extended. Pd-extended is available for Microsoft Windows, Mac OS X, and Linux. For Linux, Pd-extended comes with the binary packages for Ubuntu and Debian. At the time of writing, the latest release is 0.42.5. The beta release is 0.43.4.

The installation instructions for various platforms are:

- **Windows**: Download the file and start the installer. It will automatically install in the right Program Files folder.
- **Mac OS X**: Download the file, open the disk image, and drag the Pd-extended icon to the Applications folder. For OSX Mountain Lion users, you may need to install the XQuartz windows system first from http://xquartz.macosforge.org.
- **Linux**: Most Linux versions are Debian software package. Use the corresponding package manager in your Linux operating system to open it for installation.

Double-click on the Pd-extended application; you can expect to see the console window. In this book, I mainly use the Mac OSX version if platform differences are insignificant.

Who this book is for

Pure Data applications are mainly for real-time multimedia projects. Audio-visual performers (VJ) have been using Pure Data to create interactive imageries in their performance. Media designers with no programming experience can learn to prototype their ideas very quickly with Pure Data and GEM. In creative art/design curriculum, Pure Data and Processing (http://processing.org) are the two most popular free programming platforms to teach interactivity to art/design students. The book will also provide a comprehensive set of learning outcomes for interactive media educators.

Conventions

In this book, you will find a number of styles of text that distinguish between different kinds of information. Here are some examples of these styles, and an explanation of their meaning.

Code words in text, database table names, folder names, filenames, file extensions, pathnames, dummy URLs, user input, and Twitter handles are shown as follows: "Insert a new object called `gemwin` to create a graphics window."

New terms and **important words** are shown in bold. Words that you see on the screen, in menus or dialog boxes for example, appear in the text like this: "To create a new patch, navigate to **File | New** to make an empty patch".

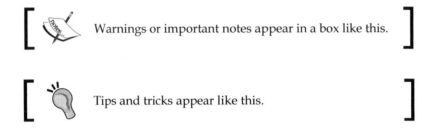

[Warnings or important notes appear in a box like this.]

[Tips and tricks appear like this.]

Reader feedback

Feedback from our readers is always welcome. Let us know what you think about this book—what you liked or may have disliked. Reader feedback is important for us to develop titles that you really get the most out of.

To send us general feedback, simply send an e-mail to `feedback@packtpub.com`, and mention the book title via the subject of your message.

If there is a topic that you have expertise in and you are interested in either writing or contributing to a book, see our author guide on `www.packtpub.com/authors`.

Customer support

Now that you are the proud owner of a Packt book, we have a number of things to help you to get the most from your purchase.

Errata

Although we have taken every care to ensure the accuracy of our content, mistakes do happen. If you find a mistake in one of our books—maybe a mistake in the text or the code—we would be grateful if you would report this to us. By doing so, you can save other readers from frustration and help us improve subsequent versions of this book. If you find any errata, please report them by visiting http://www.packtpub.com/submit-errata, selecting your book, clicking on the **errata submission form** link, and entering the details of your errata. Once your errata are verified, your submission will be accepted and the errata will be uploaded on our website, or added to any list of existing errata, under the Errata section of that title. Any existing errata can be viewed by selecting your title from http://www.packtpub.com/support.

Piracy

Piracy of copyright material on the Internet is an ongoing problem across all media. At Packt, we take the protection of our copyright and licenses very seriously. If you come across any illegal copies of our works, in any form, on the Internet, please provide us with the location address or website name immediately so that we can pursue a remedy.

Please contact us at copyright@packtpub.com with a link to the suspected pirated material.

We appreciate your help in protecting our authors, and our ability to bring you valuable content.

Questions

You can contact us at questions@packtpub.com if you are having a problem with any aspect of the book, and we will do our best to address it.

1
Getting Started with Pure Data

In this chapter, you are going to create the first ever computer program in your life, if you have not already done so. Or, if you have been working on with other text-based programming, you will be astonished by the simplicity of the **Pure Data (Pd)** graphical programming environment. In the following sections:

- We will familiarize ourselves with the terms and interfaces to work with Pure Data. We will learn how to get answers to our questions.

- By the end of the chapter, we will learn to create the first animation with the use of a counter, simple arithmetic operations, and common graphical user interface items.

If you have not installed the **pd-extended** software, please refer to the *Preface* for the installation. Pure Data is a graphical programming environment. Traditional text-based programming involves writing English-like sentences to prepare a program. In Pure Data, all you need to do is draw graphical labels on a blank window and connect those labels together to define the flow of your program.

Creating the first program

Every Pure Data program is a text file with an extension (.pd). In Pure Data's term, a program is called a patch. Electronic musicians often use cables to connect different devices to produce sound. The cables are referred as patch cables. Since Pure Data is originally a piece of software to produce electronic music, the name *patch* refers to a Pure Data program.

To create a new patch, navigate to **File | New** to make an empty patch. From the menu, choose **File | Save** to save the patch in the folder you plan to store your Pure Data material. Pure Data does not assume a default location for your patches. You can decide where to put them.

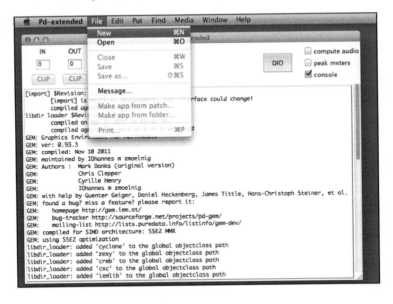

At this point, you will have an empty window with a cursor that appears to be a finger pointing to the left. Before we proceed to the notorious Hello World example, we need to go through the Pure Data interface first.

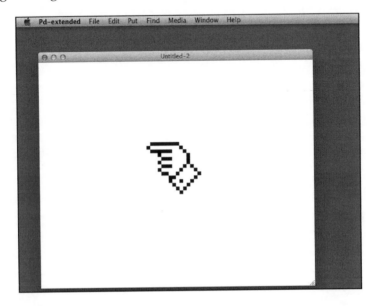

Understanding the terms and interface

There are a number of terms we need to clarify before we proceed.

- **Operation modes**: Pure Data works in two modes: **Edit Mode** and **Run Mode**. In Edit Mode, you can create and modify your program source in the patch window. In Run Mode, you execute the patch and modify data. Nevertheless, the patch will not stop playing when you switch between Edit and Run mode. You switch between the two modes by navigating to **Edit | Edit mode**. In Edit Mode, the cursor is a finger. In Run Mode, the cursor is the normal pointer. You can also use the keyboard shortcuts *Command + E* for Mac and *Ctrl + E* for Windows.

- **Programming elements**: All programming elements in Pure Data are either object or data. Objects are functional elements that mainly perform tasks. Data will be the material that objects operate with. For example, a Pure Data object print will display text messages on screen whereas the datum message will be the text to be displayed. Programming in Pure Data involves putting objects and data in the patch window—canvas, and connecting them together.

- **Input/output**: Programming in Pure Data involves connecting the output from one item to the input of another item. Nevertheless, Pure Data uses the terms **inlet** and **outlet**, instead of input and output. We'll see an example in the next section.

- **Windows**: Each Pd patch comes with its canvas window. The other window with a lot of messages is the console window. You may need to pay attention to the console window, as it will show you the error messages in case you come into problem. To clear messages in the console window, choose **Edit | Clear console**. The keyboard shortcut is *Shift + Command + L* in Mac, *Shift + Ctrl + L* for Windows.

Displaying messages

The Hello World example is straightforward. It involves one piece of data—a Hello World message, and one object to print out the message in the console window.

Create a new Pure Data patch. Save it to your folder with name `helloWorld.pd`.
Clear the console window by navigating to **Edit | Clear console**. To create anything
for your Pure Data patch, choose from the **Put** menu item.

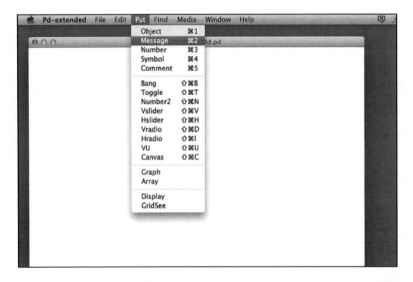

It may take a few seconds for new comers to learn the operations of the Pure Data
interaction sequence. First, we select a **Message box** (*Command + 2* or *Ctrl + 2*).
After you select **Message**, move your cursor back to the empty patch window
`helloWorld.pd`. The message icon will move along with your cursor. You can click
anywhere on the empty patch to fix the position of the message icon.

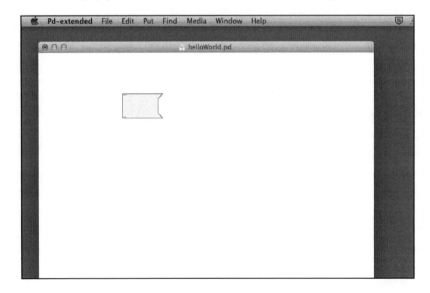

A **data entry** cursor (a blinking vertical bar) will appear in the left hand side of the message box. Now, you can type in `Hello World` inside this message box.

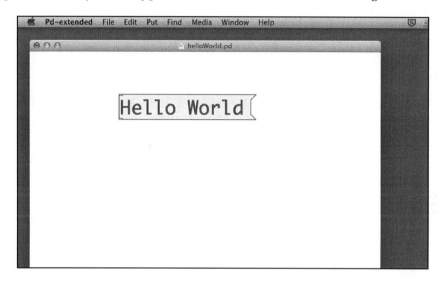

Click anywhere outside the message box to confirm the text. Note that the data entry cursor will disappear after you confirm the text. You can click on the message box again if you want to change the text later. You can also click-and-drag the message box to change its position within the patch window.

Now, we create the second item. Navigate to **Put | Object** (*Command + 1* or *Ctrl + 1*) from the menu bar to create an empty object in the patch window.

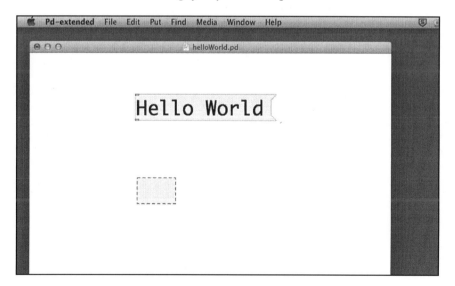

Type the word print inside the object box. Note that the empty object box is a regular rectangle with dotted outline. After you type print, click outside the object box. The object box now has a solid outline. A message box is a rectangle with a curved right edge.

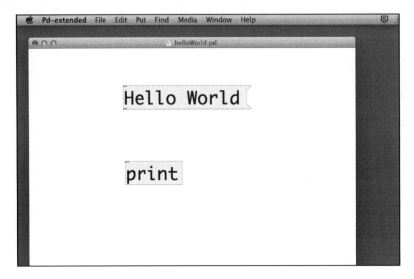

If you take a closer look at the message and object boxes, you will notice two tiny rectangles along the left edge of the message box on the top and bottom. For the object box, there is only one such rectangle on the top. They are the inlet and outlet mentioned earlier. Those on the top are inlets and those on the bottom are outlets.

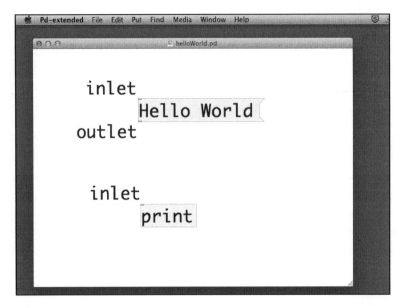

Connecting one outlet to another inlet is the programming in Pure Data. Now, we connect the outlet of the **Hello World** message box to the inlet of the **print** object box. First, move your cursor towards the outlet of the **Hello World** message box. It will turn into a small circle.

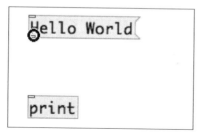

Click-and-drag to draw a line from the outlet of the **Hello World** message box. While dragging, move toward the inlet of the **print** object box. The cursor will also turn into a small circle.

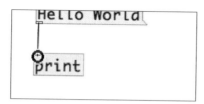

Release the mouse button to confirm the connection.

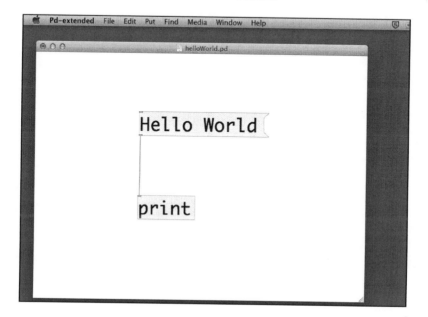

This is your first working Pure Data patch, the Hello World program. To execute the patch, we have to switch from Edit Mode to Run Mode by choosing **Edit | Edit mode** (*Command + E* or *Ctrl + E*). Note the mouse cursor changes into the regular pointer shape. Open the console window if it is hidden. You can do it by navigating to **Window | Pd window** (*Command + R* or *Ctrl + R*). Arrange the two windows side by side such that you can see the message in the console window when you work on the patch window. Move your cursor toward the **Hello World** message box. Note the cursor changes again. It is now an upward pointing arrow.

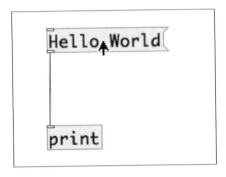

Click on the message box and note what happens in the console window. A message **print: Hello World** appears whenever you click on the message box. Yes, it is the Hello World program you have just achieved.

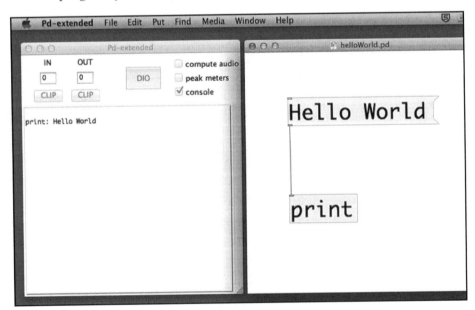

The message box in Run Mode functions like a button. When you click, it sends out the message text **Hello World** through its outlet along the connection line to the inlet of the **print** object box. A `print` object will just show the message it received onto the console window.

 In Edit Mode, you can also hold down the *Command* key or the *Ctrl* key to enter the Run Mode temporarily.

Performing arithmetic calculation

Besides the `print` object, Pure Data includes numerous objects catered to various purposes. You can check out those objects from the **Help** menu. To access the general help for Pure Data, you can choose **Help | Browser** from the menu bar.

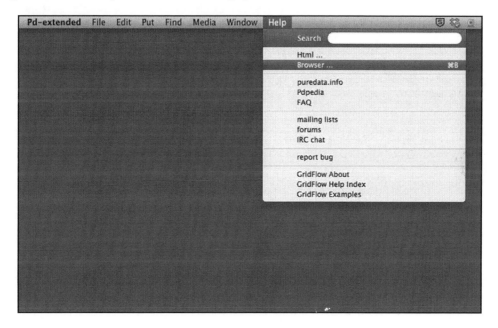

Within the help browser, you can further select the topics you would like to reference. Double-click on the title; you will call up the help menu for that topic.

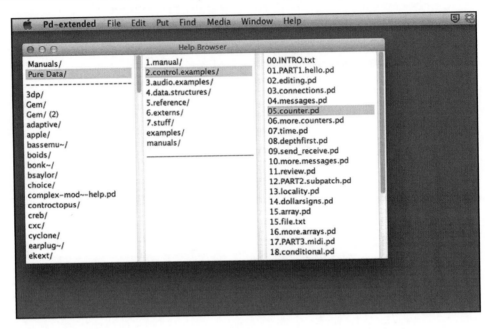

The first two items, **Manuals** and **Pure Data** are for general Pure Data reference. The rest are for external libraries shipped with the pd-extended software.

As all digital media elements are represented in numbers, the objects to perform numeric operations are essential. This section will introduce the use of common arithmetic computation. They are addition, subtraction, multiplication, and division. The programming symbols are: +, -, *, /.

Create an empty patch as described in the previous section and save it with name calculation.pd in your folder. Put a print object in the patch window. Put another object on the patch window. Type a plus sign + inside this object. Connect the outlet of this 'plus' object to the inlet of the print object.

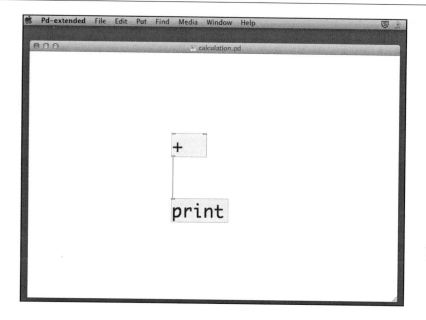

Note that the plus object has two inlets, one on the left, one on the right. It is intuitive to think that addition involves two numbers. You need to have two numbers supplied through the two inlets for the calculation. Now, we put two message boxes with two numbers onto the patch and connect them to the inlets .of the plus object box.

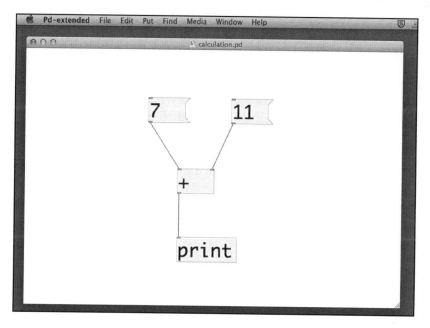

Now, switch to Run Mode by selecting **Edit | Edit mode**. Click upon the right message box first and then click on the left message box. Note the message from the console window. The order of clicking matters, which we shall be covering in the coming section.

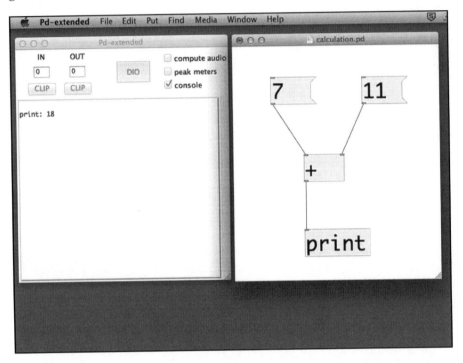

This example always adds the two numbers 7 and 11 together. Nevertheless, message boxes don't offer much flexibility when it comes to changing the numbers in real time for addition. We will replace the two message boxes with number boxes.

First, we delete the two message boxes. To delete items in Pure Data, we click-and-drag the left mouse button to draw a selection rectangle including the two message boxes and press the *Delete* key on the computer keyboard to delete them.

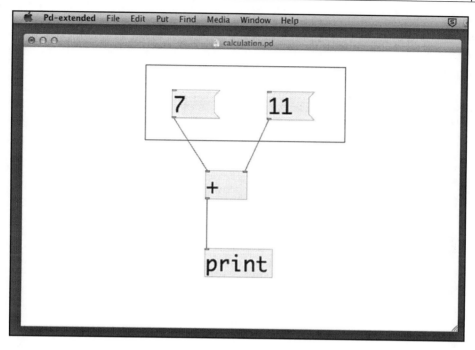

If you want to delete a connection without deleting the item, you can click upon the connection link. The cursor will change into a cross shape. Press the *Delete* key and you can delete the link without touching the two other objects.

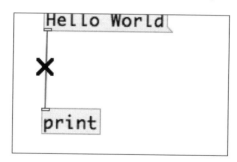

Going back to our example, we can also delete the `print` object and replace it with a `number` box. The next step is to create three number boxes from **Put | Number** (*Command + 3* or *Ctrl + 3*). Connect two of them to the `plus` object box inlets and the last one to its outlet. Note that the initial value for the number box is zero.

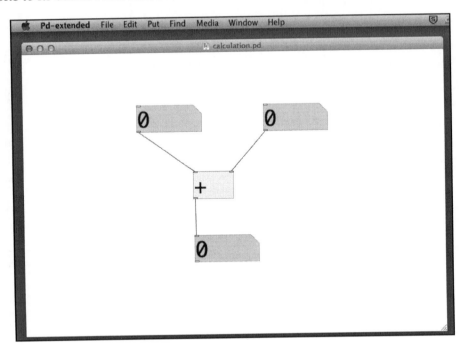

Now the addition program is ready. We can switch to Run Mode to test it. First, you click on the number box connecting to the right inlet of the `plus` object. Type in any number inside the number box; say 11. Note there are three dots after the number. Once you are fine with the number, press *Return/Enter* to confirm the number. The three dots will disappear. Note that the number box connecting to the outlet remains zero.

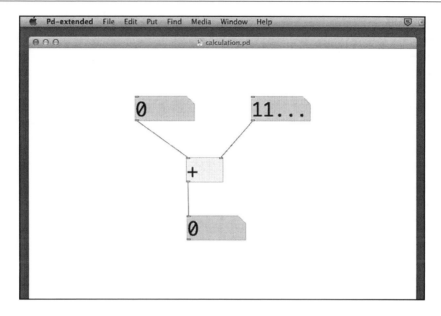

Next, you repeat the step with the left inlet number box. Type in a number and press *Return/Enter*. Note that once you press *Return/Enter*, the result number box will show you the correct result, **18** in this case.

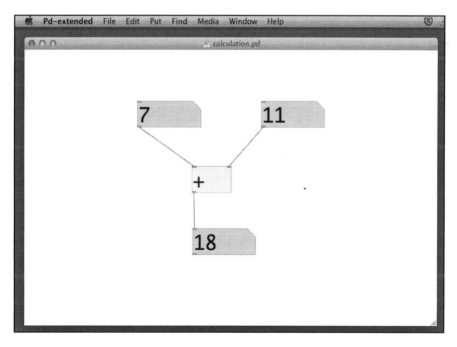

We can conclude that the plus object performs an addition operation between two numbers, one in the left inlet and one in the right inlet. The result will be in the number box connected to the outlet. Nevertheless, the behaviors of the two inlets are different, the sequence is extremely important in Pure Data programming. In Pd terminology, the left inlet is the *hot* inlet. All other inlets are *cold* inlets. Only change of values in the hot inlet will trigger the operation, which in this example is an addition process. Change of values in the cold inlet (the right one in this case) will only store the new value in the inlet without initiating an addition process.

Sometimes, it is counter-intuitive to change the number value of the right number box and wait for the left number to change too. Pure Data has another object to tackle this behavior. It is the trigger object.

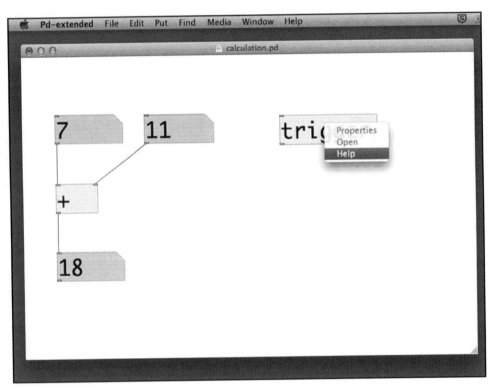

If you do not know how to use the `trigger` object, you can always right-click or *Ctrl*-click on it to display the **help** message. A `trigger` object will pass the message it receives to its outlets from a strictly right to left order.

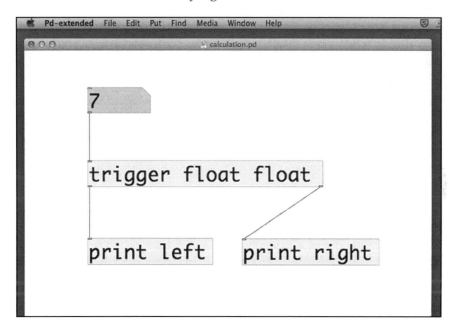

The two **float** after the **trigger** are parameters indicating that the `trigger` object will pass numeric values to its outlets. All numbers in Pure Data are floating point numbers, that is with decimal. Integer or natural number is a special kind of floating point number that it does not have digits after the decimal point. When you key in a number in the inlet number box, you will see the output from the console window. The message **right**: 7 appears before the **left**: 7.

You can also change the value of the number box by clicking-and-dragging it upward or downward to increase or decrease the value by 1. If you press the *Shift* key and click-and-drag, you can increase or decrease its value by 0.01. In all cases, the right outlet always comes before the left one. With this function, we can enhance our addition operation.

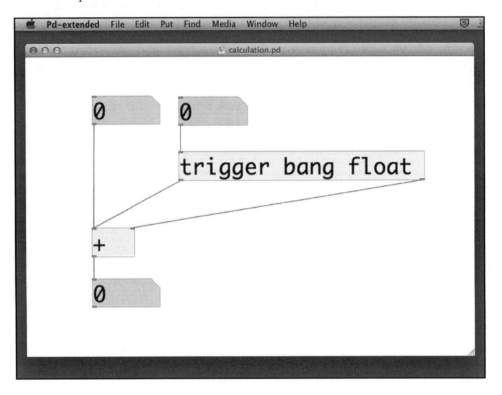

The only difference is the right number box. It goes through a `trigger` object with two parameters: `bang` and `float`. Whenever we change the value of the right number box, its numeric value (`float`) will pass to the right outlet first (right to left order) and a `bang` message will then pass to its left outlet. The right outlet goes to the cold inlet of the `plus` object first with the new number value. After that, the left outlet sends a `bang` message to the hot inlet of the `plus` object to trigger the addition process to start. It will then perform immediately without waiting for the value change in the left number box.

Once you are familiar with the object, you can write `trigger b f` or even `t b f` instead of the long form `trigger bang float`. As an exercise, you can replace the plus sign with the minus -, multiplication *, or division / signs to try them out.

Creating a counter

Most programming languages include the facility to store values in a place, and which can be referred afterward. It is usually called a `variable`. Pure Data uses a graphical object box for this purpose. The most common storage objects are `float`, `int`, and `symbol`. The objects, `float` and `int` store floating point and integer numbers respectively. The object `symbol` stores text without spacing in between, for example, **Hello**. Note that the descriptions we put next to the objects in the following screenshot are *comments*. Comments are textual descriptions for you to document your patch. You can add a piece of comment by navigating to **Put | Comment**. It is always good practice to document your patch for easy maintenance.

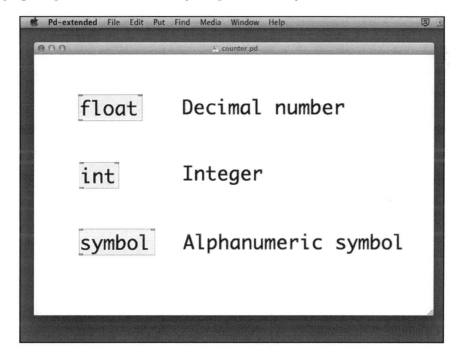

The following example will make use of a `float` object to function as a counter. Create an empty patch and save it with name `counter.pd` in your folder. Put the `float` and `plus` objects in the patch window.

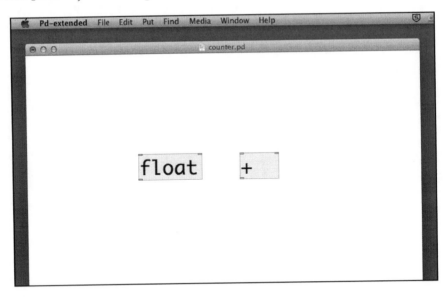

Connect the outlet of the `float` object to the left (hot) inlet of the `plus` object. Connect the outlet of the `plus` object to the right (cold) inlet of the `float` object. It looks like a cross.

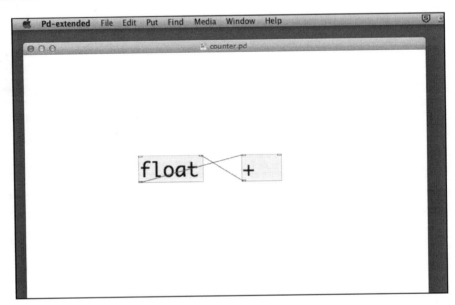

Add two more number boxes and connect one to the right inlet of the plus object and the other to the outlet of the float object. Note that the outlet of the float object is connected to two objects.

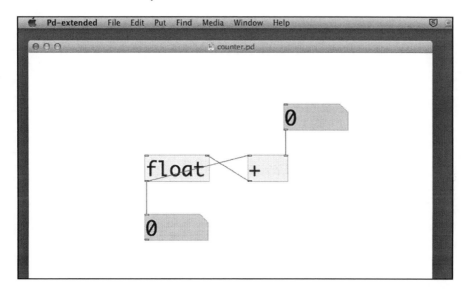

The last step is to put a bang object to the left inlet of the float object. To do this, choose **Put | Bang** from the menu bar. Connect it to the left inlet of the float object. Note that bang is one of the graphical user interface object and which functions like a push button.

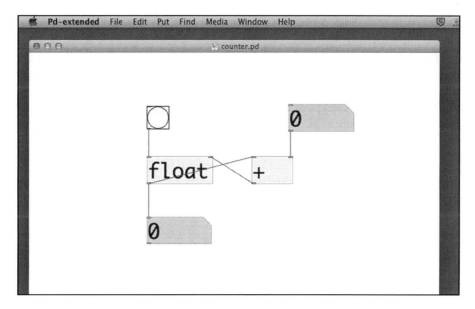

We now switch to Run Mode. Click on the right number box and type in the number 1. Click on the **bang** button a few times. Each time you click on the **bang** button, the circle turns black and the bottom number box will increase its value by 1.

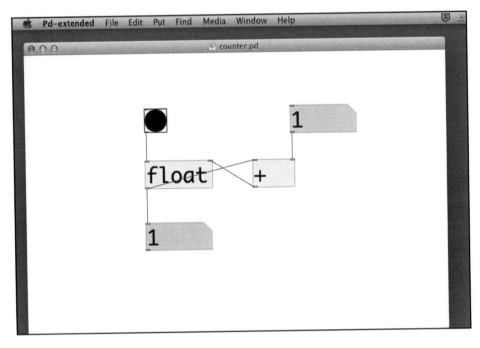

Now you can change the right number box value and click on the **bang** button again. The value determines how much the counter will increment whenever you click on the button.

When you setup this patch, the float object has an initial value of zero in its right inlet. Every time you click on the **bang** button, it sends out a bang message to the float object to output its value stored in the right inlet. That is the value in the bottom number box. At the same time, there is a connection from the float object outlet to the left inlet of the plus object. It causes the plus object to add 1 (or another value in the right number box) to it and sends the result back to the right inlet of the float object for temporary storage. The next time you click on the **bang** button, its value will increment again.

One last point to complete this counter is how you can reset the value to zero. You can achieve it by putting a 0 message to the right inlet of the float object. By clicking on this message, it sends the value zero to reset the counter. Note that we use message instead of a number box because there is no need to change the value 0.

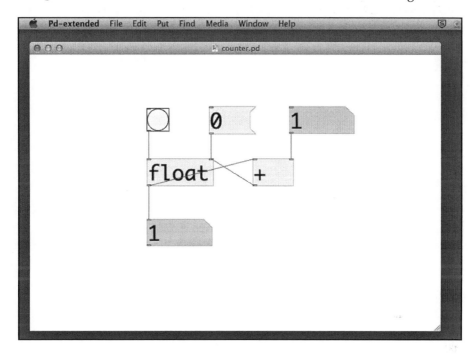

Automating the counter

As we noticed, in the last example, you need to click on the **bang** button to advance the counter. Can we do it automatically? The following example will provide you with the answer. It is another important concept in Pure Data. When you work on animation in later chapters, it requires the same technique.

Save As your last example with the name autoCounter.pd. We will now modify it with the auto-counting function. The new object we are going to use is metro. It is the metronome for counting the beat when you practice musical instruments. We add a metro object with a numeric parameter of 1000. This number is the duration of each beat, with units in millisecond. 1000 milliseconds will be one second. The second new object is a toggle box. You can choose it from **Put | Toggle**. It is another type of button, such as an on/off switch. We connect the toggle box to the inlet of the metro object and a bang box to the outlet of the metro object.

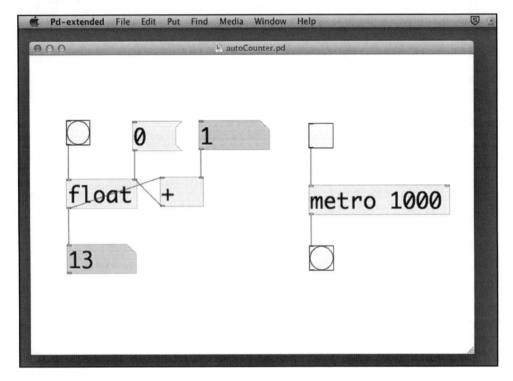

In Run Mode, click on the `toggle` box. You will notice a **cross** indicating the ON state. Note that the **bang** box flashes automatically once in every second. To stop, click on the **toggle** box again. The cross disappears.

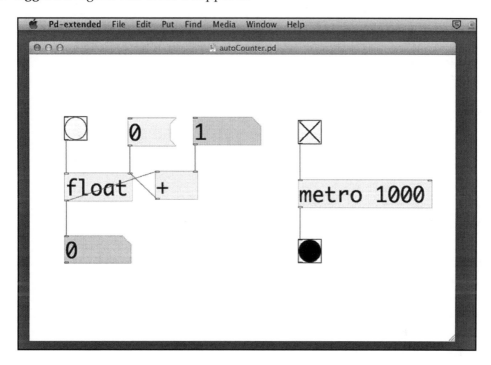

The `toggle` box starts and stops the `metro` box. A **cross** in the `toggle` box sends out a value 1. An empty `toggle` box sends out a value 0. The number next to the `metro` box is the duration in milliseconds for every count. The number **1000** means one thousand milliseconds, that is one second. For every second, the `metro` box sends out a `bang` message through its outlet. To complete the patch, we can connect the `bang` message from the `metro` box to the `bang` input for the `float` object.

We can also use a `number` box for the right inlet of the `metro` object to control the counting frequency, instead of the fixed rate of 1000 milliseconds. The smaller the value, the faster the `metro` counts.

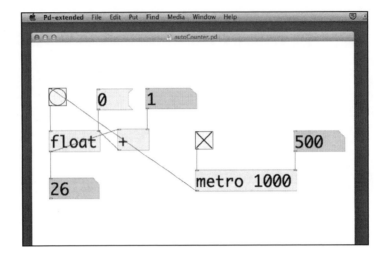

When there are more boxes in the patch window, the connection links grow messier. Pd provides a *wireless* connection for you to tidy up the links. They are the `send` and `receive` boxes. The following example makes use of `send` and `receive` boxes to eliminate the intersecting connection. The name **cnt** next to **send** and **receive** is a variable name you could use to describe the connection. You can use whatever appropriate name as long as it is unique and identical in both the `send` and `receive` boxes. You can imagine it is an invisible link connecting the `send` and `receive` boxes with the same variable name.

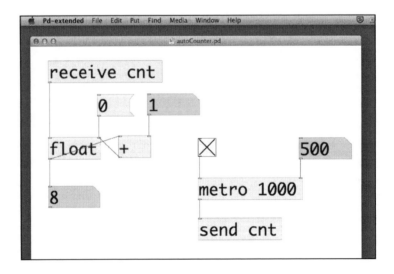

Making an animation with the interface elements

Once we have the tool to automate the counting process, we can make use of it to create an animation. Since we have not learnt to draw in Pure Data, we start by using the graphical user interface elements, such as the bang object, to create the graphics.

Save As the last example with the name animation1.pd. Simplify the patch like the following screenshot. Note that we move the **metro** box and its connections to the left-hand side and remove the send and receive objects. In this patch, we plan to animate a number of bang objects, say six of them, one by one in a sequence. This technique can be helpful when we create an animation loop later.

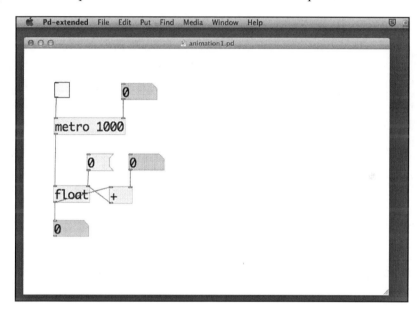

Then, we put six bang objects in the patch, arranging them in a row. To work with this, we also add a new object called **select**. It is similar to the conditional statement IF in text based programming languages.

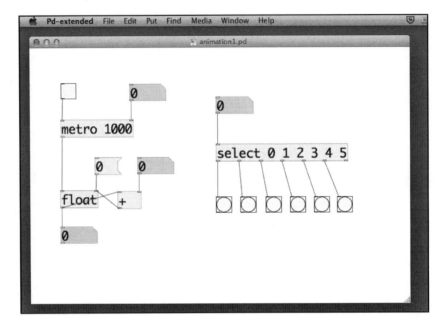

In Run Mode, if you change the value in the number box above the **select** object, you will notice the relation between the number and the behavior of the **bang** boxes under the **select** object. A number 0 will flash the first bang. A number 1 will flash the second bang. A number 5 will flash the last one. In most programming languages, we count from zero instead of one. For example, if we have a count of 5, we count from 0, 1, 2, 3, and 4. Remember that you can click-and-drag the **number** box upward and downward to change the number value.

You can consider the **select** object a multiple conditional statement. In this example, if the number from the inlet is **0**, it passes a bang to the first outlet. If it is **1**, it passes the bang to the second outlet. If it is **2**, it passes the bang to the third outlet. If it is outside the range of 0 to 5, it passes the bang to the last outlet, which is not connected to any bang box here. You can also specify non-consecutive numbers as the parameters in the **select** object. In later chapters, we will also use non-numeric parameters.

To complete the patch, we connect the counter output **number** box to the **select** object. In order to reset the counter, we also need to send the bang message to the **message** box containing the zero value, when the counter value exceeds 5.

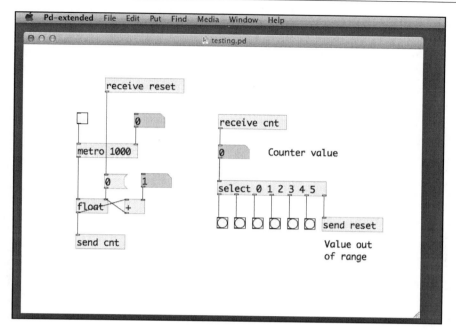

In this version of the patch, the animation runs from left to right sequentially. It is due to the counter value changing from 0 to 5. In the next example, we modify it such that we can have a random movement. Pd comes with a pseudorandom number object called random. We'll use it to generate a number from 0 to 5. If you right-click or *Ctrl*-click on it to display the help menu, you can specify other parameters to control the range of the random value.

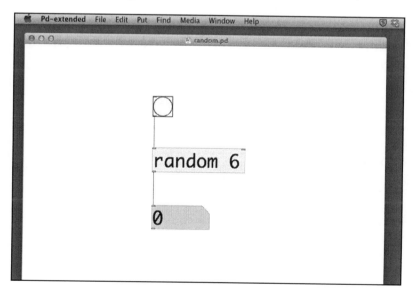

We put the number 6 here for the parameter. It will generate a random value between 0 to a number less than 6, that is 5. Again, it is common practice in programming languages for a value to start from 0, instead of 1. The next step is to combine this `random` object with the last example. It is pretty straightforward. We only need to send the `bang` message from the `metro` object to the `random` object in order to generate the next random number. The rest remains the same.

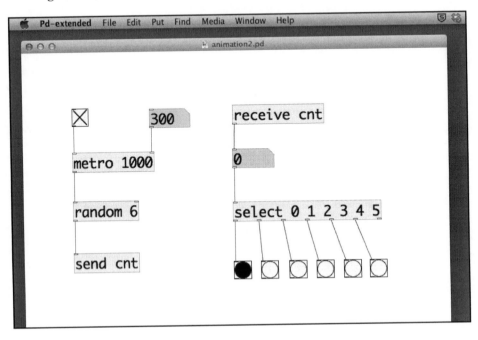

Using the graphical interface objects

In previous sections, we came across a number of graphical interface objects such as `bang`, `toggle`. The following patch will introduce the slider and radio buttons. Slider is a numeric value represented visually. You drag the handle of the slider to alter the numeric value. Radio buttons are a group of options. You can only select one among the group.

To create a slider, navigate to **Put | Hslider** or **Put | Vslider**. To create a group of radio buttons, navigate to **Put | Hradio** or **Put | Vradio**.

Hslider is a horizontal slider. **Vslider** is the vertical one. **Hradio** is a group aligned horizontally. **Vradio** aligns vertically.

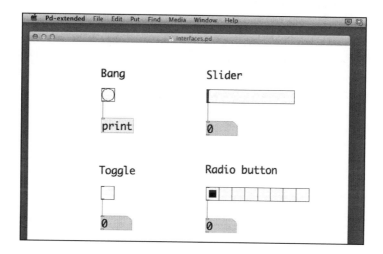

When you click on the bang object, the console window will show the bang message. When you click on the toggle object, the **number** box value alternates between 0 and 1. When you drag the **slider**, the **number** box value changes from 0 to 127, that is the default range. You can change this range by right-clicking or *Ctrl*-clicking on the slider and opening the **Properties** window to modify the output range.

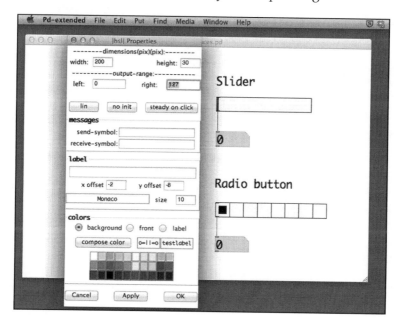

When you click on any square of the radio button group, the number box gives you a value from 0 to 7, depending on which square you click on. It is the default number of buttons in the radio group. You can also change the number of buttons by right-click on the radio button group and open the **Properties** window to modify the number.

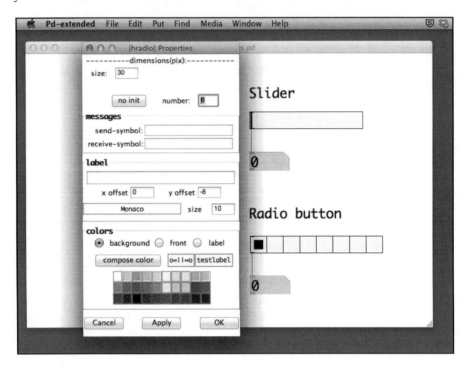

Remember that you can always right-click or *Ctrl*-click on the object to choose the help menu in case you would like to understand more about the object.

Summary

This chapter covers the basic elements in a Pure Data patch. We have discussed the use of data in Pure Data, such as floating-point number, integer, and symbol. We covered the use of simple arithmetic calculation. We introduced the use of the trigger object to synchronize the hot and cold inlets. By using the float object, we understood how to store numeric values as variables in Pd. We used the metro object to create loop in Pure Data. Within the loop, Pure Data provides the select object for conditional processing. We used the random object to create chance-based operations. The last section also demonstrates the commonly used graphical user interface elements in Pure Data. Until now, everything is number. In the next chapter, we start off our adventure in the graphics world with the GEM library.

2
Computer Graphics with the GEM Library

In this chapter, we will proceed with the **Graphics Environment for Multimedia (GEM)** library to work with computer graphics. We will start with the basics to create the GEM display window for graphics. Within the window, we will learn to draw 2D and 3D primitive shapes. We will understand the coordinates system in GEM in order to apply geometric transformations to the graphical shapes and also learn to enhance the surfaces of the graphical shapes with color information. Furthermore, we will learn to apply the lighting information to produce more realistic images. By the end, we should be able to produce a simple animation in 3D space.

GEM is an external library for the Pure Data software. It is available at `http://gem.iem.at`. Nevertheless, the version of Pure Data (pd-extended) we are using already includes the GEM library. We will use the GEM library to create both 2D and 3D graphics from scratch.

The topics that we are going to cover in this chapter are:

- Using the GEM display window
- Drawing basic 2D graphics
- Understanding the coordinates system
- Drawing basic 3D graphics
- Working with digital color
- Applying geometric transformations
- Creating animation in 3D space

To get general help and tutorials for GEM, you can also use **Help Browser** to check out the material:

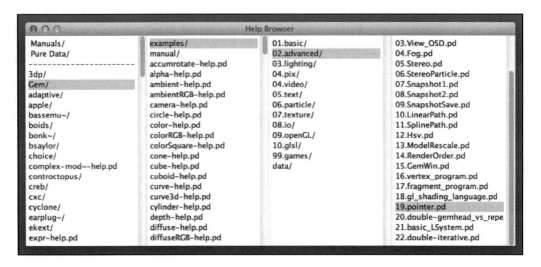

Using the GEM display window

All graphics we are going to create reside in a separate window with the main patch window. It is often called the GEM display window. We use the gemwin object to create the window. With different input messages, we can customize the properties of the display window.

Create a new Pd patch. Save it to your folder with name gem001.pd. Clear the console window by choosing **Edit | Clear console**.

Put the object gemwin onto your patch window, together with two messages and one toggle box. Connect all the messages and toggle boxes to the inlet of the gemwin object:

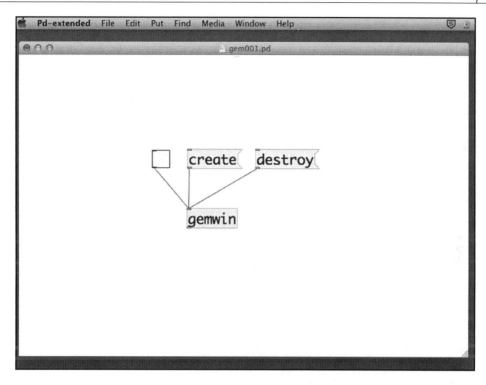

The gemwin object manages the graphics window. In this simple example, it receives two input messages:

- create: This message creates a new window for graphics display
- destroy: This message closes the graphics window

Also note the toggle box that sends the number, either 0 or 1 to the gemwin object. It is the rendering switch. Turning on the toggle will start graphics rendering within the window. Turning it off will stop it. When we work on animation by the end of this chapter, you will notice that the render switch will start/stop the playback of the animation.

Now switch to the **Run** mode. First, click on the `create` message box and then on the toggle box. You will notice a square window appearing with black background. The default title of the window is **GEM**. And the default size of the window is 500 x 500 pixels, as shown in the following screenshot:

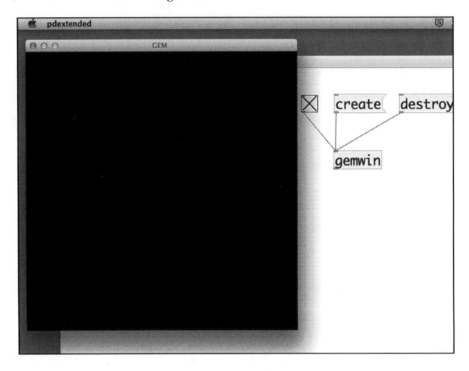

To close the window, switch off the render toggle and click on the `destroy` message box. If you right-click or simultaneously press *Ctrl* and click on the `gemwin` object and display the help menu, you can click on more items to check out the detailed operations of window management in GEM. We'll try out a few more options before we start drawing on the window.

To change the size of the window, we use the dimension message. The correct form is `dimen 640 480` to change the size to 640 x 480 pixels. The first number is the width and the second one is the height. Both are measured in pixels. Also bear in mind that you have to first click on the `dimen` message before clicking on the `create` message and toggle:

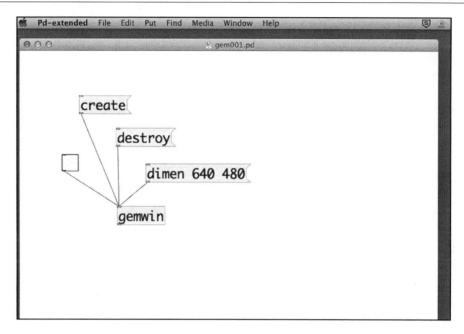

To change the window title, we use the `title` message. Note that the title text cannot have space characters. Otherwise, it just takes the first word. Again, you need to first click on the `title` message before clicking on the `create` message:

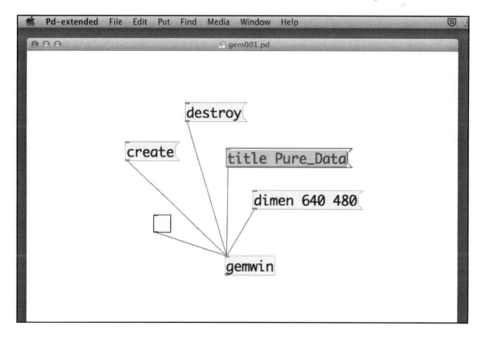

To change the background color, of course, we use the `color` message. It is a bit tricky because we have to understand how we can specify color in GEM. You may have known that digital display color can be represented by the three primitive colors: red, green, and blue. All other colors are different combinations of the three primitive colors. GEM uses three numbers to denote the red (*R*), green (*G*), and blue (*B*) colors. The range of the numbers is from 0 to 1. For example, a red color is 1, 0, and 0; a yellow color is 1, 1, and 0. The first number is red, the second is green, and the third is blue. You can also have decimal numbers for the color values, such as 0.5, 0.1, and 0.1. The following example changes the window background to white, with the color combination as 1, 1, and 1:

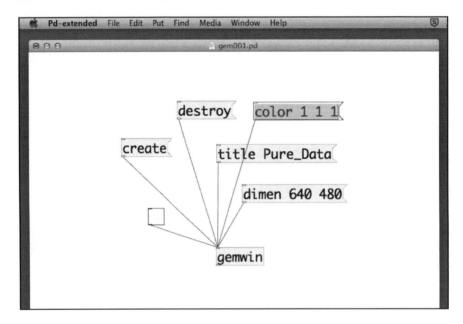

To resume the system default of the window properties, a `reset` message will do:

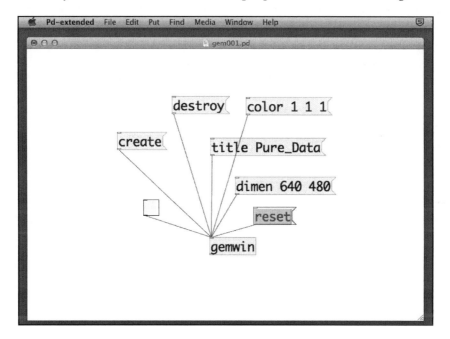

Drawing basic 2D graphics

Before exploring more advanced properties of the window, we start working on 2D graphics. The GEM library comes with a number of 2D primitives such as `circle`, `curve`, `polygon`, `rectangle`, `square`, and `triangle`.

Create a new `Pd` patch. Save it to your folder with name `gem002.pd`. Clear the console window by choosing **Edit | Clear**. Create a default graphics window with the `gemwin` object, `create` message, `destroy` message, and the toggle render box as shown in the last section.

We will first create a 2D square in this exercise. Put an object named `square` onto the patch window. If you switch to the **Run** mode and create the window to start rendering, nothing happens. In order to render the square object, we need one more GEM object, `gemhead`:

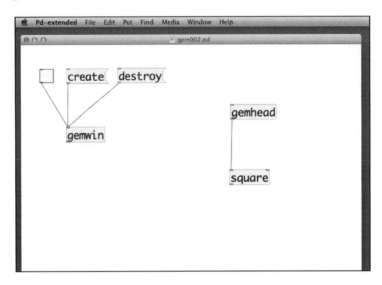

The `gemhead` object defines the path that GEM library uses to produce the graphics. When the GEM window starts to render any graphics, it searches all the `gemhead` objects in the patch. Starting from each `gemhead` object, it goes down the connection from `gemhead` to the object that defines the graphics, in this case, a `square` object:

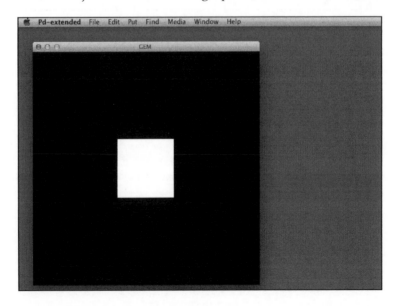

You will see that the `square` object has two inlets. The first one is connected to the outlet of the `gemhead` object that defines the rendering path. The second one defines the size of the square. We can put a number box to it to try it out:

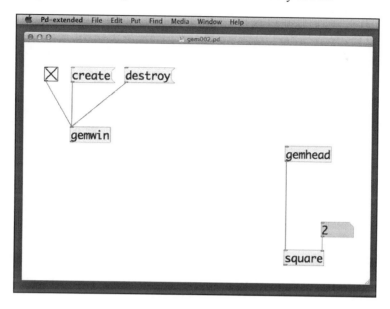

In the **Run** mode, try changing the value of the number box. Remember that you can click on a number box to type a new number value or click-and-drag it up or down to increase or decrease the value of the number:

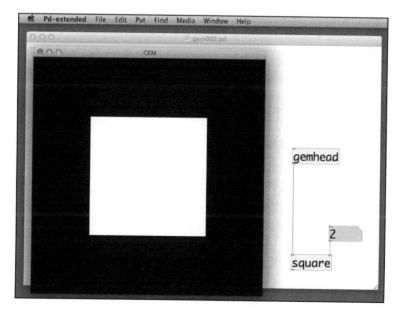

You will see that the size of the white square changes according to the value of the number box. The default size is 1. When you change the number value to around 4, it occupies the whole GEM window.

The normal rendering is the white solid fill color. You can also use outline and corner point to render them. By attaching messages with the text `draw fill`, `draw line`, and `draw point` to the square object, in real time we can alter the rendering method. In the **Run** mode, clicking on the messages will change the rendering method. The default one is `draw fill`:

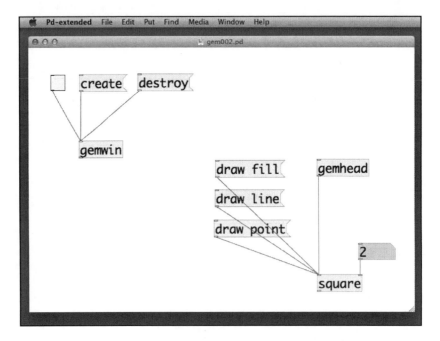

Here is the `draw line` image (shown in the following screenshot):

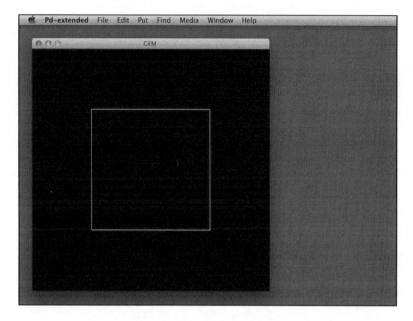

And here is the `draw point` image (shown in the following screenshot):

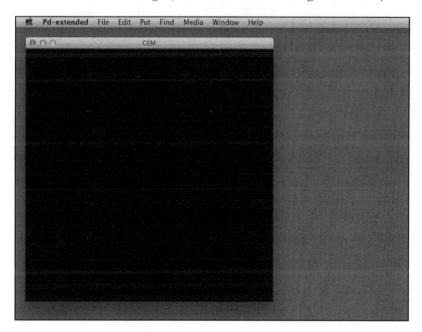

The square object has only one parameter, its size. For other shapes, there will be more parameters to control the dimension. Next, we take a look at the rectangle object. It has two parameters, width and height. We use two number boxes to control them:

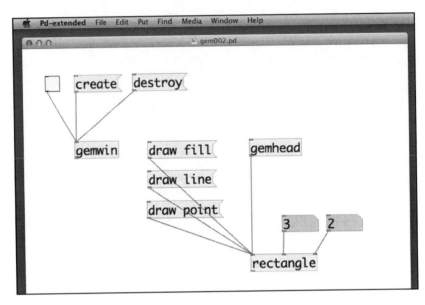

The triangle object will draw an equilateral triangle. It has only one parameter to control its size:

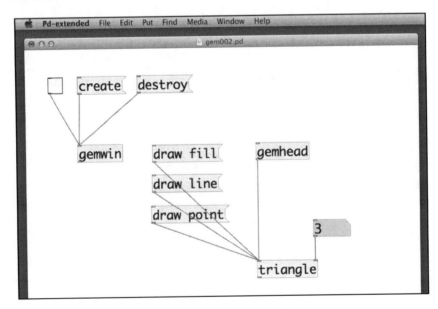

The `circle` object is also straightforward. It has only one parameter for its size:

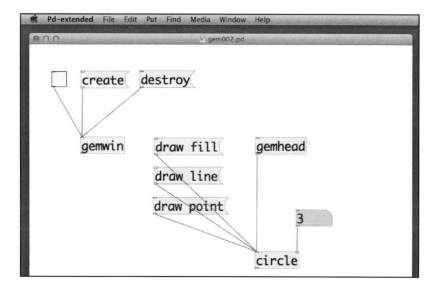

The next shape, `polygon`, is a bit complicated. It has one parameter inside the object box, that is, the number of edges. The following example is a polygon of five edges. Besides the left-most hot inlet, it has five other inlets. Each of them defines one corner of the polygon. A corner is a message of three numbers, representing the x, y, and z co-ordinates of the point. The center of the window is the origin of the coordinates system (0, 0, 0). We are going to cover the coordinates system in the next section in more detail.

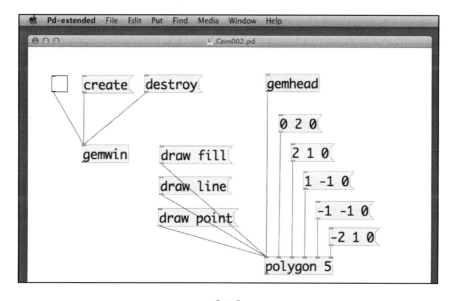

Note that the coordinates are in three-dimensional space, even though we are preparing 2D graphics. All the points here have z values equal to zero. The polygon shape it generates is shown in the following screenshot:

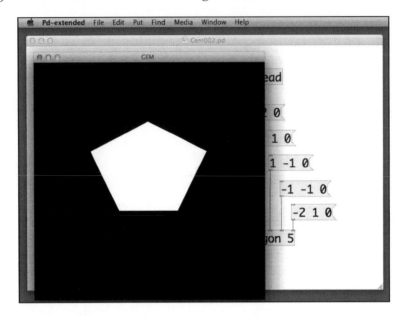

Similar to the `polygon` object, the next object (`curve`) also requires us to put in the points to define the curve line. With just two control points, it draws a straight line:

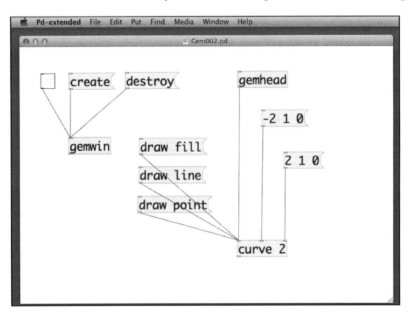

The drawing is a straight line from the endpoint (-2, 1, 0) to (2, 1, 0):

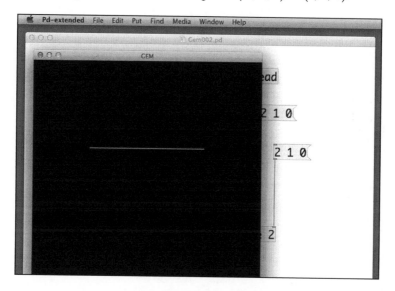

The curve object defines bezier curve. If we have three points, the first and third points are the endpoints of the curve. The second one is the anchor point that defines the curvature of the line:

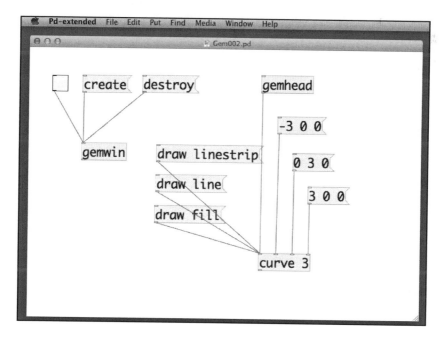

Note the use of the message draw linestrip here. The messages draw line and draw fill will produce a closed shape. If you want an open curve line, draw linestrip will do:

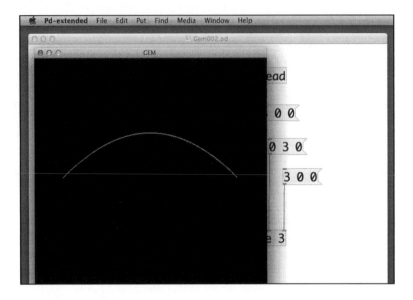

When you add more anchor points to the curve object, you can come up with a more complicated curve. It is an example of a curve with five points, two endpoints, and three anchor points:

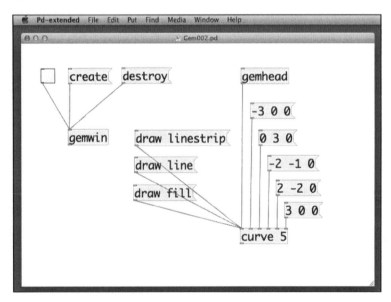

The first and the last messages are the two endpoints. The middle three points trace the curvature of the overall curve:

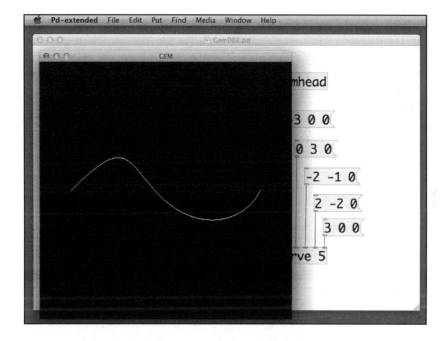

Understanding the coordinates system

In the last section while working on the size of the graphical shapes, we understood that when a `square` object with size 4, it will cover the whole GEM window. In the `polygon` and `curve` examples, we learned that each point in the GEM window corresponds to a point in three-dimensional space.

The GEM window is a two-dimensional projection plane of a three-dimensional space. The origin (0, 0, 0) is the center of the window. The horizontal axis is the x axis. Toward the right-hand side is the increasing value of x. The vertical axis is the y axis. Moving upward increases the value of y. For the z axis, you have to imagine a line moving from the center of the GEM window toward your eyes:

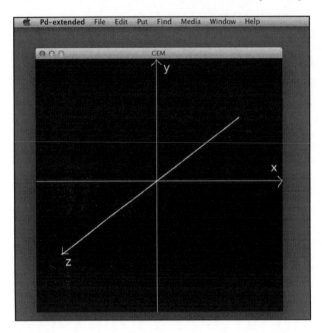

If we consider all the points with z value equal to zero, it will form a flat surface parallel to the GEM window. On this surface, when we move from the left-hand margin to right-hand margin, the x value changes from -4 to 4. When we move from the bottom margin to the top margin, the y value changes from -4 to 4. The measurement is due to the default settings of the GEM window view properties and is independent of the window's dimension in pixels.

Drawing basic 3D primitive shapes

All the 2D graphical shapes can work in the 3D environment. In addition, GEM provides a number of 3D primitives, such as cone, cube, cuboid, curve3d, cylinder, disk, sphere, teapot, torus, and tube. Let us learn it step-by-step by following a similar procedure.

Create an empty patch and save it with name gem003.pd in your folder. Put the gemwin object, create and destroy messages, and the toggle box for rendering.

We start from the simplest 3D object, cube. Put the gemhead and cube objects and connect them together. Similar to 2D shapes, we can also have the draw fill and draw line messages. Here is the patch and the resulting window. By using the draw line message, the 3D perspective projection of the cube is more obvious:

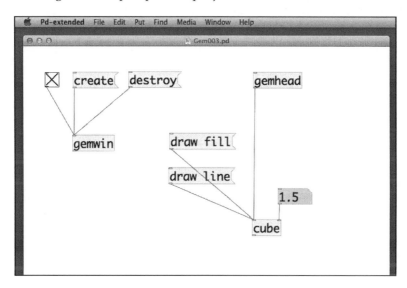

Here is the wire-frame rendering of the cube in the three-dimensional space:

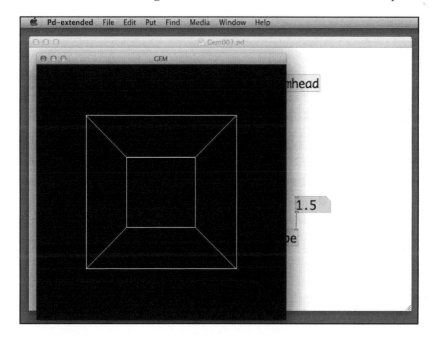

Control for the `cube` object is simple. It has only one number inlet for its size. The next object is `sphere`. It has two parameters. One for the size and another for the resolution, that is, the number of straight line segments to form the circle. If you have an extremely small value for the last inlet, such as three or four, you may end up with a polygonal 3D object, instead of a `sphere` object:

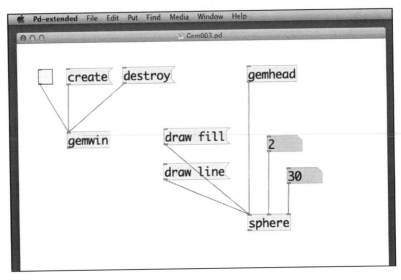

Here is the wire-frame rendering of the sphere. Note that the last inlet of the sphere object defines its resolution:

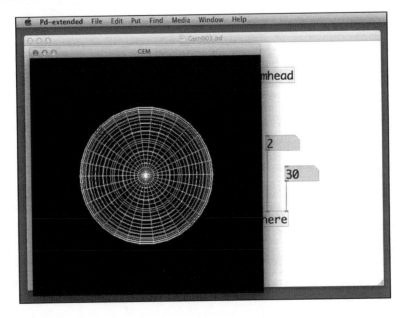

In order to show the 3D rendering of the sphere, we can make use of lighting. In the `gemwin` object, we can turn on the lighting effect by the message `lighting 1`. To turn it off, specify the message `lighting 0`. We also introduce a new object `world_light` to light up the environment.

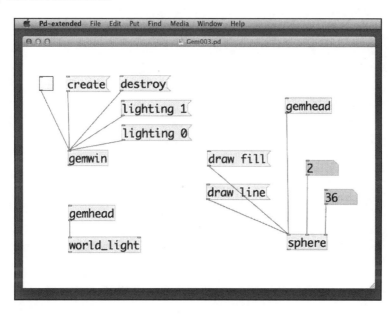

Here is the result without turning on the lighting:

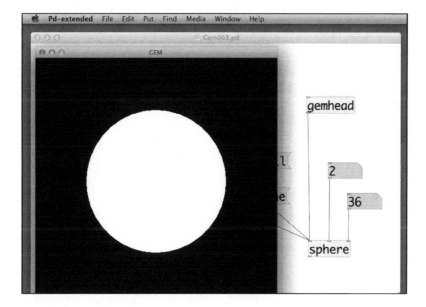

Here is the result with lighting turned on:

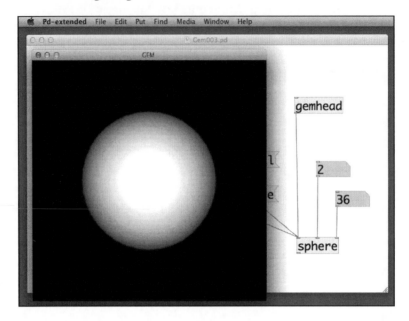

In the patch, we have to use two messages to turn lighting on and off for the GEM window. Actually, we can simplify it with one message and a toggle box. In the message box, we type `lighting $1`, instead of putting 1 or 0, and then we connect a toggle box before it:

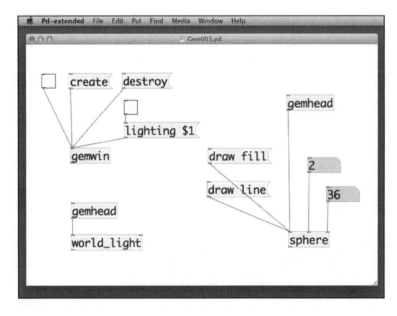

In the previous chapter, we learned that a toggle box sends out either 0 or 1. The lighting $1 message has one argument, similar to the use of function arguments in other programming language. The notation $1 is the first argument. This message box will package the text lighting together with 0 or 1 from the toggle box and send it out to the gemwin object to control the lighting effect.

The world_light object defines a point light at infinity distance to the scene. Without the light, your scene will be invisible once you turn on the lighting message. Note that the world_light object has another gemhead object for it. You can also add color information in the second inlet of the world_light object. Again, the color is the RGB number values, ranging from 0 to 1:

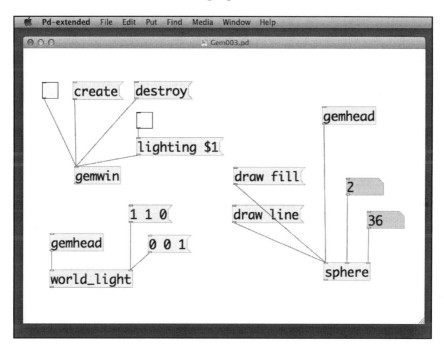

Working with digital color

We have seen how to specify the window background color and the world light color. For all the 2D and 3D graphics, we can also individually specify the color information with RGB values. The coming example will show us how to specify color for the primitives.

Create an empty patch and save it with name gem004.pd in your folder. Put the gemwin object, create and destroy messages, and the toggle box for rendering. In addition, put a gemhead object with a sphere object.

Between the gemhead and the sphere objects, insert a color object. For color specification, it will be a message of three numbers: red, green, and blue. Clicking on the message will change the color of the sphere:

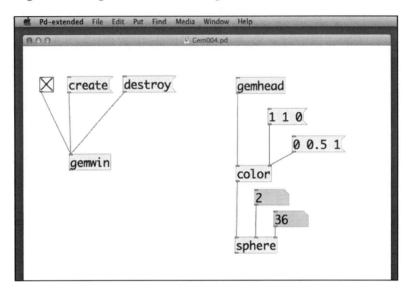

We can also use another object colorRGB to specify color for the graphical shapes. It requires three (RGB) to four (RGB and alpha) number boxes to specify the color. Remember that each number ranges from 0 to 1. If you press the *Shift* key and click-and-drag a number box upward or downward, you can alter the number in decimal point, in a step of 0.01:

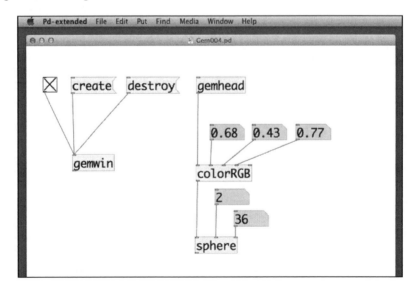

Color specification is straightforward in GEM. By using `color` or `colorRGB`, you alter the default color (white) according to the number values. You can also use both the `world_light` color and the object color together:

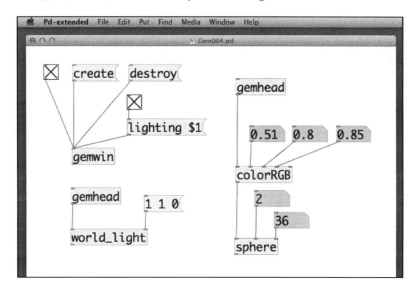

Some color input requires three individual numbers. Some color input requires a message list of three numbers. We can combine them together such that the user interface is consistent, that is, three number boxes:

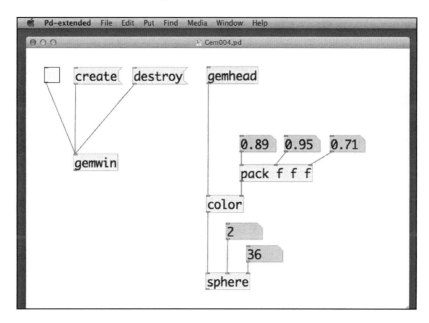

The new object is pack. It simply packs three numbers together. Note the parameters
f f f. Each f represents a floating-point number. The number of f corresponds to
the number of inlets of the pack object. In this example, three numbers are packed
together to form a list for the right-hand inlet of the color object. Nevertheless, this
patch is not perfect. If you play around with the number boxes, you will notice that
only the red color box (hot inlet) will send out the color list message. The rest (green,
blue) will just store the new values and wait until there is a change in the red number
box. If you remember how we handled the synchronization of hot and cold inlets, we
make use of the trigger object:

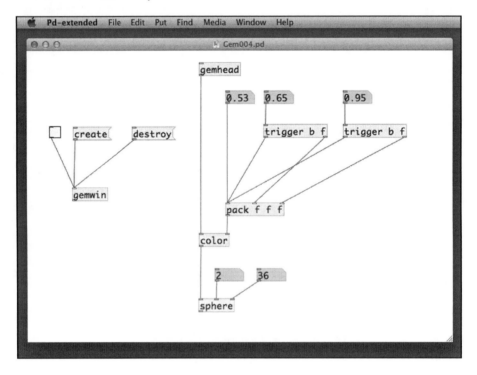

For the green and blue color number boxes, they send out the number to a trigger
object, trigger b f. Each trigger box will first send out the number to the
corresponding number inlet of the pack object and then send out a bang message to
the hot inlet of the pack object to output the color number list to the color object.
In this case, changes in the green and blue numbers will also go immediately to the
sphere object without waiting.

Applying geometric transformation

In this section, we start to move the graphical shapes in the 3D space. The operations are translation, rotation, and scale. Each operation comes with two versions. They are: `translate`, `translateXYZ`, `rotate`, `rotateXYZ`, `scale`, and `scaleXYZ`. In this book, we focus on the use of `translateXYZ`, `rotateXYZ`, and `scaleXYZ`. Readers can use the help menu to check the usage of `translate`, `rotate`, and `scale`.

Performing translation, rotation, and scaling

Create an empty patch and save it with name `gem005.pd` in your folder. Put the `gemwin` object, `create` and `destroy` messages, and the toggle box for rendering. In addition, put a `gemhead` object with a `cube` 3D object.

Between the `gemhead` and the `cube` objects, insert a `translateXYZ` object. The `translateXYZ` operation moves the object along each of the three axes. The three number boxes control the magnitude of the movement:

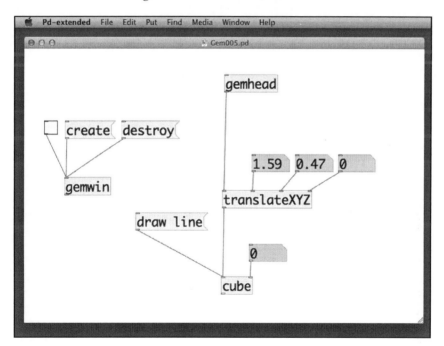

Note that the cube changes position and renders with a perspective view:

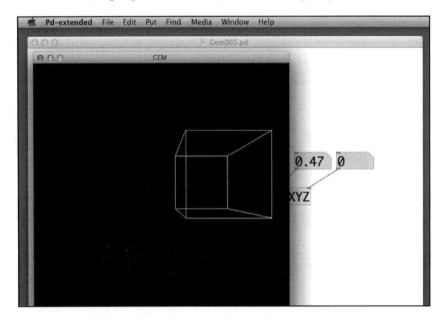

For rotation, insert the rotateXYZ object to replace the translateXYZ object in the last example. It also requires three number boxes for the rotations in three axes. The unit is in degree:

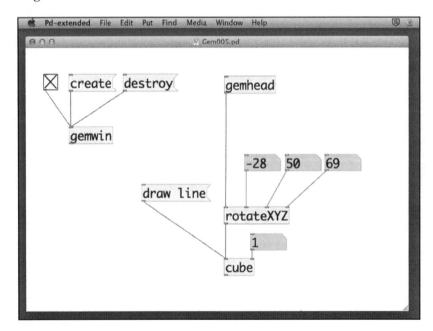

Here is the result of the cube with the rotation in three axes:

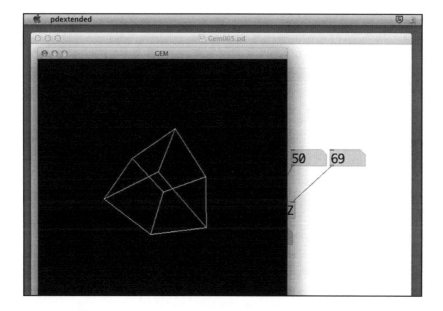

For scaling, use the object scaleXYZ. It changes the size (scale) of the cube in the X, Y, and Z dimension. The number 1 is the original size:

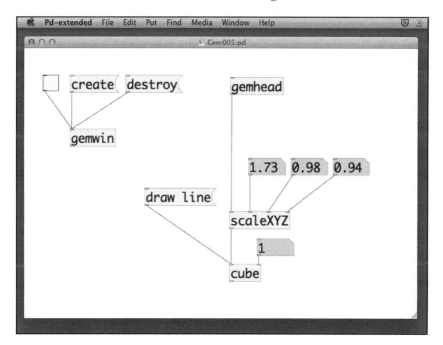

Here is the cube with different scaling factors in the three axes:

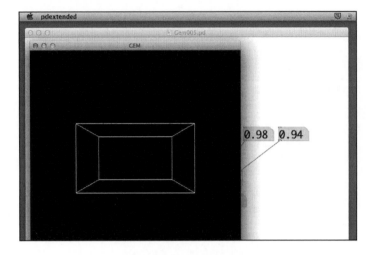

It is easy to understand the operations of translateXYZ, rotateXYZ, and scaleXYZ in GEM. By changing the values in the number boxes, you control the amount of transformation in the particular coordinates axes.

Checking the margins of the window

By using the translateXYZ object, we can verify the margins of the window, as shown in the last section about the coordinates system. Note that when the cube is translated to the x value of -4 or 4, half of it will be outside of the frame:

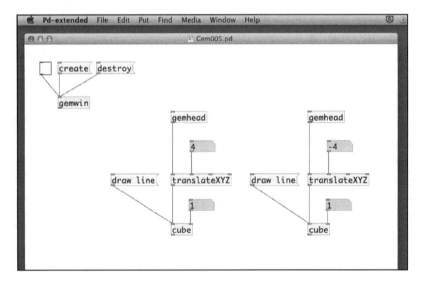

Here are the two cubes translated to the left-hand and right-hand margins of the GEM window:

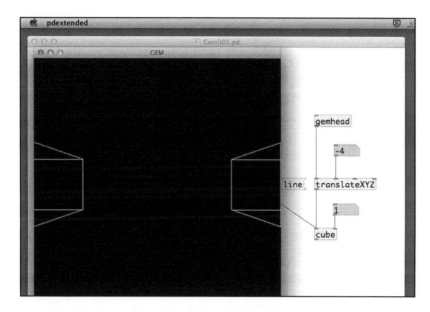

You will observe that when we translate a cube towards the margins of the window, it looks distorted due to the perspective projection. In some game applications, we may want to maintain the 3D shape no matter where it travels across the screen. In this case, you might consider using the ortho (orthogonal) projection object. All graphical shapes under the ortho object will use parallel projection instead of perspective projection:

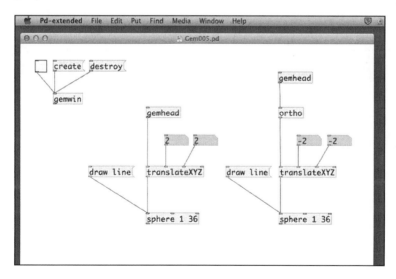

Here is the resulting image (shown in the next screenshot) where you will notice the difference between the orthogonal and perspective projection:

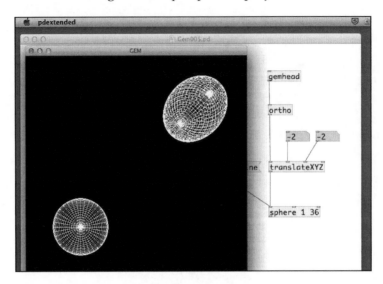

Order of transformations

Another issue we would like to cover is the order of transformation. We have covered only one transformation for each graphical shape. In fact, we can have a number of transformations for each shape. The following example illustrates how the order of transformation matters in some cases. The first one has a translation before a rotation along the y axis. The cube translates to the position (1, 1, 0) in the 3D space and then rotates around its own y axis:

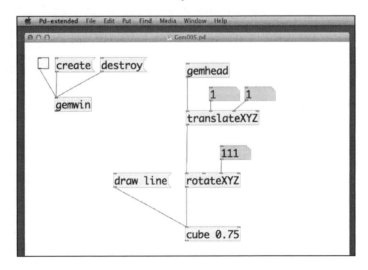

The second example has the same rotation along y axis first and then a translation to the same position (1, 1, 0). The cube rotates along the y axis of the window with a displacement from the center by one unit along the x axis and one unit along the y axis. By clicking-and-dragging the number box for the rotateXYZ object, the result is more obvious:

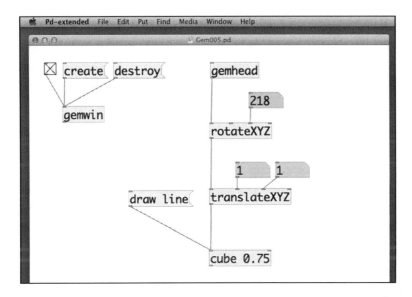

Creating animation in 3D space

In *Chapter 1, Getting Started with Pure Data,* we have used the metro and random objects to create an animation of the graphical interface object (bang button). With the introduction of the GEM library, we can replace the bang button with other graphics. We have also used a float object to implement a counter. Actually, in pd-extended, we have another counter object that we can directly make use of.

Create an empty patch and save it with name Gem006.pd in your folder. Put the gemwin object, create and destroy messages, and the toggle box for rendering. In addition, create a metro object with a toggle box and connect it through a counter object.

For the `counter` object, it requires a number of input parameters. The three inlets we are using are for setting the minimum value, counter value, and the maximum value. In this case, I have used three message boxes for the purpose. The output of the `counter` object will be a number box:

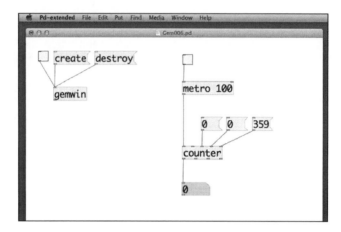

Before turning on the `metro` object, we need to click on the three message boxes to set up the minimum (third inlet), maximum (fifth inlet) values of the `counter` object, and reset the current count (fourth inlet) to the minimum value. Once we start counting, the number value will count from 0 to 359 and back to 0 again. We are going to use this value to control rotation of a graphical shape.

We combine the `counter` patch with one of the geometric transformation example to test the result. The `counter` number box output will be connected to the y axis rotation parameter for a `rotateXYZ` object:

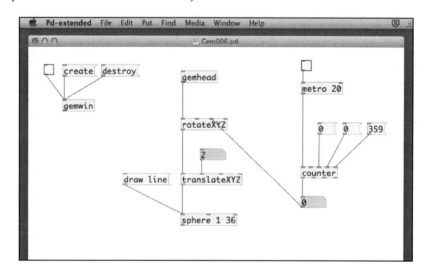

In the next example, I have added one more `sphere` with different size into the animation. Under the same `gemhead` link, there are now two `sphere` objects. I also put in a `trigger` object to send out the graphic information to both spheres in synchronized fashion. Note the parameter for `trigger a a`. The letter `a` stands for any, that is, any type of data:

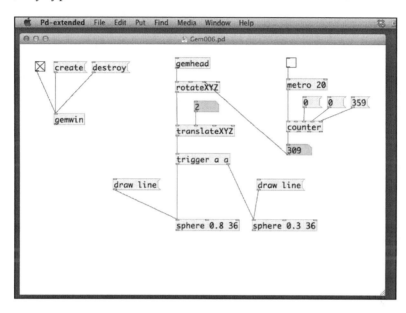

The resulting graphics are shown in the following screenshot:

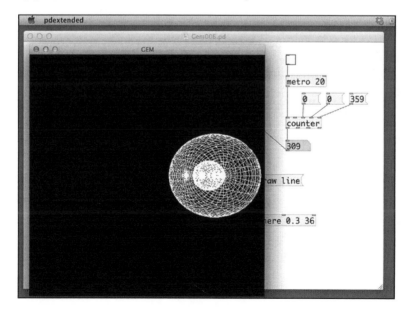

In this case, the smaller sphere object is inside the bigger one. What if I want them to be separate? One easy method is to put a translateXYZ object for one of the sphere object. Let's try. Refer to the following screenshot:

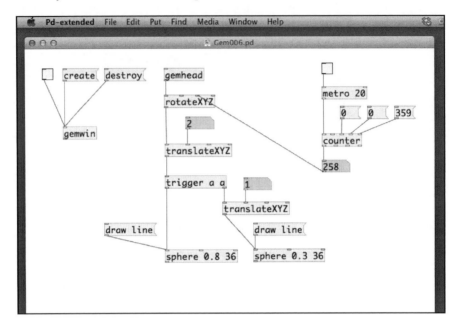

No matter how much you change the x value of the second translateXYZ number box, the two spheres always rotate together. In GEM, the transformations are common to all the graphical shapes under the same gemhead rendering path. The way to separate them is to add a new object, separator. After the trigger object, the rendering signal splits into two. While one goes directly to the sphere object, another one goes to a translateXYZ object first. Since the two sphere objects are isolated by two separators, transformations applied on the smaller sphere will be local to it. The transformations above the separators are applicable to both spheres:

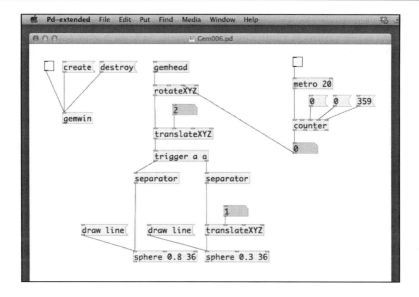

After we have introduced the two `separator` objects, the `translateXYZ` object for the smaller `sphere` object now works properly. Now, what if I want the smaller sphere to rotate around the bigger one? An additional `rotateXYZ` object will do, as shown in the following screenshot:

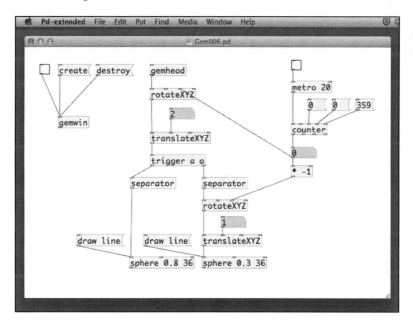

Note that we can use a multiplication object with value -1 to change the direction of rotation.

To finish, we can use lighting and color change effects for the two spheres for a nicer result, as shown in the following screenshot:

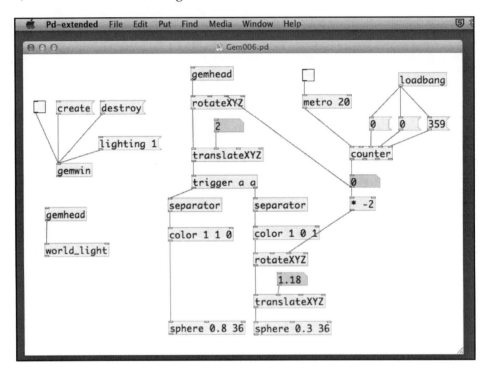

In the upper-right corner, there is a new object loadbang. This object will generate a bang message when you first open the patch from hard disk. If you have any initialization that you would like to do before running the patch, it is a good practice to use a loadbang object to send out the message. In this case, I have used it to initialize the minimum, maximum, and current count values of counter:

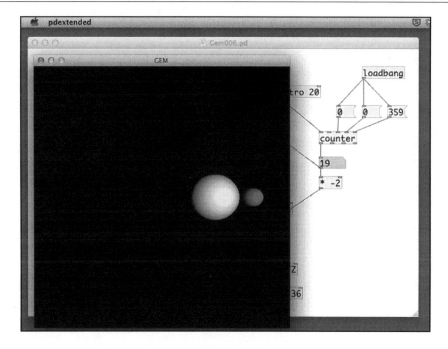

By using a metro object, we set up a timeline for the whole scene to follow. The previous examples use the time to control the rotation of two spheres. Of course, we can use it to control translation, scaling, or even the color of the graphical shapes. The key point is how we can make use of the counter values to map into the meaningful range of numbers for the visual effects. For example, rotation is between 0 and 359 degree, translation can be between -4 and 4, color is the RGB value between 0 and 1.

Summary

This chapter explains how to create 2D and 3D graphics in the GEM library, using primitive shapes, applying geometric transformations, such as translation and rotation, and how to make use of automation to create animation. So far, we have only used the basic color rendering and world lighting for the graphical shapes. In the next chapter, we are going to import external images into the GEM window.

3
Image Processing

Besides drawing the graphics from scratch, we can also obtain images from external sources to work in the GEM environment. *Chapter 3, Image Processing*, will illustrate the step-by-step process for incorporating digital images, videos, and live streams into existing Pure Data applications. We will also cover advanced topics such as background removal and background substitution effects. The topics included are as follows:

* Obtaining images from external sources
* Applying image filters
* Layering multiple images
* Working with time
* Performing background removal
* Working with chroma key
* Experimenting with advanced effects

Obtaining images from external sources

The first step is to create an empty patch with the basic GEM window setup. Create a new Pure Data patch. Save it to your folder with name `Image001.pd`. Put in the `gemwin` object, with the `create` and `destroy` messages. Use a `toggle` box to control the rendering. To work with the examples, you also need a few digital image files in formats such as JPEG, PNG, a few video clips in QuickTime (MOV) or MP4 formats. For live video, you also need a working webcam connected to your computer.

The following screenshot is the patch content:

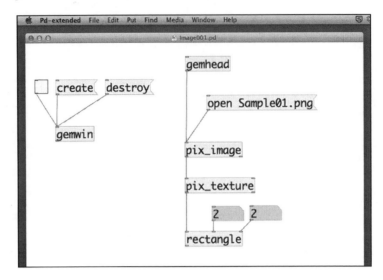

In the patch, we need a gemhead object. We also have a new object—pix_image. And then, we connect another new object—pix_texture, finally to a rectangle object. There is a message box for the pix_image object. It is a message to instruct the pix_image object to open an external file with name Sample01.png that resides in the same folder with the Pure Data patch. If the PNG file does exist and is a valid image document, the image will show up after you click on the message box. If the image does not exist, an error message will show up in the console window.

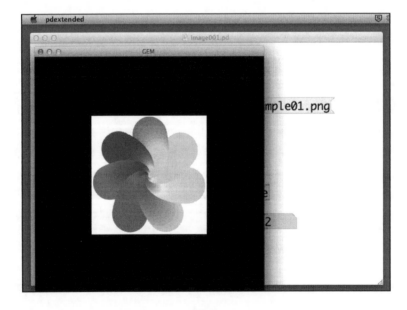

Actually, the image can be in a different folder. In this case, we have to specify the path of the file. In a later section, we can also choose the file interactively with an openpanel object.

The GEM library comes with a number of commands with pix as prefix. They are the pixel objects that handle image processing at pixel level. The pix_image object is an object that reads in a digital image file, such as JPEG, PNG, TIFF, GIF, and stores it in memory. The next object—pix_texture, will enable texture mapping with the digital image stored. Finally, the texture will map into the rectangle object.

Imagine you have a cloth printed with the image loaded from an external file, and wrap it around a rectangle. If you want to load another image file, you have to put in another message box with another file name. Alternately, we can use an openpanel object to interactively select the file from a file browser dialog box. Click on the **bang** object of the openpanel object. Select an image file from the location you put there. Confirm your selection. You can also observe the message from the console window to check if the loading is successful or not.

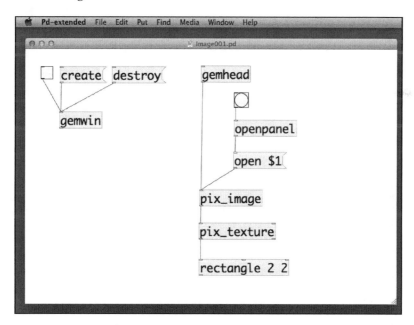

Besides using a `rectangle` object to hold the image, you can also experiment with 3D primitives, such as cube, sphere, and so on. To highlight the 3D effect, the example also uses a `rotateXYZ` object to have a perspective view of the `cube` object.

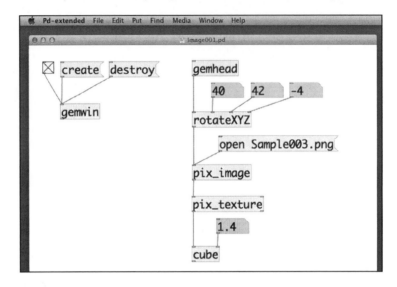

The following screenshot is the result of an image file texture-mapped onto a `cube` object. With the perspective projection, you will notice the X, Y, and Z dimensions of the cube surface.

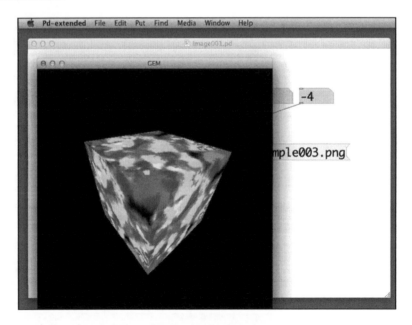

If you replace the `cube` object with a `sphere` object, you will have an image similar to the following screenshot:

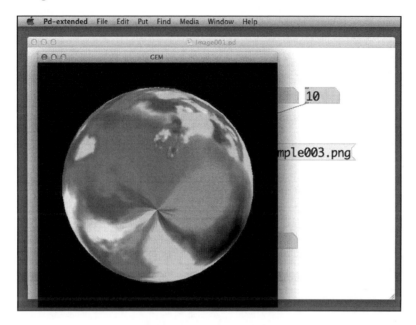

After we play around with loading external still images, we can proceed to work with digital videos. The logic is the same but the object is different. It will be the `pix_film` object instead of the `pix_image` object.

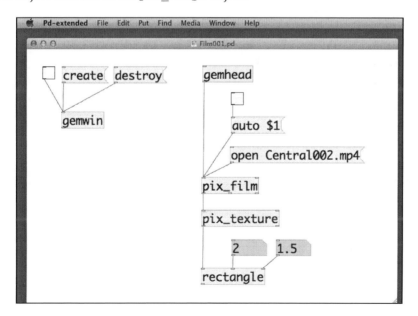

Similar to the still image, the digital video appears on top of the rectangle object. We can adjust the size of the rectangle object to cater to the aspect ratio of the video. The size of the rectangle object in the example is 2 x 1.5, which is the common 4 x 3 aspect ratio. You can also put the size inside the object such as rectangle 4 3.

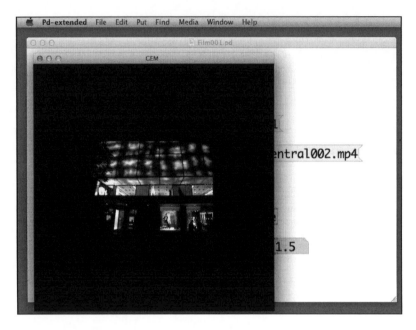

To play back a digital video, the pix_film object uses the same open message to load the external video in the same folder with the patch. In this case, we use an MP4 video here. The video format depends on the operating system. For Mac OSX, it will mainly be QuickTime, MP4, and WMV, if you have the **Flip4Mac** (http://www.telestream.net/flip4mac/) software installed. For Windows, it will be AVI, WMV, and MP4. For Linux, it depends on the video libraries installed. You can expect GEM to playback AVI, QuickTime (MOV), and MPEG. Note that the pix_film object displays only the video channel, not the audio channel.

 To play sound along with the video, you have to first extract the audio track from the video and use audio objects (to be covered in *Chapter 7, Audio Programming*) to playback the sound separately.

In addition to the open message, the object also requires an auto message. As shown in the following screenshot, we have connected a toggle box to the auto message with a $1 parameter, such that the 0 or 1 message will pass to the auto message. The message will enable and disable the automatic playback of the video. You can use it to start and stop the playback.

The pix_film object has two extra outlets, as shown in the following screenshot. The middle outlet is a list of three numbers. We use a new object called unpack to extract the list into three floating-point numbers. The first number is the number of frames in the video. The second number is the frame width. The third number is the frame height. An unpack object will split a list into different items, depending on their data types. Note the three f parameters, that indicate the unpack object, will split the list into three floating-point numbers. The right outlet of pix_film is a bang message that indicates the end of the video.

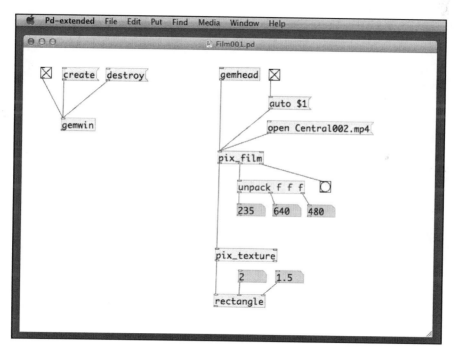

One of the uses of the end-of-video `bang` message is to stop the playback after it plays once. Normally, with the `auto` message on, the video loops. We can connect the outlet of the `bang` message to the inlet of the `toggle` box for the `auto` message. Once the video reaches its end, it sends a `bang` message to change the `toggle` box to 0.

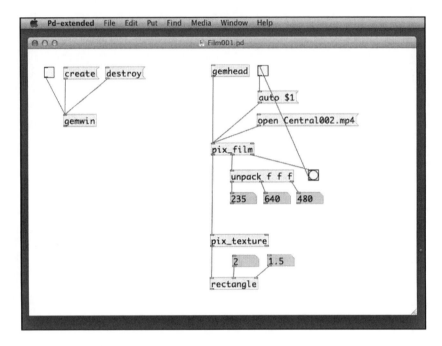

The preceding patch works only in the Version 0.42.5. The behavior of `pix_film` changes in the new Version 0.43.4. The video does not loop when the `auto` message is on. We have to reset the frame number to 0 in the right inlet of the `pix_film` object in order to loop the video. The following patch `Film002.pd` demonstrates the usage in Version 0.43.4.

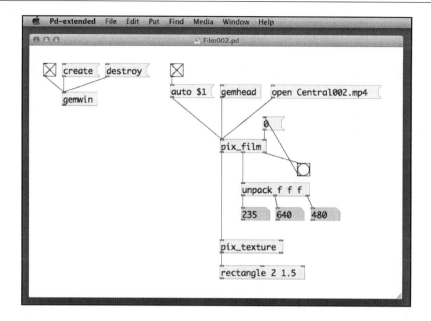

After image and video processing, we will proceed to live stream video with a webcam. The new object is `pix_video`. It will pick up the default video source from your computer system. For Mac OSX, you can use the `dialog` message to select other video source. For Windows and Linux, you can click on the `enumerate` message to list the available video devices and use the radio button to select the device.

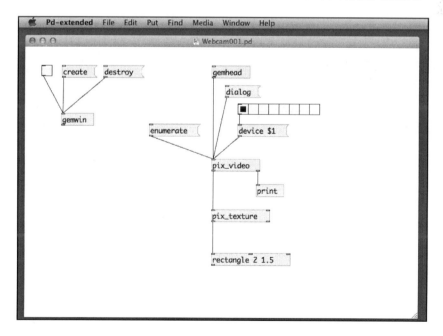

With this patch, your default live webcam image will be mapped on top of the `rectangle` object as shown in the following screenshot:

As a review, we can group all the image, video, and webcam into one single patch. Try arranging them in a row by using the `translateXYZ` or `translate` object. Here is an example. You can create a video wall if you have a number of videos to arrange in different layout.

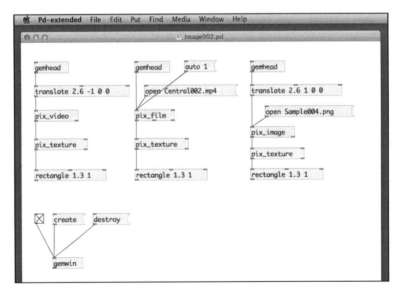

This example has three images, one still photo on the right-hand side, a digital video in the center, and the live webcam image on the left-hand side. Each of them is mapped on a separate `rectangle` object. The `translate` object works similarly with `translateXYZ`. It takes two parameters. The first one is a number denotes the scaling factor. The second parameter is a list of three numbers indicating the direction in X, Y, and Z dimensions. The total translation value will be the scaling factor that multiplies the X, Y, and Z direction values.

The next image is the expected result from this patch, `Image002.pd`:

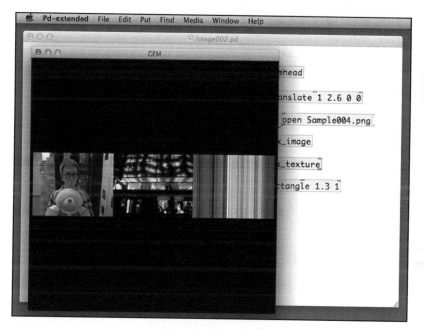

Applying image filters

After we load the external images as input, we can start to apply effects to the images. The first few effects are image filters similar to what you can find in software such as Photoshop. We will explore a few of them.

The first one is the **invert** filter. It inverts the color for each pixel in the image. For testing, you can use image, video, or live stream. In the example, we use a `pix_image` object. The object to perform the invert filter is `pix_invert`. The invert filter will compute the new color for each pixel and for each RGB value by using 1 to subtract the original color value. The dark area becomes light. And the light area becomes dark.

For example, if the original pixel color is red, (1, 0, 0) in RGB, the inverted color will be (1-1, 1-0, 1-0) or (0, 1, 1). It is the color cyan.

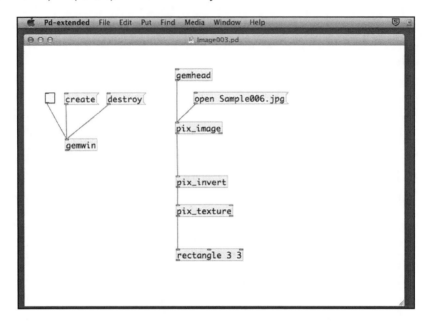

Here is what you would expect with the use of the `pix_invert` object. It is the same as the invert filter when you work with Photoshop.

The next object is `pix_2grey` that converts the original image into grey tone. Here is the patch with `pix_2grey`:

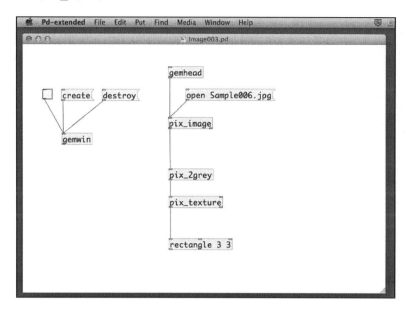

The `pix_2grey` object will convert the original RGB image into grayscale as shown in the following screenshot:

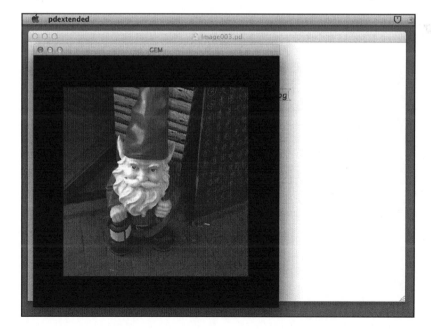

The `pix_flip` object is also straightforward. It flips the image either horizontally or vertically or both. The controls are the `none`, `horizontal`, `vertical`, and `both` messages.

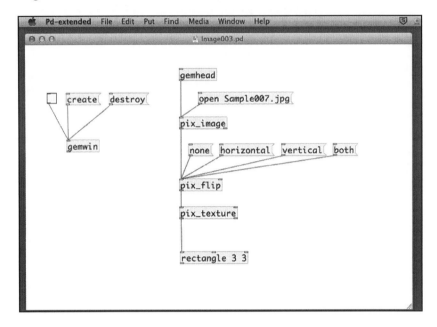

Here is an example with the vertically flipped image:

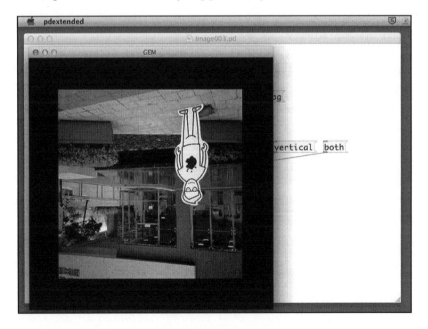

The next effect—`pix_metaimage`, is very interesting and useful. It makes use of a smaller copy of an image to create a mosaic of the original bigger image.

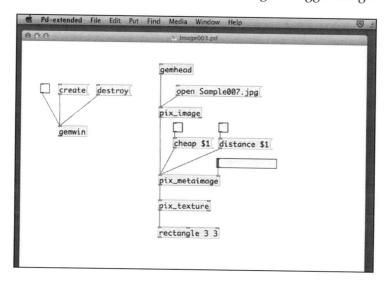

There are three parameters for the `pix_metaimage` object. The `cheap` message will enable or disable smoothening when scaling the image. A value 1 for cheap will disable smoothening. The `distance` message will use 3D or 2D scaling of the image. A value 1 for distance will use 3D distance to scale the image. The last parameter is a `horizontal slider`. You have to change the range of the slider to a value between 0 and 1. Put 1 in the right box of the slider property.

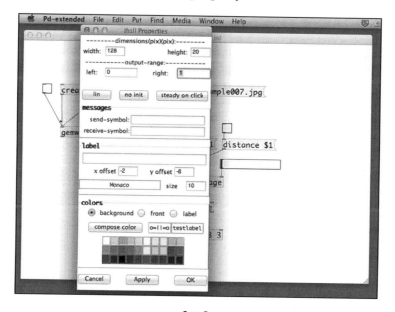

Here is the resulting image you would expect with the typical usage of a `pix_metaimage` object:

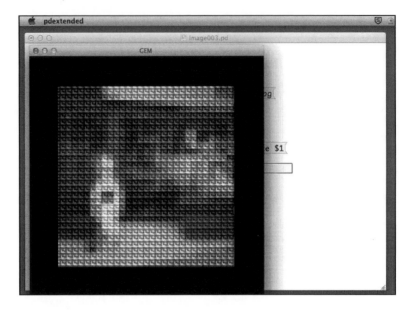

The next effect is the `pix_lumaoffset`. It uses the brightness of the image to create an illusion of depth. The first parameter—the `fill` message, determines whether it uses color fill or color line to render the image. The second parameter—the `smooth` message, turns on and off smoothening. The third parameter—the `offset` number box, determines how much to offset the color lines. The last parameter—the `gap` number box, is the spacing between each color line.

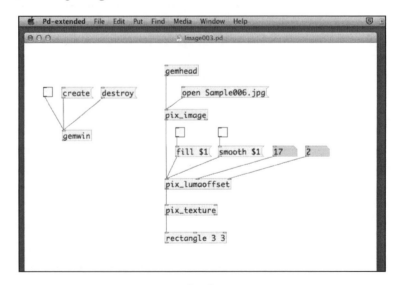

Note the illusion of depth created by the horizontal lines that changes according to the brightness of the image.

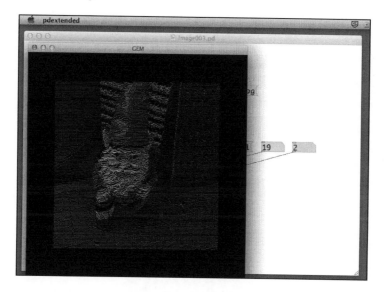

Layering multiple images

The filters we learned in the previous section use only one input source. There are other GEM pixel effects that combine two images together. The logic is similar to the layer option in Photoshop layers. They are the `pix_add`, `pix_subtract`, `pix_multiply`, and `pix_diff` objects.

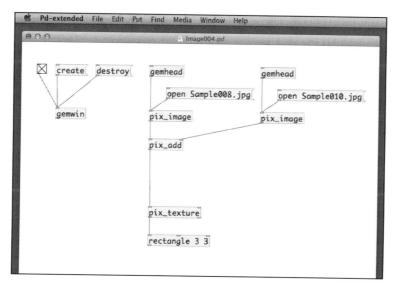

The following first example uses the `pix_add` effect that combines two images together according to their pixels' color values:

Note that the object requires two input images. The patch has two `gemhead` objects. Each `gemhead` will use a `pix_image` object to load its image. In the end, there is only one `pix_texture` object to map the resulting image to the rectangle. The `pix_add` object adds the color pixel values of the two images, with result clamped between 0 and 1. The `pix_subtract` object subtracts the color pixel value of one image by the others. The `pix_multiply` object multiplies the color pixel value of the two images. The `pix_diff` object computes the absolute value of the color pixel value difference between the two images.

You have to use two images of the same size for these objects. Again, you can use digital videos or webcam live stream instead of digital images.

The next object we look into is the `pix_mix` object. In addition to the two input images, the `pix_mix` object has the third inlet that is a number between 0 and 1. We use a horizontal slider with the output range from 0 to 1. You can refer to the last section about specifying the range.

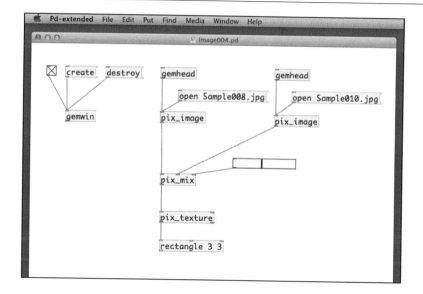

Following is the resulting image with the `pix_mix` object. Note that the semi-transparent effect of the images.

When you push the slider to the left-hand side, that is with a value closer to 0, you see more of the left image. When you push the slider toward the right-hand side, with value closer to 1, you see more of the right image. It is a cross-fading effect. Again, you need two images of the same size.

All the images we displayed are rectangular in shape. If we want to have an irregular shape image, how can we do this with GEM? The following example will make use of the `pix_mask` object. It defines an alpha channel mask, similar to Photoshop, for another image. Here is the patch:

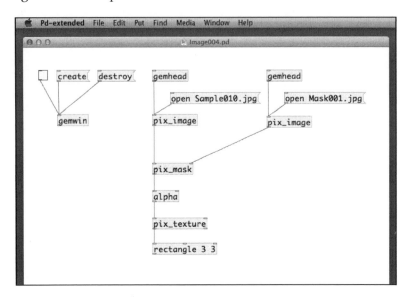

The `pix_mask` object also takes in two images through its inlets. The one on the left-hand side is the original image. The one on the right-hand side is the mask. It is a black and white image of the same size as the original one. The white area will be transparent. You can also have gradient, that is feather edge, too. You can use Photoshop or other image editing software to create the mask image file. We use another new object, `alpha`, to enable alpha blending in the final result.

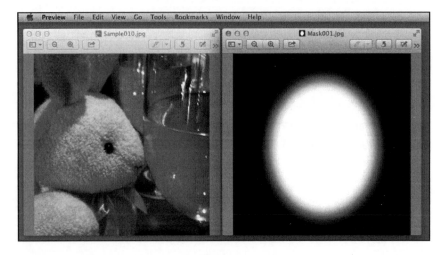

The resulting image in GEM window is shown in the following screenshot:

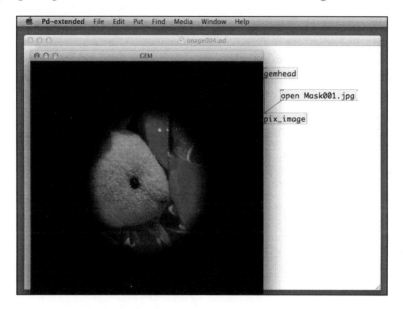

Working with time

The effects we have learned so far work with spatial arrangement in a frame. There are a few objects in GEM to facilitate us to work with frame in the time domain. For example, the following patch can delay the playback of a frame. It is the `pix_delay` object. The parameter in the right inlet is the number of delayed frames.

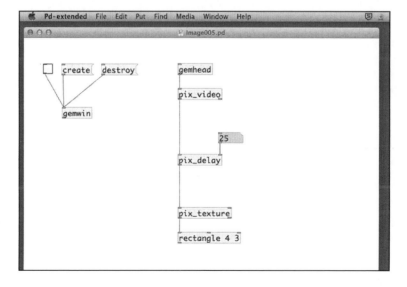

GEM also has another group of objects to store and retrieve images. They are the `pix_buffer`, `pix_buffer_read`, and `pix_buffer_write` objects. Imagine that you can define a number of empty boxes by using the `pix_buffer` object. Once the boxes are ready, you can deposit image frames onto the empty boxes using `pix_buffer_write`. When you need the frames, you can retrieve them by `pix_buffer_read`. In the following example, We define a buffer named `temp` of size 1 frame to store the image:

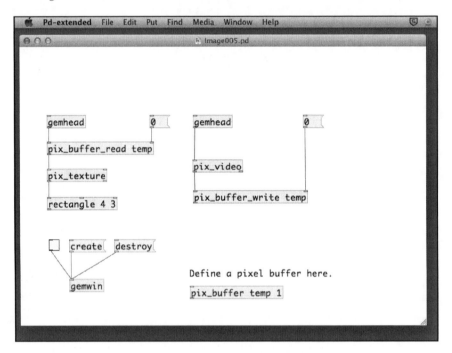

The `pix_buffer temp 1` object defines a pixel buffer `temp` of size 1 frame. The `pix_buffer_write` object receives the image frame from `pix_video`. Note that the `pix_buffer_write` object has a right inlet with a message 0. It is the index number of the storage in the buffer `temp`. The index starts from 0, similar to the array index in other programming language. If you need to 'write' the image to the buffer, you first have to click on the message 0 for `pix_buffer_write`. For the `pix_buffer_read` object, it works in the same way. If you need to retrieve the image from the buffer `temp`, you also click on the message 0 for `pix_buffer_read`. We do not have other index numbers in our case because the buffer has only one element. The `pix_buffer_read` object will then pass the image to `pix_texture` for texture mapping onto the `rectangle` object. The operation will be: first click on the message for write, and second click on the message for read. We can automate it by using the `metro` object.

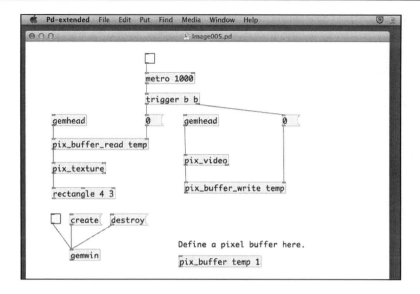

In this case, we can create a stop-motion effect for your digital movie or live stream video.

Performing background removal

The GEM library includes image-processing objects for us to isolate the foreground and background of a scene. The logic is simple. It takes a snapshot of a background image first. When the subject enters into the scene, it compares the current frame with the stored background image. Only the pixels with change in the color are highlighted in the resulting image. Those areas without any changes remain black.

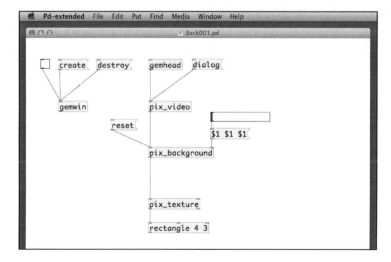

The object is `pix_background`. It has a parameter in its first inlet, a `reset` message. Clicking on this message will store a copy of the current frame as the background image. The second parameter is the list of three numbers in the right inlet. In this example, we have used a horizontal slider with a range between 0 and 1. The three numbers `$1` are the red, green, blue values forming the threshold that will turn black after the frame comparison.

To operate this patch, first point your webcam to a static background, such as a wall. Click on the `reset` message. Move the slider from left to right to a point that the GEM window image just turns black. Wave your hand in front of the webcam. You will notice the GEM window image shows only your hand and the background remains black. The quality of the background removal depends on the specification of your webcam, the lighting condition. The result will not be comparable to those professional video effect switchers.

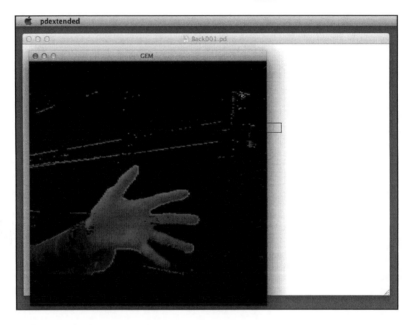

Working with chroma key

Chroma key is the post-production technique to combine two videos by making a range of color hues transparent in foreground video to reveal the background video. In modern movie-making, you may have seen an actor/actress performing in front of a huge blue or green screen. In post-production, the blue/green background is removed and substituted by other image. The GEM library has similar function and of course the quality depends upon the camera and lighting condition. The following patch is quite straightforward:

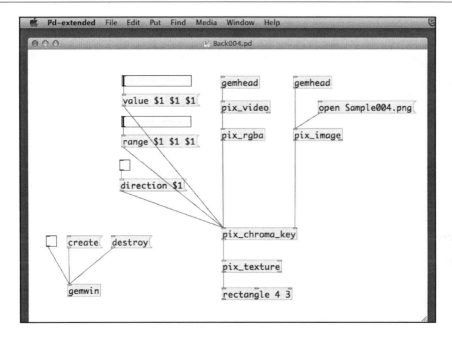

The object is `pix_chroma_key`. It accepts two inputs. They can be digital image, digital video, or webcam live stream, of the same frame size. In addition to the two images, the object requires a number of control data. The `value` message determines the color value or that we want it to be transparent. The `range` message defines the range of tolerance for the color value. The `direction` message determines which image, left or right, will be transparent. The number range for the horizontal sliders are between 0 and 1. And we use the same value for red, green, and blue for simplicity. We also use a `pix_rgba` object to ensure the webcam video stream is RGB. To illustrate the working mechanism, we include the original left and right images for reference.

Here is a snapshot of the webcam input:

Here is the background still image.

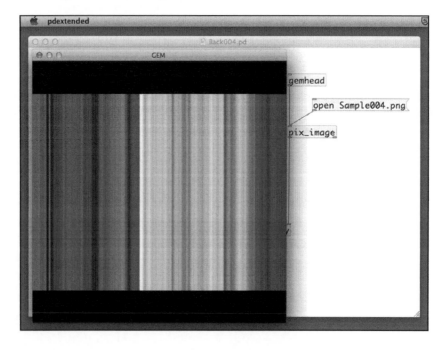

In this example, we have pushed the `value` slider closer to the right hand side, in order to make the white area transparent. Here is the chroma key effect in action. The white area is transparent. It uses the still image as the background.

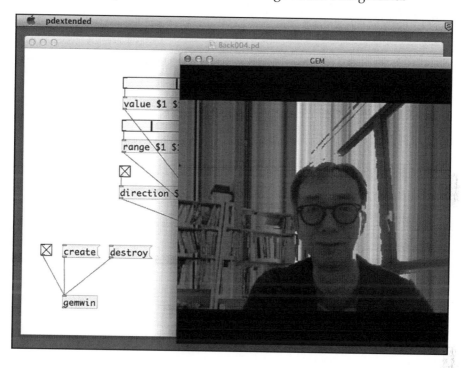

Experimenting with advanced effects

In this last section, we will explore a number of objects to tackle some common interactive art/design situations. Most of them involve more advanced knowledge of the GEM library.

Layering with gemhead

In a lot of design scenarios, we have a background image, instead of just the black background. In this case, we can use two gemhead objects, one for the background and the other for the foreground graphics. The gemhead object has a parameter to determine its render order.

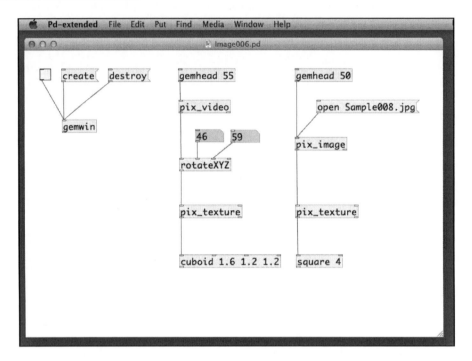

If you have multiple gemhead objects in your patch, the render order depends on its render number, that is the number parameter in its specification. The default number is 50. The higher the number, the later it renders. In this example, the gemhead object with 50 renders first. The gemhead object with 55 renders later. In effect, the gemhead object 50 will be in the back, as a background layer. The gemhead object 55 will be in the front, as a foreground layer.

Coloring pixel data

The `color` and `colorRGB` objects we learned in *Chapter 2, Computer Graphics with the GEM Library*, can also apply to the pixel data. Here is a very simple example to colorize the original image into different color values:

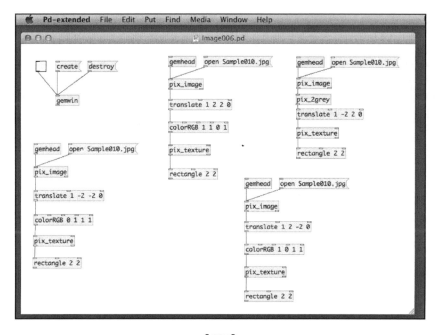

Here is the resulting image where we layout the four copies of the same image with different color tints:

Creating painterly effect

The final example of this chapter will be a bit difficult. It involves a live stream image and the way to convert it into a mosaic like painting. We shall demonstrate the process in a step-by-step way. Here we go. The first thing is to understand the number of buffers in a GEM window. Normally, a GEM window has double buffers. For every frame, new graphics are drawn at the alternate buffer and swapped for display to create an illusion of movement. We create animation in this way. To create a painting, however, we want to retain the graphics from previous frames until we explicitly clear the buffer. Hence, we switch to single buffer mode. A `buffer 1` message to the `gemwin` object will do.

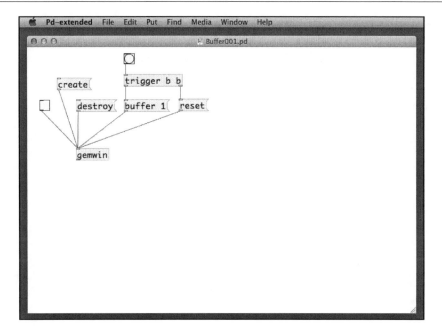

We used a `trigger` object to first send a `reset` message and then a `buffer 1` message, to change into single buffer display for the GEM window. You can click the `create` message after you click on the `bang` object. The next step will be the regular display for a `pix_video` object.

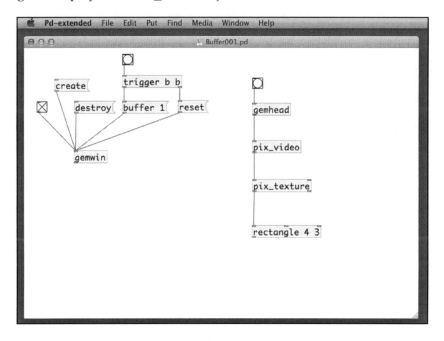

Note that we have a bang box before gemhead. In single buffer mode, you need a bang object to force rendering the new frame from the pix_video object. To continue, we have to retain the color information for each pixel of the video image. It is the pix_data object that does the job. Given a pixel image, it will return the RGB color information for a pixel, with the X and Y co-ordinates in a range of 0 to 1. It also requires a bang message to trigger the sending of color information.

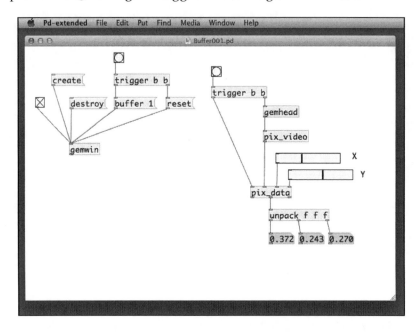

In the preceding patch, we have used two sliders of range 0 to 1 to define the X and Y coordinates. The results are three numbers representing the red, green, and blue values for that pixel located by the two sliders. Next, we replace the two sliders with a pair of random numbers that locate a random pixel within the video image and display the color with a circle.

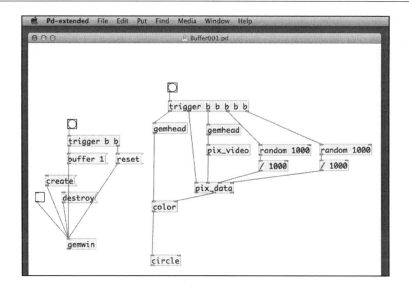

The two `random` objects are with a parameter of 1000. They will return random numbers in the range of 0 to 999. After a division by 1000, they return two random numbers within the range of 0 to 1. They are the coordinates of a random point within the webcam video image. The color information is sent to the `color` object of the circle in the second `gemhead` object. After you create and initialize the GEM window, you can click on the second `bang` box, above the two `gemhead` objects, to notice the change in the color of the circle. In the next step, we also change the position of the circle according to the two random numbers. Remember that in the previous chapter, we have experimented that the width and height of the GEM window are from -4 to 4.

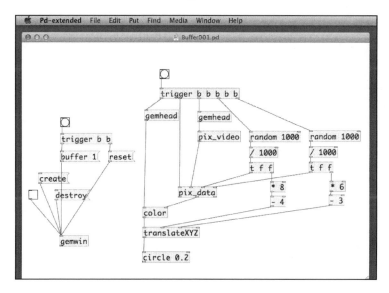

We send the two random numbers to two `trigger` objects. Note that `t f f` is the short form for `trigger float float`. The coordinate values ranging from 0 to 1 are scaled to -4 to 4 for X-axis and -3 to 3 for Y-axis. It is due to the aspect ratio of the webcam video being 4:3. When you click on the second `bang` box, a color dot appears at random location in the screen corresponding to a color pixel at that position in the webcam image. The next natural step is to automate the process with a `metro` object.

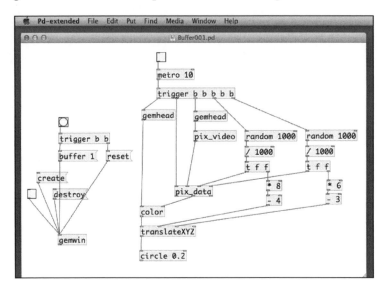

And the resulting image is like the following one. For other use of the `pix_data` object, we will re-visit it in *Chapter 5, Motion Detection*.

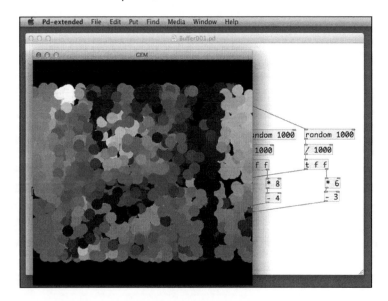

Summary

In this chapter, we covered the common image processing objects in the GEM library. We understood how to combine the 2D and 3D graphics with digital images, videos, and/or live streams, using texture mapping. Similar to imaging software such as Photoshop and GIMP, we learned to apply filters to digital image, and combine multiple images with various effects. Other than the spatial effects, we also worked with temporal effects with delay and stop motion. Within one frame of image, we also learned to make sense of the content by performing background removal, or replacing part of the image with others using the chroma key effect, and producing a creative rendering of live stream video. Having learned some of the basic image processing techniques, we are now prepared to proceed with advanced image processing features on motion tracking and color tracking, that will be covered in further chapters.

4
Interactivity

In this chapter, we start to learn about the creation of interactive computer graphics, that is the use of interactivity in Pure Data. In previous chapters, we have experimented with the use of built-in graphical interface objects, such as slider, button, and so on. Imagine the scenario where we are working with a performance or an installation where we need to go back to the patch window and work with those interface elements. We would not want the audience to see the patch window. In this case, we have to enable the use of the mouse and keyboard within the GEM window. In this chapter, we will learn:

- To obtain the mouse position within the GEM window and respond to the keyboard interaction.

- With these skills, we will learn to create graphical buttons or hotspots.

- Combined with the image processing techniques in the previous chapter, we can make a simple video-jockey instrument with the computer keyboard. Finally, we can create an interactive animation, similar to a pong game.

Obtaining the mouse position

First of all, create an empty patch with name `Mouse001.pd`. Put in the `toggle` box, the `create` message, and the `destroy` message for the `gemwin` object. From now on, we refer it as the `gemwin` basic setup. The object to report the mouse position is `gemmouse`. In order to make `gemmouse` work, you have to click on the GEM window to make it active. The `gemmouse` object will not work if your patch window is the active window.

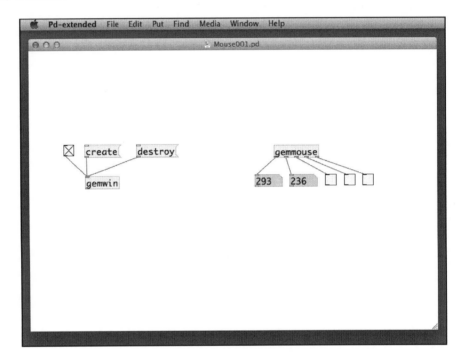

When you move the mouse inside the GEM window, the first two number boxes return the mouse position in X and Y coordinates. By default, the GEM window size is 500 by 500. As long as the GEM window is the active window, `gemmouse` will report the X and Y coordinates of the mouse, even if it extends beyond the window itself. The remaining three `toggle` boxes correspond to the left, middle, and right mouse buttons, respectively. When you click upon a button, the `toggle` box returns a `1` message, that is with a cross. When you release the button, it returns a `0` message.

It is often convenient to have a fixed range of the mouse position even with different GEM window size. If we specify two numbers after the gemmouse object, such as shown in the following screenshot, with gemmouse 1 1, the X position will be normalized to the first number 1 and the Y position will be normalized to the second number 1.

 Normalization is the process to map a value into a fixed range, usually between 0 and 1. For example, the original X position value is between 0 and 500 pixel. If we divide this number by 500, we can obtain a value between 0 and 1.

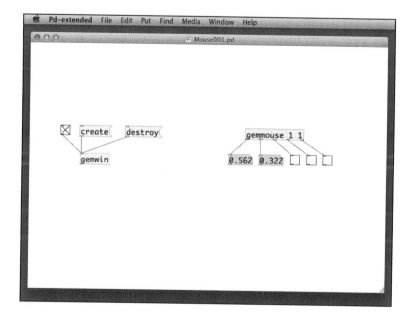

It will be a good idea to display the numbers in the GEM window instead of the number boxes in the patch window. The GEM library includes the text2d and text3d objects to display text on screen. For the text2d object, it mainly requires a text message. For example, if you want to display the text **Hello World**, you put a text Hello World message to the left inlet of the text2d object. The alias $1 message specifies if we want to have anti-aliasing (edge smoothening) effect for the text display.

A value 1 in the `toggle` box will turn on anti-aliasing while a value 0 turns it off.

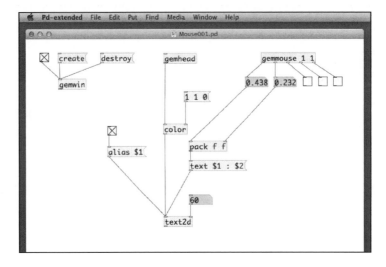

The `text2d` object takes one `text` message to display. In this example, the text has two input parameters, $1 and $2, separated by a colon :. Before the message, we use a `pack` object to combine the two numbers representing the X and Y coordinates to form a list. And the two numbers will go to the two parameters, $1 and $2.

The `number` box connecting to the right inlet, is the font size of the text measured in points. You can check out more parameters for the `text2d` object by right-clicking or *Ctrl*-clicking on it to show the **help** menu. The result of the sample patch is as follows:

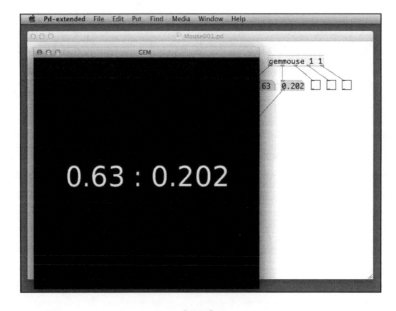

For the `text3d` object, we do not have the anti-alias option. We can have geometric transformation in three-dimensional space, such as rotation. Here is the sample patch and the result display.

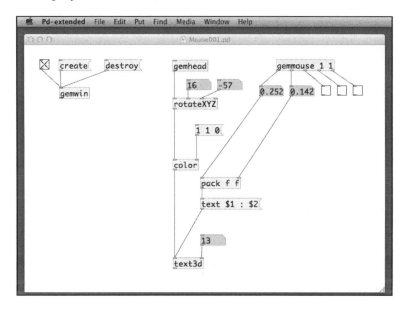

The result image will be similar to the previous example except that we have the rotation in the three-dimensional space.

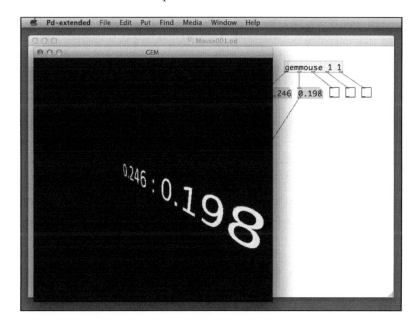

Knowing the mouse position, we can create our first interactive patch by making a graphical shape to follow the mouse. Create another patch `Mouse002.pd` with the GEM window basic setup. In the patch window, we create a `gemhead` object with a small `square` object with size 0.2.

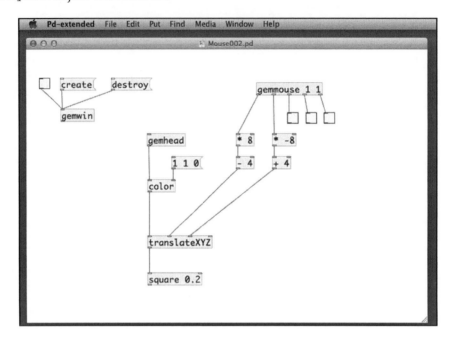

The patch makes use of a `translateXYZ` object to follow the mouse cursor. Remember that in *Chapter 2, Computer Graphics with the GEM Library*, we understood that the width and height of the default GEM window in terms of its measuring units are both ranging from -4 to 4. That is, both width and height are 8 units, with origin (0, 0) at the center. In order to convert the normalized mouse position to the GEM window unit, we have to scale the interval from (0, 1) to (-4, 4). In the patch shown in the preceding screenshot, there are two sets of calculation. The first `*` 8 and `–` 4 are for the X direction. The second `*` `-8` and `+` 4 are for the Y direction. We need to multiply the mouse position by 8 and subtract it by 4. For the Y-axis, the direction is reversed. Mouse position is zero on the top margin and one on the bottom margin, while the graphics is 4 on the top margin and -4 on the bottom margin. In this case, we need to multiply the mouse position by -8 and add 4 to it.

So far, we have not taken into account the mouse button. In the next example, we make use of the left mouse button to change color of the square. We create another patch Mouse003.pd to save the result.

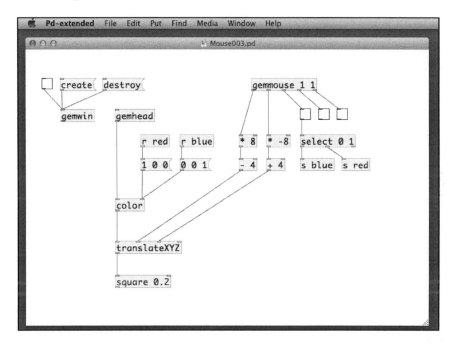

In the preceding screenshot of the patch, the third outlet of the gemmouse object is the indicator for the left mouse button. A value 1 indicates the button being pressed and a value 0 indicates the button released. We use a toggle box under the third gemmouse object outlet to show this status. Below the toggle box is the select 0 1 object. It checks the status of the toggle box. If it is 0 (button released), it sends a bang message to the blue color message, through the s blue object. If it is 1 (button pressed), it sends a bang message to the red color message, through the s red object. Since the square always follows the mouse, it has an illusion that you are clicking on the square.

In the previous example, the color change responds to the *press* and *release* actions of the left mouse button. In the following next example, Mouse004.pd, it implements a toggle switch. Clicking on it once changes to blue and remains blue even you release the mouse button. Clicking on it again changes to red and remains red until you click again.

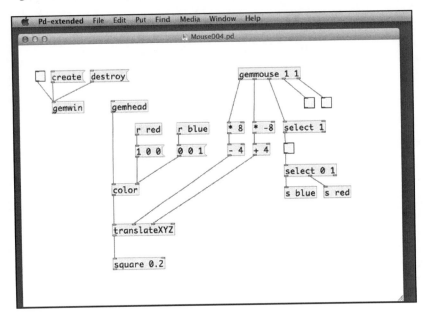

Note the use of a toggle box between two select objects. It is like an indicator that stores the status of the button. Depending on whether it is 0 or 1, the second select 0 1 object will send out a bang message to blue or red messages.

In the previous examples, Mouse004.pd we saw how the square object always follows the mouse cursor. The next challenge will be a patch to implement the mouse drag action. The square only follows the mouse cursor whenever the left mouse button is pressed down. When you release the button, the square stops following the mouse.

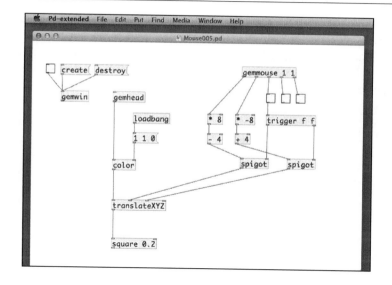

The patch in the preceding image makes use of a new object — spigot. It is a gate. When its right inlet is non-zero, the left inlet message will pass through the object to the outlet. When its right inlet is zero, the left inlet message will be blocked. In this case, the mouse position information will only send to the translateXYZ object whenever you are clicking down the left mouse button.

If we combine the previous example in the *Chapter 3, Image Processing*, on the topic of single buffer, we can implement a simple drawing program. With single buffer, we use the mouse position and the left button to leave marks on the GEM window, and the right button to clear the screen.

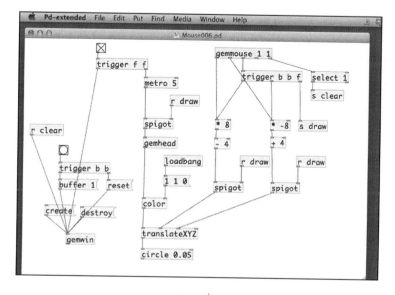

Here is a sample image where we can use the mouse to draw in the GEM window.

The key object is the `spigot`. It is very useful in handling logic. In this example, it relies on the left mouse button status. A value one (mouse button pressed) will turn on the `gemhead` object rendering with the position update for the tiny circle.

 Note also the `loadbang` object to initialize the color for the circle.

Responding to keyboard events

Apart from the computer mouse, the keyboard is the other common interface that we work with a computer system. In GEM library, there are two objects: `gemkeyboard` and `gemkeyname`. In the following patch `Keyboard001.pd`, we take a look at the behavior of the two objects. Similar to `gemmouse`, we have to click upon the GEM window to make it active first, before the keyboard events can be detected.

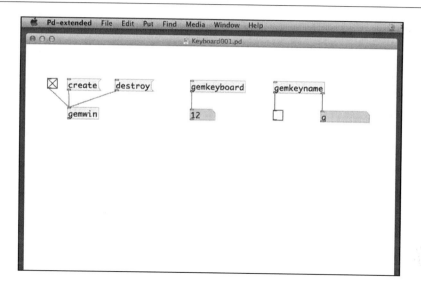

The first object—gemkeyboard, will return a number when you press a key on your keyboard. It detects the key down event, not the key up. The number is the key code representing that particular key in GEM library. Please note that different operating systems, such as Windows, OSX, and Linux may have different key codes for the same key. You need to test the number before porting a patch from one platform to others.

The second object—gemkeyname, will return a symbol when you press a key. It is the actual symbol itself, for example, the character a, b. The first outlet is a `toggle` box. Pressing any key gives 1. Releasing any key, it gives 0. In this case, this object can detect both key down and key up events. We can add the `bang` boxes to illustrate this.

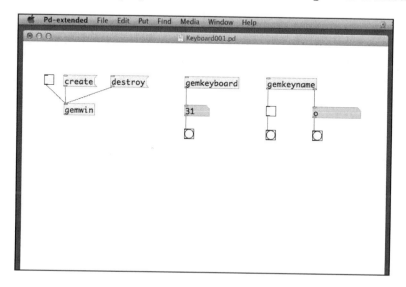

The `bang` box under `gemkeyboard` flashes only once when you press and release a key. Pressing-and-holding the key will not generate further `bang` messages. For `gemkeyname`, both the `bang` boxes flash twice when you press and release a key, one for the key down and one for the key up. Again, we can use the `text2d` or `text3d` objects to display the key we have pressed on the keyboard. We are going to try it in another patch, `Keyboard002.pd`. We display the key symbol directly through a `text2d` object. Using the `toggle` box for key down and key up events, we use it to change the color of the text.

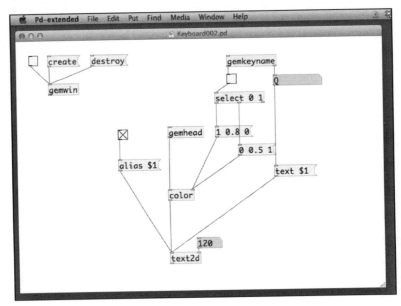

In the next example `Keyboard003.pd`, we use the *left arrow* and *right arrow* keys to decrease and increase a number. The key numbers we use are for Mac OSX 10.8. The number is displayed in the GEM window through a `text2d` object.

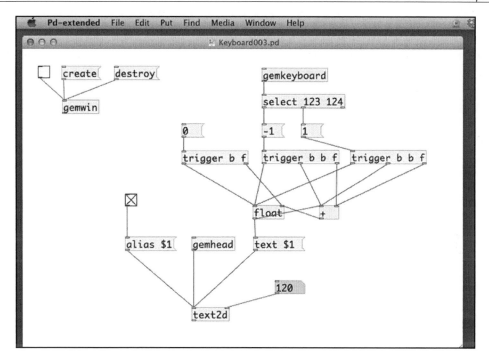

Remember the counter example in *Chapter 1, Getting Started with Pure Data*. The float and plus objects implement a recursive adding operation. The only difference here is that we use two message boxes (right inlet) for the plus object. It can either be -1 or 1, depending on which key you press, *left arrow* or *right arrow*. The two trigger objects below the -1 and 1 messages are essential. They first route the number to the right inlet of the plus object. And they send a bang message first to the plus object to add the existing number with either -1 or 1. Finally, they send another bang message to the float object to pass the result to the text $1 message for display. We also include a 0 message to reset the number to 0.

With this keyboard-controlled counter, we can use it to rotate a 3D shape. You can see how it works in this following example Keyboard004.pd. We increase the numbers to -5 and 5 for more obvious effect.

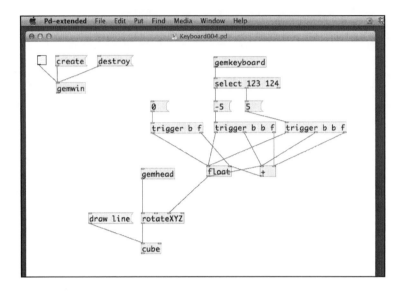

You may find that it is necessary to repeatedly press-and-release the key to rotate the cube object continuously. The preceding patch does not take care of press-and-hold action for a keyboard event. To handle it, we create another patch in Keyboard005. pd. Again, we have to make use of the metro object to rotate the cube object continuously when you hold down the key.

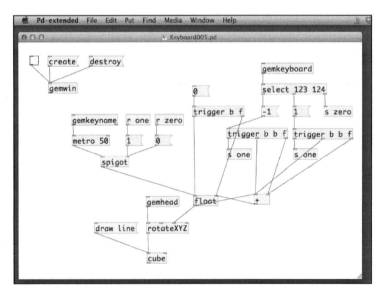

We take advantage of the `toggle` output from the `gemkeyname` object. The `spigot` object under the `metro` object will route through the `bang` message to the counter (the `float` object) when either the *left arrow* or *right arrow* key is pressed.

Creating a graphical button

In this section, we prepare a graphical button that responds to a mouse click action. From previous sections, we understand how to use `gemmouse` and its outlets to check if buttons are clicked or not. To create a graphical button, we need to indicate if the mouse click is within the proximity of the button in the GEM window. To make it simple, we start with a square button in this `Button001.pd`.

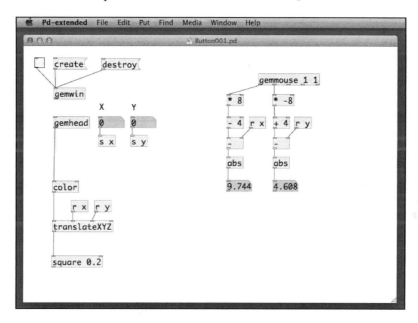

The first thing we have to check is the proximity. It is actually the distance between the center of the button and the current mouse position. In the patch, we use the GEM 3D space coordinates. The calculation following the `gemmouse` object is the same as the previous section. The scaling from the range of 1 to the range of 8 is dependent on the window size. In the default square window of 500 by 500 pixels, we are using the window margins from -4 to 4.

The two number boxes with label X and Y are the location of the button. The patch computes the difference between the X position of the button with the X position of the mouse, and also the difference between the Y position of the button with the Y position of the mouse. It takes the absolute values `abs` of the differences, since we do not concern the direction.

The formulae are:

Difference in X position = abs(X position of mouse - X position of square)

Difference in Y position = abs(Y position of mouse - Y position of square)

Now try moving the mouse toward and away from the square button. Notice the changes in the two number boxes below the abs objects. If the mouse is within the boundary of the square, both number values will be less than 0.2. In this case, we can make a comparison with a threshold, say 0.2. We can use the comparison operators, such as, <, >, <=, or >=.

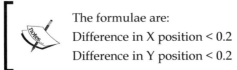

The formulae are:

Difference in X position < 0.2

Difference in Y position < 0.2

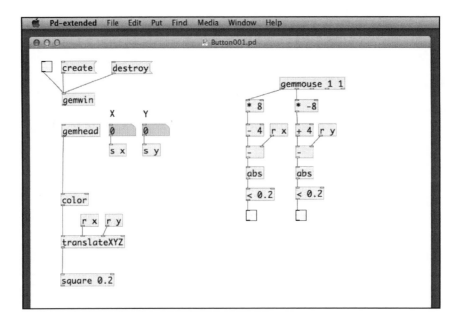

We use a toggle object to display the comparison result here. You will find that both the toggle boxes need to be 1 (true) for the mouse pointer to be inside the square button. In this case, we need the logical operators to combine the result of the two toggle boxes. The common logical operators are && and ||. The && is the logical AND operator. It returns 1 if both inputs are 1. The || is the logical OR operator. It returns 1 if either one input or both are 1. In the example, we need the logical AND operator. We need both values to be less than 0.2.

The formula is:

(Difference in X position < 0.2) && (Difference in Y position < 0.2)

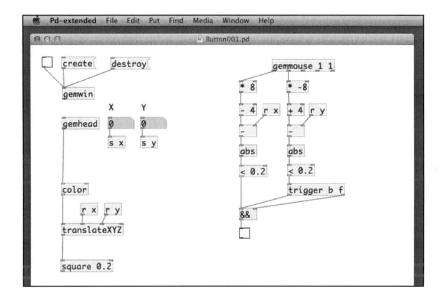

Finally in the following image, we combine the proximity checking with the pressing of the left mouse button with a spigot object. The last toggle box is the general status of the button.

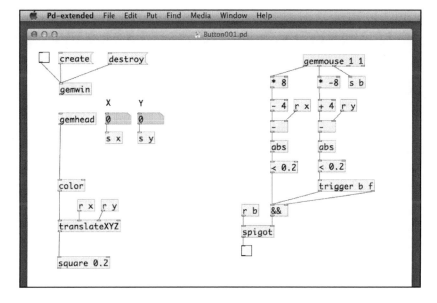

One more feature with the button is the status feedback. We can give different colors to the square to indicate its status. In the following patch, we have three messages for the color object: white, yellow, and red. After the logical AND operator, &&, we have a `select 0 1` object to detect if the mouse position is outside or within the square button. A result 0, that is outside the square, will send the white message. A result 1, that is within the square, will send the yellow message. In addition, the left mouse button status, sending through the s b object, will go to the `spigot` object. When the mouse position is within the square and the left button is down, the second `select 0 1` object will then send the red message to the color object.

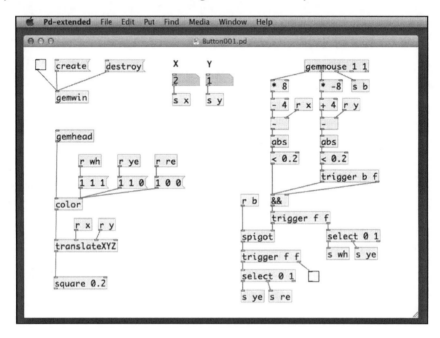

Preparing a video-jockey instrument

In this section, we are going to create a simple video controller tool that is similar to common video jockey equipment that mixes videos and applies effects in real time. Take a look of what we have done in the *Chapter 3, Image Processing*, when we worked with digital video with `pix_film`.

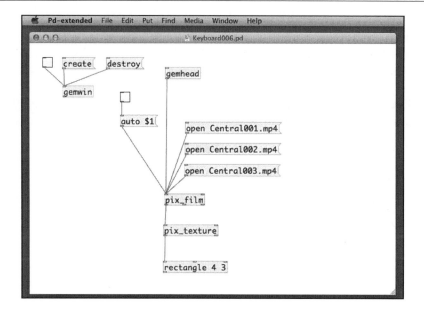

If we want to change the video playing, we have to click on the **open** message. When we are working in a live performance, we would like the audience to immerse into the visual imagery. It is not a good idea to switch back and forth to the patch window to click on the messages. In this case, we can make use of the keyboard object, such as the gemkeyboard.

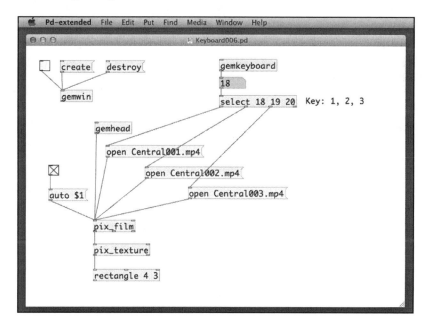

In the patch, we have assigned the numeric keys, 1, 2, and 3 to select different videos for playback. If we repeatedly press the same key, we will notice that the same video will playback from beginning again and again. In some applications, you may not want this. To handle it, we introduce another object — change.

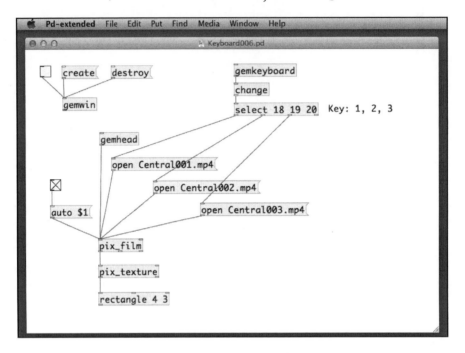

The change object passes its input to the outlet only when it changes. If you repeatedly press on the same key, only the first message will pass through the change object. In this patch, the same video will play continuously. When you press a new key, it then sends the signal through. In the next version, we use the pix_mix object we have done in *Chapter 3, Image Processing*, to mix two videos together.

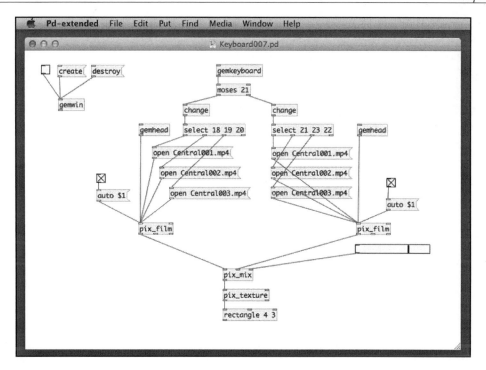

As shown in the previous example screenshot, the `pix_mix` object needs two pixel data inputs. The last inlet is a number ranges between 0 and 1. For this, we have created a horizontal slider that ranges from 0 to 1. Note that there is a `moses` object in the beginning of the patch. It is a routing object that sends the signal to the left outlet if the incoming signal is less than the parameter, which in this case is 21. If the incoming signal is larger or equal to the parameter, it sends the signal to the right outlet. We use it to route the left and right video signals. The numeric key *1*, *2*, or *3* controls the left video. The key *4*, *5*, or *6* controls the right video. Note also that the key code representations for key *4*, *5*, and *6* are 21, 23, and 22, respectively in the Mac OSX version of Pure Data. The rest of the patch is similar to the last version.

To improve this version, we have to replace the horizontal slider because it requires users intervention to switch between the GEM window and the patch window. We can use the gemmouse object to take care of it.

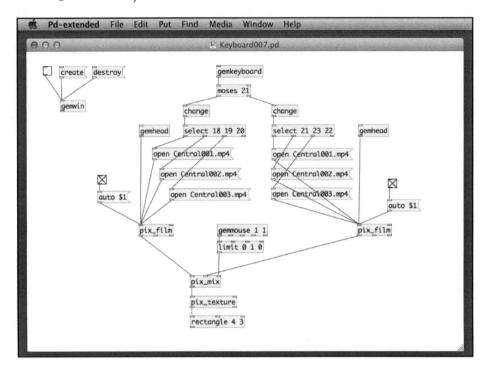

We can also use a limit object to clamp the range of the gemmouse object to strictly within 0 and 1. Moving the mouse left and right will mix the two incoming videos, similar to a cross-fader in the VJ instrument.

In the next patch, Effect001.pd, we are going to explore the ways to implement a live switching effect controller. It makes use of the pixel effects we have come across in *Chapter 3, Image Processing*.

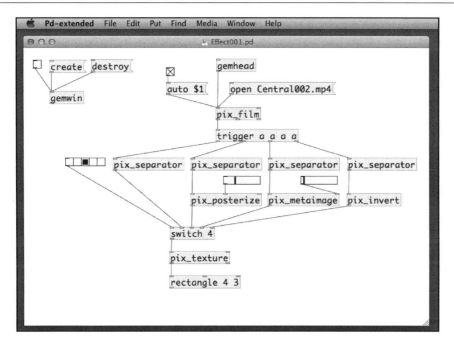

The effects are `pix_posterize`, `pix_metaimage`, and `pix_invert`. In *Chapter 3*, *Image Processing*, we have learned how to use the `pix_metaimage` and `pix_invert` objects. The `pix_posterize` object produces a **color posterization effect** (color depth reduction) for the incoming image. In the preceding patch, it needs a horizontal slider with range between 0 and 1 to control the posterization amount. We use a `pix_separator` object to isolate each branch of the pixel effects. It is similar to the `separator` object that we learned in *Chapter 2*, *Computer Graphics with the GEM Library*. If we do not isolate them, the pixel effects will mix together. The core logic of the patch is the `switch` object. It depends on the number received in the left inlet, that is the horizontal radio buttons in the example, to determine which other inlets to send through to the outlet.

The improved version is to get rid of the radio buttons and uses keyboard to control the effect switching. The solution is the combination of the `gemkeyboard` and `select` objects again.

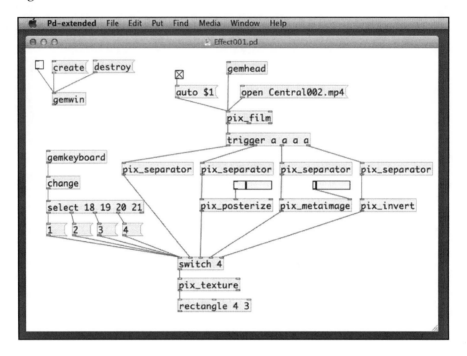

In this section, we have tried out basic functions of VJ instrument. It will be nice to combine the video switching, video mixing, and effects switching into one single patch for live performance. As an exercise, interested readers can attempt to integrate the three patches into one.

Creating interactive animation

In the last section of this chapter, we are going to create an interactive animation. It is a simplified version of the classic *Pong Game*.

Before we get on with the Pure Data patch, we first draft a brief plan about the steps we have to do.

- Animate the moving ball
- Bounce the ball on the four margins
- Create the paddle control
- Keep and display the score

Animate the moving ball

We start with a ball that bounces around in the GEM window. Remember that we use the `metro` object to animate graphics in the *Chapter 2, Computer Graphics with the GEM Library*. To make a ball move, we change its position within the GEM window by using the `translateXYZ` object. Here is the first version of the patch `Pong001.pd`.

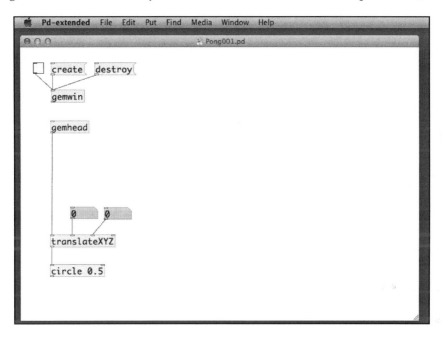

Changing the two number boxes for the `translateXYZ` object will move the ball around. In order to create an animation, we need to use the `metro` object to automate the changing of the numbers. In *Chapter 2, Computer Graphics with the GEM Library*, we have used a `counter` object to create the movement. To create a more flexible motion, such as changing speed, changing direction, we may need to use a variable to store the current position of the ball. We then add a value to the variable to increase or decrease its value, and thus create an illusion of motion. For example, if the ball is in the center of the window (0, 0) and we add 0.1 to its X position for every frame controlled by the `metro` object. We can create an animation of the ball moving from the center to the right-hand side with a step of 0.1 units per frame.

In this case, we need a variable—the `float` object, to maintain the current X position of the ball and another number to store the step.

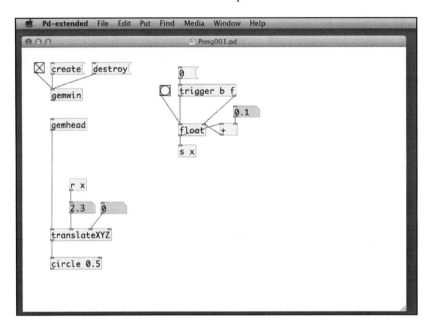

Bouncing the ball on the four margins

Every time you click on the **bang** button, the ball moves toward the right margin by 0.1 units. The 0 message box and the `trigger` object are for the purpose of resetting the X position to 0. You can click on the **bang** button until the X position reaches 4 when half of the ball is out of the right margin. We have to plan how we can let the ball rebound when it hits the right margin. Better still, we can start the bouncing process when the X position reaches 3.5, that is that the surface of the ball hits the right margin. The bouncing process is just the reversed movement of the ball. Instead of moving to the right, we have to let the ball move toward the left, once it hits the right margin. In this case, we have to decrease the X position of the ball, instead of increasing it. We can, however, add a negative number (-0.1) to the X position every time we click on the **bang** button.

The logic involves a decision. It has to check the current X position of the ball. If it exceeds 3.5, it has to change the step from 0.1 to -0.1. We use the 'greater than' comparison object, >.

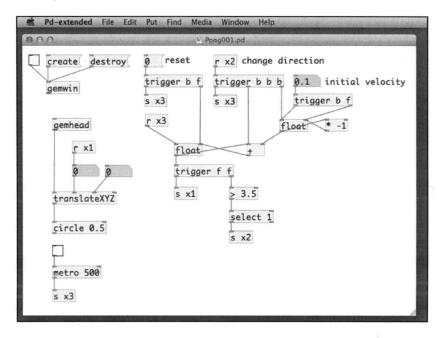

This one looks complicated. We have two variables. The first one (left) is the X position of the ball. The second one is the velocity in X direction. Both are implemented by the `float` object. The X position variable will add the X velocity variable in every frame. It also checks the condition if it is greater than 3.5 or not. If it is, the `select` object will send a `bang` message to the X velocity variable to multiply itself with -1. Note the comment **change direction**. Essentially, the X velocity changes from 0.1 to -0.1. In later frames, the direction changes from right to left (negative). The `0` message resets the initial X position to 0. The number box next to the comment **initial velocity** sets the initial velocity of the movement. We type `0.1` in this number box. Note also the `trigger` object under **change direction**. We have to make sure that the multiplication, addition, and sending out of the X position are all completed in one frame.

When you switch on the `metro` box, the circle moves from the center to the right margin and bounces back to the left margin. Upon hitting the left margin, it disappears. Remember that we only implement the hit test for the right margin. We have to include the left margin in the next version.

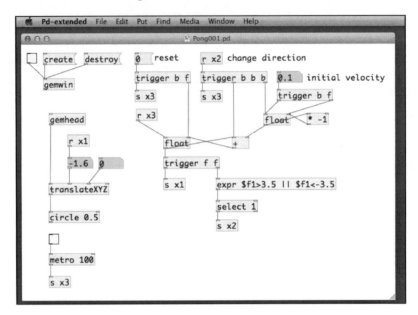

Other than using two individual comparison objects, We combine the two into one single object—the `expr` object. It is the expression object. We can specify any mathematical expression as the parameter of the `expr` object. If you require external parameters outside the object, you can use the notation $f1, and which is the first extra inlet. If you have more than one parameter, you can have $f2, $f3, and so on. In our case, we have only one. The expression we have is a logical one. It first compares if the current X position is greater than 3.5 or not. It then compares if the current X position is less than -3.5 or not. If any or both of the conditions are true, that is a logical OR, it returns true (a number 1). The subsequent `select` object will trigger the direction change if it receives 1 from the expression.

Now, we have a ball that can bounce between the left and right margin. We can duplicate the whole set for the Y direction. Remember to change all the labels for the send and receive objects from x to y.

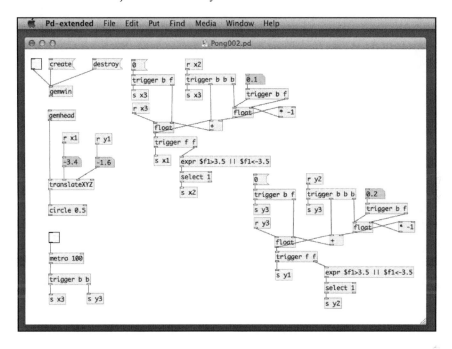

You can key in different values for the initial velocity of X and Y directions. In the example, we use 0.1 and 0.2. Start the metro object and observe the movement of the ball across the GEM window. You can adjust the parameter of the metro object to change the speed.

If we would like to introduce more interactive behavior of the ball, the patch grows too complex. The connection lines become messy. Pure Data has two ways to simplify the patch. The first one is sub-patch. The second one is abstraction. The abstraction is more versatile and we are going to look into it now. The concept is similar to the subroutine or function in other text based programming languages. To illustrate the use of abstraction, We define a simple task:

- Create a patch Test002.pd to contain this abstraction
- Give it two numeric inlets
- Add one to the left inlet to produce the left outlet
- Subtract one from the right inlet to produce the right outlet

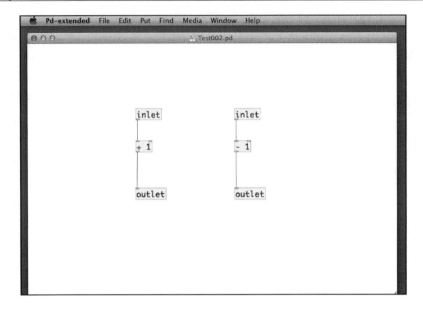

There are two new objects: inlet and outlet. The abstraction will have a name Test002. We can use it just like a common object as long as it is in the same folder with your other patches. The inlet object defines an input for the abstraction Test002. Note that the order of the inlets matters. The left one corresponds to the left inlet. The right one corresponds to the right inlet. If we have more than two inlets, the order matches with the left to right position of the inlet objects. The following patch is different from the previous one in the order of the inlets.

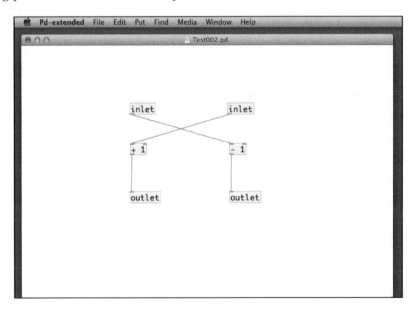

Similarly, the order of the outlets matters too. The left outlet will be the left outlet of the abstraction, the right one be the right outlet. Here is the patch `Test001.pd` that makes use of the `Test002` abstraction. Observe how the input numbers relate with the output numbers.

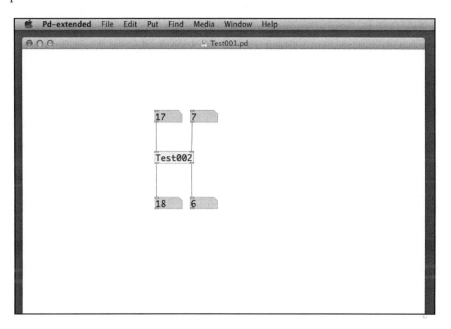

Using the concept of abstraction, we move out the details of the moving ball into an external patch named `Ball.pd`. The design of an abstraction is an art. We need to consider what to put inside the abstraction and what inlets and outlets to interface with the outside calling patch. We use a number of `send` and `receive` objects for the bouncing ball example. The labels x1, y1, and so on may cause trouble if you have the same labels in your calling patch. In this case, the labels inside the abstraction will have a special prefix $0-. The label x1 becomes $0-x1.

For each patch, the $0 will be replaced with a unique 4 digits number. If you have multiple instances of an abstraction that contains the label $0-x1, they will essentially be different. The following patch will display the value of $0 for each instance of the same abstraction.

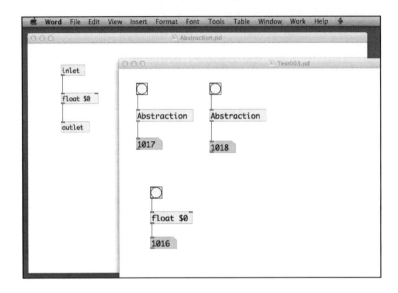

Let us go back and take a look of the Ball abstraction.

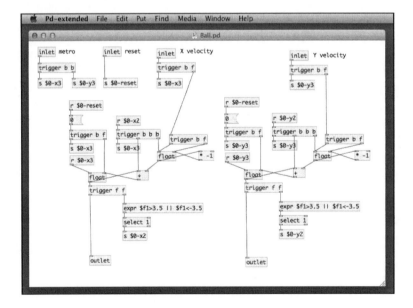

The abstraction `Ball` has four inlets. The first one is the clock `bang` message from `metro`. The second is another `bang` message to reset the initial position to the center (0, 0). The third and the last inlets are velocity in X and Y directions. All labels now have the prefix `$0-`. To use the abstraction, we include the `gemhead`, `translateXYZ`, and `circle` objects to display.

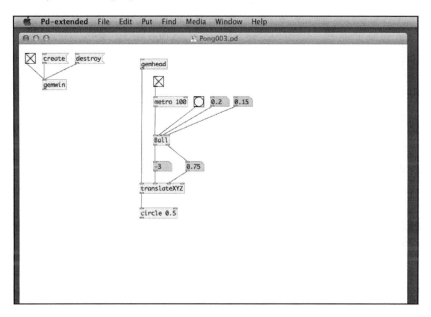

The first inlet is the `bang` message from `metro`. It causes the updates of the X and Y positions of the ball in every frame. The second inlet is the `bang` message to reset the ball to the center. The last two number boxes are the X and Y velocity. It greatly reduces the complexity of the main calling patch. Nevertheless, our abstraction `Ball` is not perfect. It makes a number of assumptions. The first is the GEM window size, that is a square with margins from -4 to 4. The second is the size of the ball, 0.5 units for the radius. Actually, we can use more inlets to take in the size of the window and the ball. At this point, we settle for this version.

If you would like to introduce one more ball in the GEM window, you can just duplicate the whole gemhead group. By using different color and initial velocity, we can have two balls moving around in the window.

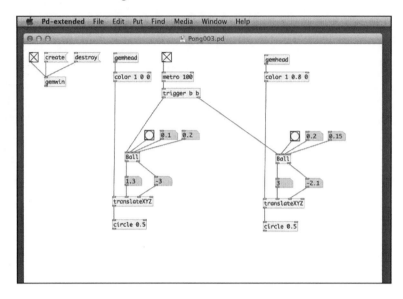

Here is the result GEM window display with two instances of the Ball abstraction.

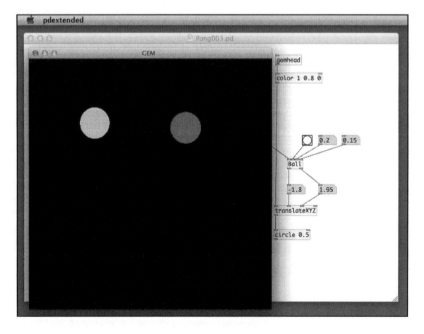

Creating the paddle control

In the previous example, the bouncing ball moves by itself. To introduce interactivity, we add another graphic for it to hit upon. To simplify the logic, we add a rectangular block that moves left and right along the bottom margin. We use the keyboard *left arrow* and *right arrow* keys to control the movement.

From the keyboard event section, we understand the key codes for the *left* and *right* keys are 123 and 124, respectively. Again, we need a temporary storage—variable to keep the current position of the rectangular block. It needs a `float` object again. Pressing the *left* key will add a negative number to the `float` object. Pressing the *right* key will add a positive number to the `float` object. A `translateXYZ` object will pick up this floating-point number to change the X position of the block. Here is the part of the patch that handles the moving rectangular block.

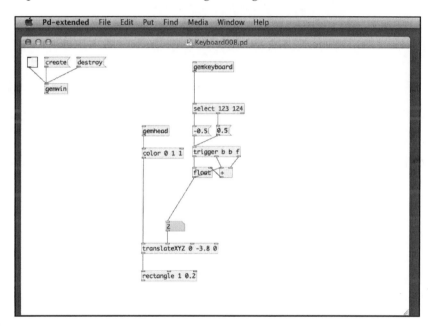

The GEM window display of the paddle will be such as the following screenshot:

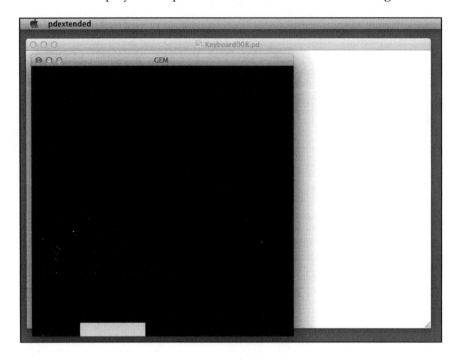

Now we combine the patch with the bouncing ball one. The difficult part is to detect when the ball hits upon the top of the rectangular block. This application is a simple version as it only performs hit test on the bottom of the ball and the top of the block. Since the block only moves left and right, we can just test the following two conditions:

- The bottom of the ball hits upon the top of the block. That is, the center of the ball is less than a certain number.

- When the center of the ball is less than that number, the ball is within the range of the rectangular block. That is, the center of the ball is within a certain range in X direction, determined by the X position of the block.

In the combined patch, we click-and-drag the Y position number box for the ball until it just touches upon the rectangular block. The value is around -3.1.

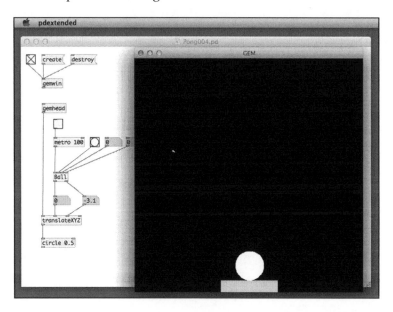

Now we can click-and-drag the X position number box for the ball to test the range in X direction of the rectangular block. The center of the block in X direction is zero. Here is the left most position for the ball. The value is -1.

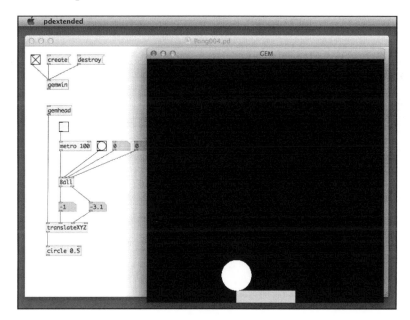

Here is the right most position for the ball. The value is 1.

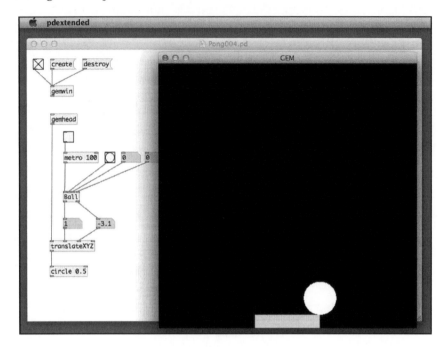

By using the figures, we rewrite the previous two conditions.

- The Y position of the ball is less than -3.1
- The X position of the ball is within the range of -1 to 1 relative to the X position of the rectangular block

To put it in Pure Data terminologies, we further rewrite the conditions.

- The Y position of the ball is less than -3.1
- The absolute value of the difference between the X position of the ball and the rectangular block is less than 1

In the following patch Pong004.pd, we put in the two conditions in one single expr object. The first parameter comes from the absolute value of the difference between the two X positions. The second parameter is the Y position of the ball. The toggle box after the expr object indicates whether there is a hit or not. You can observe the status of this toggle box when you play around with the keyboard controlled rectangular block.

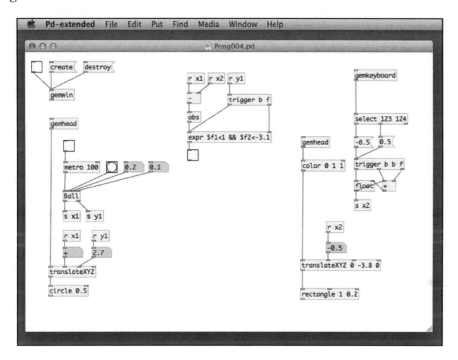

In game programming, this is called collision detection. After we implement this, the remaining part is the collision response. That is how the two graphical objects behave after the collision. In our example, the ball will bounce upward upon collision. In other words, it changes its Y direction. To achieve this, we have to modify the Ball. pd abstraction to cater for such action. Changing direction is already catered for within the abstraction. We multiply a -1 to the existing velocity. The two receive objects with labels, $0-x2 and $0-y2 are the entry points to receive a bang message for changing the X and Y directions respectively. The only missing thing is the inlet to interface with the calling patch.

The patch `Pong004.pd` needs to send a `bang` message to the `Ball.pd` abstraction to initiate a Y direction change when the ball hits upon the rectangular block. To achieve this, we add two more inlets for the X and Y direction changes. In our case, we only use the Y direction for the current example.

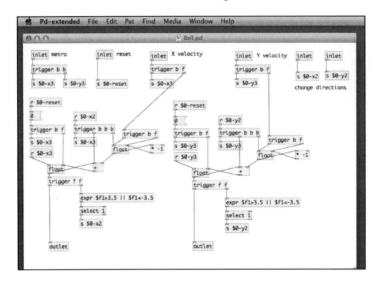

To use the two new inlets, it is very simple. In the patch `Pong004.pd`, after we compute the conditional expression, we use a `select` object to detect the value 1. And use it to send out a `bang` message to the Y direction change inlet (right most) of the new `Ball.pd` abstraction. We also modify the patch to assign two random values for the initial velocity in X and Y directions.

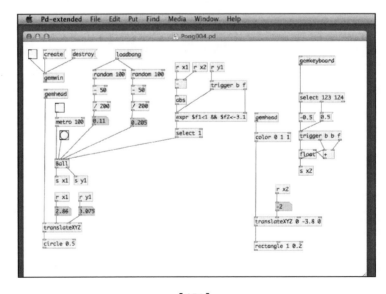

Keeping and displaying the score

One last thing you can add is a score. In the next patch `Pong005.pd`, we put another `float` object to store the score. Every time there is a hit, the `select` object sends out a `bang` message to increment the number by 1. We use another `text2d` object to display the number on the GEM window.

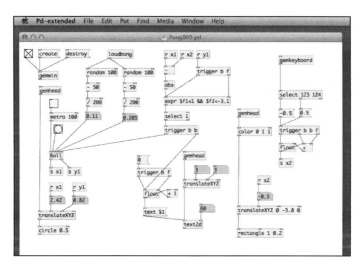

You can use the number box (right inlet) of `text2d` to control the display size of the score. To reset the score, you can click on the **0** message above the **text $1** message. You can also modify the number boxes for the `translateXYZ` object for the `text2d` object to relocate the position of the score display.

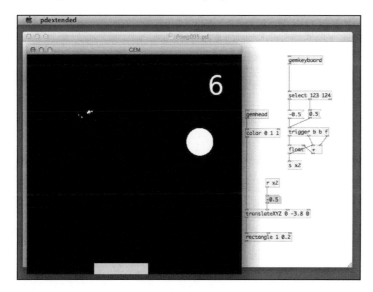

Summary

In this chapter, we start to explore interactivity by using the common interaction devices, the mouse and the keyboard. By using the `gemmouse` and `gemkeyboard` objects, we implemented graphical buttons, a controller for a video-jockey application, and a cross-fader for mixing videos. We also created interactive animations that demonstrate game-like features. To avoid being too complex in one single patch, we took advantage of the abstraction in Pure Data to use a separate patch file for commonly referenced objects. The interactive features we explored so far limit to the keyboard and mouse. In *Chapter 5, Motion Detection*, we start using the webcam to detect whole body interaction with motion tracking features in GEM.

5
Motion Detection

In this chapter, we plan to extend the interactivity beyond the use of mouse and keyboard. Motion detection needs the computer webcam to capture and detect the body movement of users. In *Chapter 3*, *Image Processing*, we worked with the `pix_video` object to obtain the live video stream. So far, we only displayed the video or applied effects on it. We have no idea about what is happening within the video image. In the coming sections, we try to make sense of the image.

In a video frame, all we know is the width, height of the frame, the number of pixels, and the red, green, and blue color components of each pixel. We have no idea whether there is a bird or pig in the frame. And we do not know whether the subject in the video frame is moving or not. In order to identify movement, we have to compare a frame with another reference frame. The following sections will introduce a number of topics including:

- Obtaining the frame difference
- Detecting presence
- Detecting motion
- Creating a motion detection animation
- Comparing colors
- Performing color detection
- Making an air drum

To work with the examples, you need to have a webcam installed on your computer.

Obtaining the frame difference

To begin with, we create a patch with name `Frame001.pd`. Put in all those elements for displaying the live webcam image in a rectangle. We use a `dimen 800 600` message for the `gemwin` object to show the GEM window in 800 x 600 pixels. We plan to display the video image in the full size of the window.

From *Chapter 2, Computer Graphics with the GEM Library*, we understood that a square of size 4 x 4 occupied the default GEM window. The aspect ratio of the current GEM window is now 4:3. We use a rectangle of size 5.33 x 4 (4:3 aspect ratio) to cover the whole GEM window:

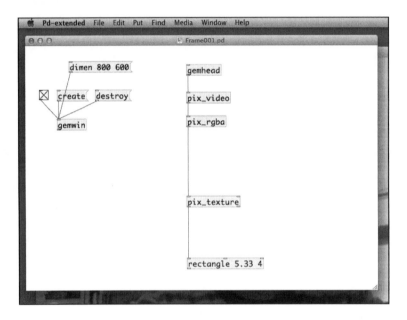

Now we have one single frame of the video image. To make a comparison with another frame, we have to store that frame in memory. In *Chapter 3, Image Processing*, we learned the use of the `pix_buffer` object. We can store a frame by using `pix_buffer_write` and retrieve it for comparison by using `pix_buffer_read`. In the following patch, you can click on the bang box to store a copy of the current video frame in the buffer. The latest video frame will compare against the stored copy, as shown in the following screenshot:

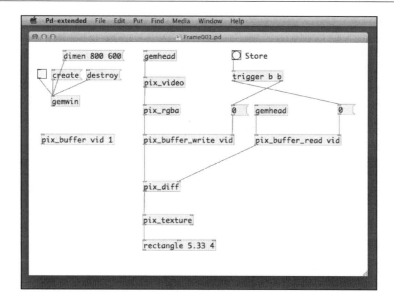

The object to compare two frames is `pix_diff`. It is similar to the **Difference layer** option in Photoshop. Those pixels that are the same in both frames are black. The color areas are those with changes across the two frames. Here is what you would expect in the GEM window:

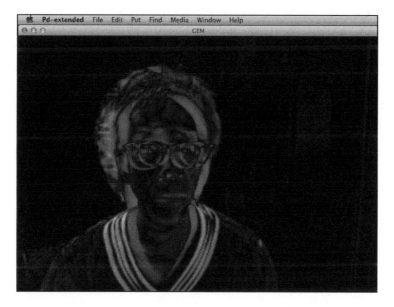

You may remember that the effect is similar to what we have done with the pix_
background object in *Chapter 3, Image Processing*. To further simplify the image, we
can get rid of the color and use only black and white to indicate the changes:

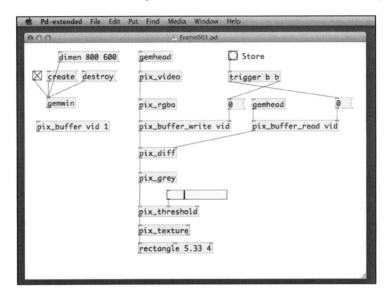

The pix_grey object converts a color image into grey scale. The pix_threshold
object will zero out the pixels (black) with color information lower than a threshold
value supplied by the horizontal slider that has value between 0 and 1. Refer to the
following screenshot:

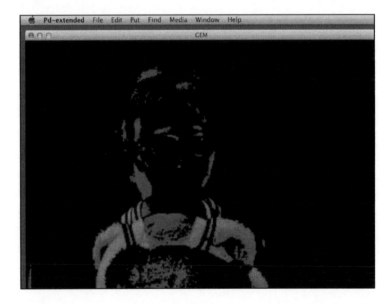

Note that a default slider has a value between 0 and 127. You have to change the range to 0 and 1 using the **Properties** window of the slider.

In this case, we can obtain the information about those pixels that are different from the stored image.

Detecting presence

Based on the knowledge about those pixels that have changed between the stored image and the current video image, we can detect the presence of a foreground subject in front of a static background. Point your webcam in front of a relatively static background; click on the bang box, which is next to the `Store` comment, to store the background image in the `pix_buffer` object. Anything that appears in front of the background will be shown in the GEM window. Now we can ask the question: how can we know if there is anything present in front of the background? The answer will be in the `pix_blob` object:

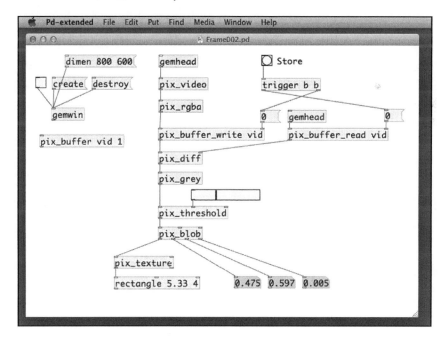

The `pix_blob` object calculates the centroid of an image.

The centroid (http://en.wikipedia.org/wiki/Centroid) of an image is its center of mass. Imagine that you cut out the shape of the image in a cardboard. The centroid is the center of mass of that piece of cardboard. You can balance the cardboard by using one finger to hold it as the center of mass.

In our example, the image is mostly a black-grey scale image. The `pix_blob` object finds out the center of the nonblack pixels and returns its position in the first and second outlets. The third outlet indicates the size of the nonblack pixel group. To detect the presence of a foreground subject in front of the background, the first and second number boxes connected to the corresponding `pix_blob` outlets will return roughly the center of the foreground subject. The third number box will tell how big that foreground subject is.

If you pay attention to the changes in the three number boxes, you can guess how we will implement the way to detect presence. When you click on the store image bang button, the third number box (size) will turn zero immediately. Once you enter into the frame, in front of the background, the number increases. The bigger the portion you occupy of the frame, the larger the number is. To complete the logic, we can check whether the third number box value is greater than a predefined number. If it is, we conclude that something is present in front of the background. If it is not, there is nothing in front of the background. The following patch `Frame002.pd` will try to display a warning message when something is present:

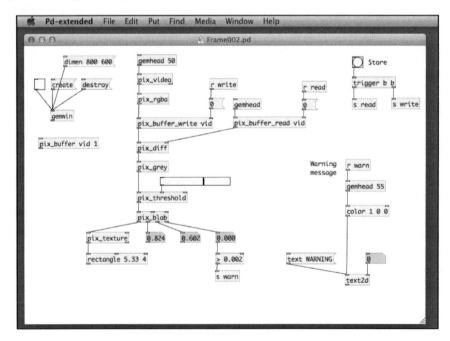

A comparison object > 0.002 detects the size of the grey area (blob). If it is true, it sends a value 1 to the gemhead object for the warning text to display. If it is false, it sends a value 0. We'll use a new technique to turn on/off the text. Each gemhead object can accept a toggle input to turn it on or off. A value 1 enables the rendering of that gemhead path. A value 0 disables the rendering. When you first click on the store image bang button, the third number box value drops to 0. Minor changes in the background will not trigger the text message:

If there is significant change in front of the background, the size number box will have a value larger than 0.002. It thus enables the rendering of the text2d message to display the **WARNING** message.

After you click on the **Store** bang box, you can drag the horizontal slider attached to the pix_threshold object. Drag it towards the right-hand side until the image in the GEM window turns completely black. It will roughly be the threshold value. Note also that we use a number in each gemhead object. It is the rendering order. The default one is 50. The larger number will be rendered after the lower number. In this case, the gemhead object for the pix_video object will render first. The gemhead object for the text2d object will render afterwards.

In this case, we can guarantee that the text will always be on top of the video:

If you remember that the `pix_background` object in the *Chapter 3, Image Processing*, the logic is the same. Actually, you can replace the previous version with a single `pix_background` object. A `reset` message will replace the bang button to store the background image. In the following patch, it will show either the clear or warning message on the screen, depending on the presence of a subject in front of the background image:

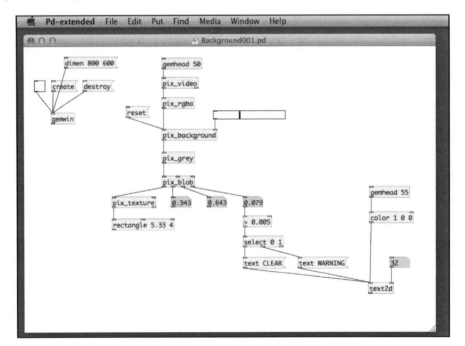

The GEM window at this moment shows only a black screen when there isn't anything in front of the background. For most applications, it would be better to have the live video image on screen. In the following patch, we split the video signal into two – one to the `pix_background` object for detection and one to the `pix_texture` object for display:

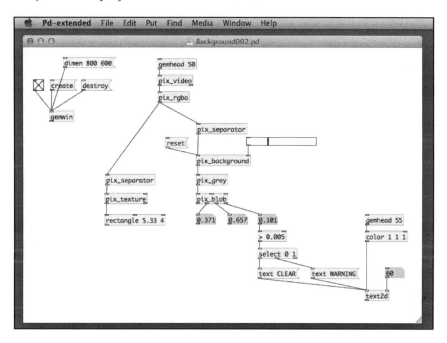

The patch requires two `pix_separator` objects to separate the two video streams from `pix_video`, in order not to let one affect the other. Here is the background image after clicking on the `reset` message:

The `warning` message shows up after the subject entered the frame, and is triggered by the comparison object `> 0.005` in the patch:

We have been using the `pix_blob` object to detect presence in front of a static background image. The `pix_blob` object will also return the position of the subject (`blob`) in front of the webcam. We are going to look into this in the next section.

Detecting motion

We compare the current video image with a predefined background image to detect presence. To detect motion, we compare the current video image with a previous frame. To achieve this task, we have to make use of the `pix_delay` object to delay a video frame:

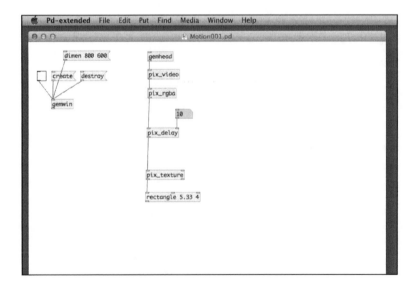

The number box in the right-hand inlet of the `pix_delay` object specifies the number of frames to delay. The patch `Motion001.pd` delays the video image for a number of frames and displays it on the GEM window. To make comparison, we use the current video frame and the delayed frame with the same `pix_diff` object:

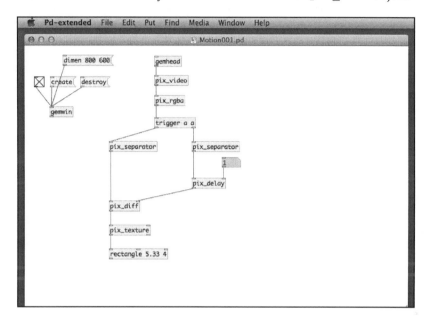

Usually, we use the value 1 in the number box for the `pix_delay` object to retrieve the previous frame. The guideline is to track faster motion, use a smaller number (for example, 1) to track slower motion, use a bigger number. The image in the GEM window is the frame difference between the two frames:

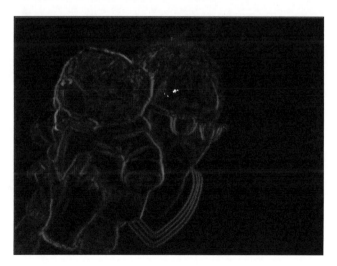

With this image, we can again apply the `pix_blob` object to obtain the tracking information:

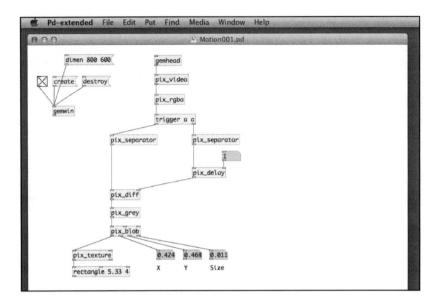

When you move in front of the webcam, notice the changes in the three number boxes, especially the first and second for the X and Y values. The two number boxes indicate the position where motion is detected. The range of values is between 0 and 1. In the GEM library, we can use the `pix_movement` object to serve the same purpose for motion detection:

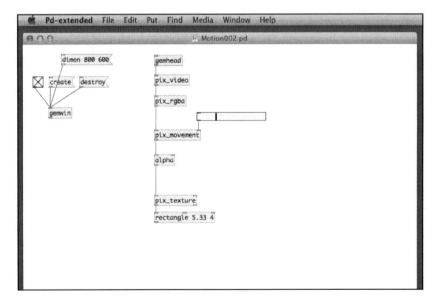

The right-hand inlet for `pix_movement` is a threshold number between 0 and 1. When color change between two frames is less than the threshold, the resulting pixel color will be black; otherwise, the resulting pixel color will be the difference between two frames. We can use a horizontal slider here. If you push the slider to the left-hand side, you can expect more imagery. When you push the slider to the right-hand side, you eliminate the imagery. You have to try out various positions to have just enough imagery for the tracking. It can depend on the lighting condition and the speed of the movement.

The `pix_movement` object detects movement between two frames and keeps the different image in the alpha channel of the pixel information. Note that we have to enable alpha blending by the alpha object to display the result. To obtain the details about the movement, we go back to the `pix_blob` object again:

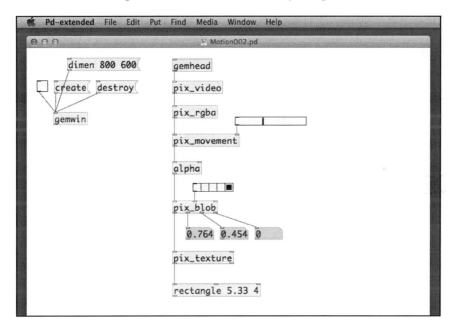

Note that the `pix_blob` has one more inlet that we can specify. It is a horizontal radio button with five options. The first option (default) with value 0 is using grey scale for the `blob` tracking. The next three options (values 1, 2, 3) correspond to red, green, and blue channels for tracking. The last option (value 4) is the alpha channel. Since the `pix_movement` object puts the different image in the alpha channel, we have to specify the last option in the radio button to use the alpha channel for movement tracking. Pay attention to the value that changes in the first two number boxes from the outlets of the `pix_blob` object. Try to relate the values with your movement in front of the webcam. The values are the X and Y position of the center of movement.

In most cases, the X value is flipped because the webcam image is not a mirror image of your own. You can handle it by using a `pix_flip` object to flip the image horizontally:

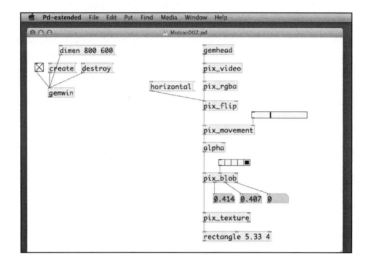

You can verify the tracking by waving your hand from the left-hand side to the right-hand side. The first number box value, X position, will increase. If you wave your hand from top to bottom, the second number box value, Y position, will increase. The range of numbers is between 0 and 1. We now finish the first motion-tracking patch. The next challenge will be replacing the two number boxes with a graphical shape to follow the movement. That is the fun part. We work on it in the next patch `Motion003.pd`. Refer to the following screenshot:

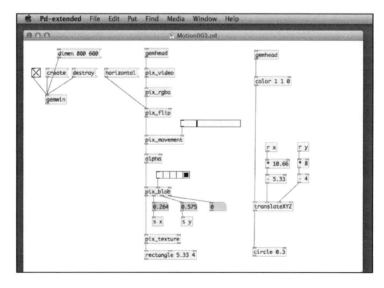

The patch is simple. The X and Y position returned from `pix_blob` will be the X and Y position of another graphic (a circle in this example). Before we send the values to `translateXYZ`, we have to convert the range between 0 and 1 to the screen size in GEM's measurement unit. The screen is not a square in this example. In examples from previous chapters, a square window has its coordinate values from -4 to 4. For the current window of size 800 x 600, we have the measurement of 10.66 x 8 (which is a 4:3 ratio). Based on this piece of information, we map the 0 to 1 values into the GEM's window-measurement units using a division and a subtraction object:

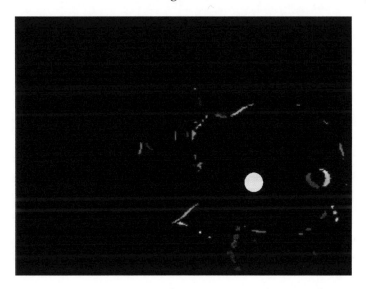

The yellow circle follows the movement of the subject in front of the webcam. The position is the center of gravity of the moving `blob` object. If you have movements in every corner of the screen, the center is still in the middle of the window. If your movement is localized in a particular region of the window, the tracking will be more accurate. The yellow circle moves in a very jerky manner. To enhance the motion, we can use a new object, `smooth`. This object will smoothen the incoming value by averaging with former values. Its right-hand inlet is a horizontal slider with value between 0 and 1, to control the smoothness of the output value. Smaller value will provide smoother result.

Refer to the following screenshot:

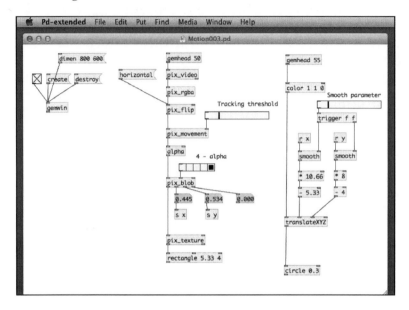

Both the X and Y position values use the smooth object. It smoothens the incoming numbers, and output it for the yellow circle to follow. The next step will resume the normal video display by splitting the video signal into two – one for the pix_movement object to track the motion and another one for the pix_texture object to display:

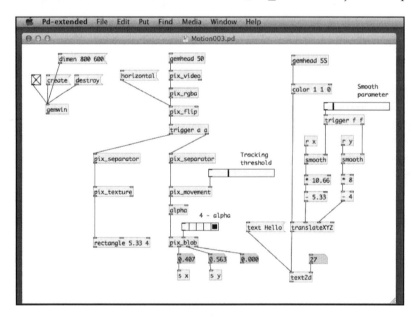

In this version, we use a piece of text to follow the movement, instead of a circle. The rest is the same as the former one for detecting presence:

Creating a motion detection animation

So far in this chapter, we learned the basic tools to detect presence and motion. Detecting presence is like a binary switch that indicates the presence or absence of a subject in front of a predefined background. Detecting motion indicates the position of the center of the moving `blob` object. We have tried using a graphical shape and a piece of text to follow the movement. In the following patch `Motion004.pd`, we use an image with the `pix_image` object:

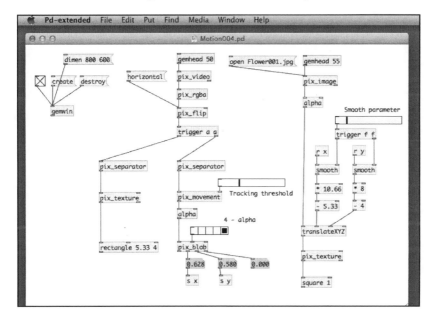

There is no new technique here. Use the `pix_image` object with an `open Flower001.jpg` message to open the image file in the same folder with the patch. You also need the `pix_texture` object to map the image onto the square. In this case, the image will follow your movement:

The image is itself a square. It has a white background color. In some applications, you may want to have an irregular shape with a transparent background. We have learned the use of the `pix_mask` object to handle it in *Chapter 3, Image Processing*. We can also directly make use of the alpha channel of the PNG or TIFF file to remove the background. In Photoshop, you can delete the background of an image and save the transparency information in the alpha channel. GEM library supports such image files with alpha channel. Remember to enable alpha blending with the `alpha` object. In the following example, the image `Flower002.png` that `pix_image` opens has a transparent background:

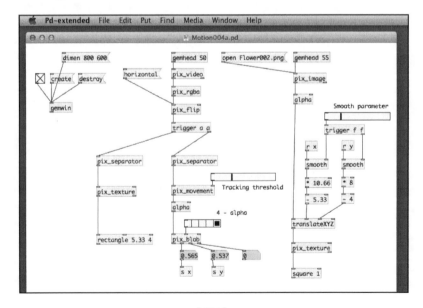

Note that the flower does not have the white background color here:

The next thing we can do is to analyze the direction of movement. The `pix_blob` object returns the X and Y positions of the moving `blob` object. To find out the direction, we have to know the X and Y positions of two consecutive frames and compute their difference. That means we have to store a pair of X and Y positions for the previous frame. We use the `float` object again for storage purpose:

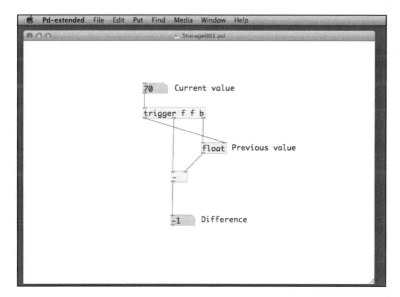

The patch computes the difference of a value that changes per frame. The `float` object keeps the previous value. The first number box is the current value. When it changes, it first sends a bang message to the `float` object to output its stored value, that is, the previous value. It then sends the current value to the subtraction object to compute the difference. Finally, it sends another copy of the current value to the right-hand inlet of the `float` object to be used in the next frame. The next patch `Difference001.pd` will use this logic to compute the changes in X position:

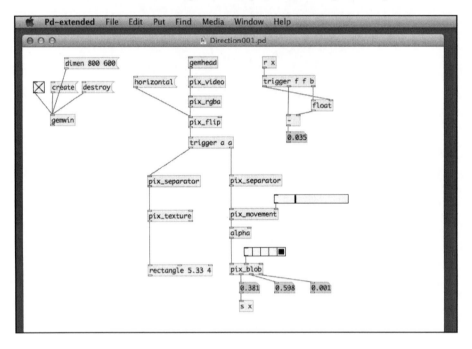

You will observe that the value changes in the number box after the subtraction operator. When you move toward the left-hand side, the number becomes negative. When you move toward the right-hand side, it will be positive. We are going to make use of this relation to create an interactive animation in the next patch `Direction002.pd`:

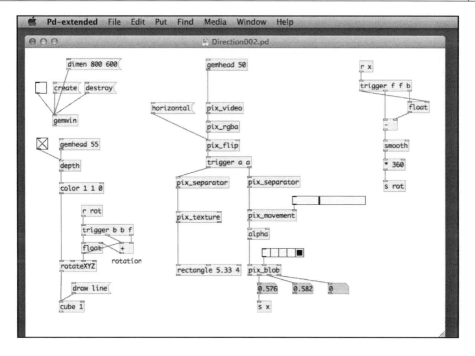

On the right-hand side of the patch, where we compute the difference in positions between two frames, we use the smooth object again to smoothen the value. We also need to increase this number as it is originally within the range of 0 to 1. In this case, we multiply it by 360, corresponding to the 360 degrees in a complete rotation.

On the left-hand side of the patch is a cube. We use the draw line message to enable the wireframe view. It is also necessary to disable the depth test by using the depth object. The horizontal movement will drive the cube to rotate along its y axis. The float object above the rotateXYZ object stores the current rotation value. The number sent from the r rot object is the amount we add to the current rotation value. It can be negative or positive, depending on which direction you wave your hand. We use a trigger b b f object because it is necessary to send the number, add it to the current value, and route the result to the rotateXYZ object in one step:

Comparing colors

The next technique to detect motion is by comparing colors across different frames. Firstly, we identify a pixel in the video frame. We store the pixel color information in the Pure Data patch. In the subsequent frame, we compare the color of that pixel with the stored information. If the colors change significantly, we assume there is movement in that area. To work with these tasks, we have to know the pixel color information. The `pix_data` object does it. We have briefly introduced it in *Chapter 3, Image Processing*, in the image-processing examples. Now we make use of it for interaction design:

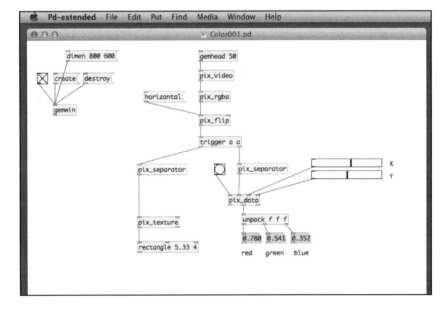

We need to provide four inlets for the `pix_data` object. The first one is a bang message to trigger the reading of the pixel color. The second is the video image. The last two are the X and Y positions of the pixel in the range between 0 and 1. We use two horizontal sliders for the X and Y positions. The position (0, 0) is the top-left corner. The position (1, 1) is the bottom-right corner. The output is the second outlet that is a list of the red, green, and blue colors, also in the range between 0 and 1. It needs an `unpack` object to split the list into three numbers.

The next challenge is to compare two colors. We cannot check if the two colors match exactly because there will be noise in the video signal. We can only check if the two colors look similar. The similarity is a numeric threshold. In this case, we have to find a way to measure the distance between two colors. Whenever the distance is shorter than a predefined threshold, we claim that the two colors are similar.

Each color is a combination of three primary colors: red, green, and blue. We think that each color is actually one point in a three-dimensional space with the three axes: red, green, and blue. The range of each axis is from 0 to 1. To compute the distance between two points in a three-dimensional space of X, Y, and Z, we use the *Pythagorean theorem*:

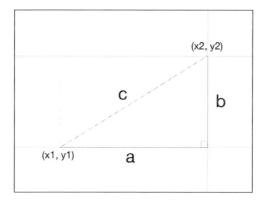

When we learned mathematics in school; for a right angle triangle with three edges as shown earlier, we understood that the length, a, b, and c have the relation:

$c^2 = a^2 + b^2$

For the two points (x1, y1) and (x2, y2) in a 2D plane, we can also make use of this relation to measure the distance between them:

$a = x2 - x1$

$b = y2 - y1$

The value of *c* will be the distance between point (x1, y1) and point (x2, y2). We can have this formula:

$$c^2 = (x2 - x1)^2 + (y2 - y1)^2$$

$$c = \sqrt{((x2 - x1)^2 + (y2 - y1)^2)}$$

We can generalize the case in 3D space. Assume we have two points (x1, y1, z1) and (x2, y2, z2) in space and the distance between them will be $\sqrt{((x2-x1)^2 + (y2-y1)^2 + (z2-z1)^2)}$. If we replace the X, Y and Z with R, G, and B, the two colors are (r1, g1, b1) and (r2, g2, b2). The distance between them will be $\sqrt{((r2-r1)^2 + (g2-g1)^2 + (b2-b1)^2)}$. Now we put the formula into an abstraction patch `colorDistance.pd`:

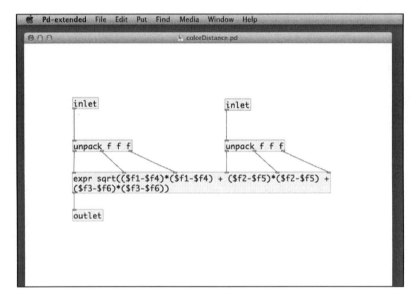

The `expr` object implements the formula of the square root of the sum of the differences between the red, green, and blue components of the two colors. To validate the patch, we can use a very simple patch to check the result, which is shown in the following screenshot:

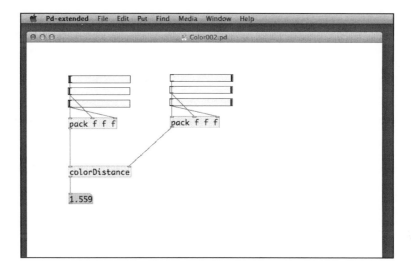

Each slider has the range between 0 and 1. Each `pack` object will compile a list of the red, green, and blue and send to the `colorDistance` abstraction. At this moment, only the red component is the hot inlet. It does not matter as we just use it for validating the `colorDistance` result.

Now we know how to obtain the color pixel information. We understand how to compare two colors. The remaining task is to find a way to store a copy of the pixel color and compare it with the latest pixel color from the video frame. We use the `spigot` object. The switching function of the `spigot` object can allow us to store the color information or pass it for comparison. Let's have a look at the patch `Color003.pd`:

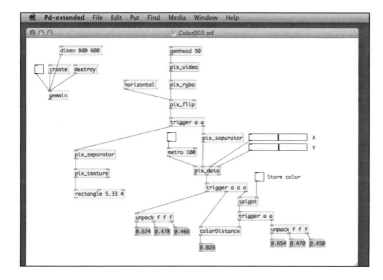

In the patch, we put six number boxes to indicate the pixel color information. The three on the left-hand side are the current pixel color from the video image. The three on the right-hand side are the pixel colors stored for comparison. To work with the patch, click on the dimension message, create the GEM window, start the rendering, and flip the video image horizontally. Push the sliders roughly towards the center of the X and Y range. It will be a position in the center of the window. Turn on the toggle for the metro object. The three number boxes on the left-hand side will change continuously. They are the current red, green, and blue values of the pixel selected by the two sliders. To store the current pixel color for comparison, turn on the toggle labeled **Store color**. The three number boxes on the right-hand side start changing. They are now the same as the three on the left-hand side. Uncheck the toggle labeled **Store color**. The three numbers on the right-hand side will stay there. And the number box after the colorDistance abstraction will indicate the distance between this stored color and the current pixel color in the latest video frame. We can test this number with a comparison operator to see if there is significant change in that particular area of the video image.

Performing color detection

Based on the material in the last section, we continue to explore color detection. In the previous patch, we do not know exactly which pixel in the window we are checking. To provide a visual feedback, we can use a small square to indicate the position. We also remove most of the number boxes to enhance performance. One of the easy ways to improve performance of a Pure Data patch is to remove the unnecessary graphical interface units, such as bang, number box, and toggle. It takes CPU time for Pure Data to update those items in the patch window. The Color004. pd patch is a working version for performing color detection. The result will be the final number box from the colorDistance abstraction:

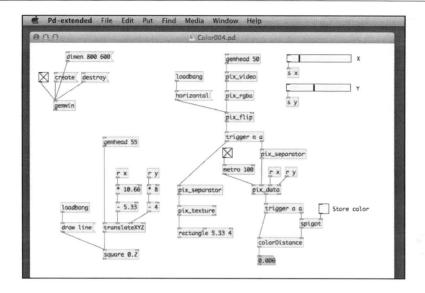

The patch uses the same mapping logic to map the range between 0 and 1 to the width of 10.66 units and the height of 8 units. The center of the white square is the pixel we use for checking:

Note that when you click on the toggle to store color, the resulting number box reduces to 0. When you click off the toggle, the number increases again. If there are no significant changes in square area, the number remains small, such as 0.035 in our example. The value depends on lighting condition, the webcam quality, and so on. When you point your finger inside the square, the number may suddenly increase significantly. It also depends on how different is the color between your finger and the original background.

In our example, the number box value increases to 0.867, which is significantly larger than the original 0.035 value. After a number of experiments, you can determine what the threshold value will be. And we use the threshold to determine whether something appears in the square with color different from the original background color:

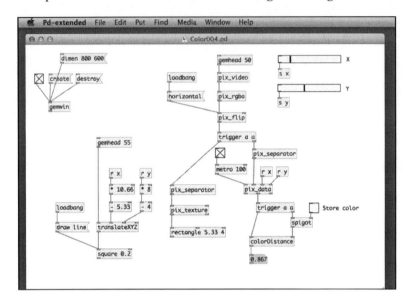

We need a comparison operator, for example, a < or > object. After the comparison, we place the result in a toggle box. We can also improve it by using a change object to send message only when there is a change in the result:

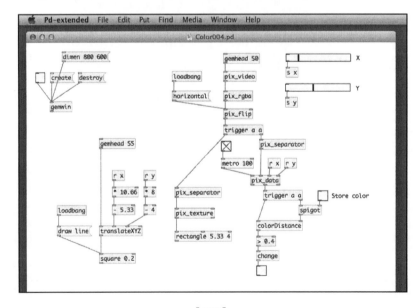

The patch window can get crowded. It is good practice to put reusable items into an abstraction. We name the abstraction `hotSpot.pd`:

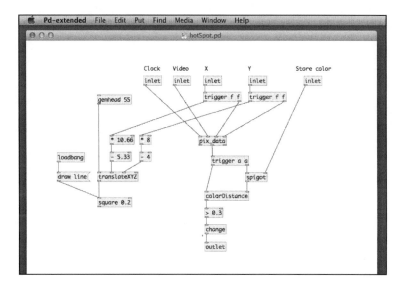

The abstraction `hotSpot` has five inlets. The first one is a stream of bang messages from the `metro` object. The second one is the video image. The third and fourth ones are the X and Y positions of the pixel to track. The last inlet is the toggle switch to store the color. The following patch `Color005.pd` will make use of this abstraction. You can use your finger to change the size of a circle in the GEM window:

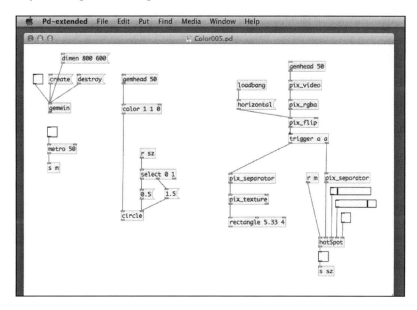

Create and render the GEM window. Turn on the `metro` object. Use the sliders to position the square to a position for interaction. Turn on the toggle for the `hotSpot` abstraction to store the background color. Turn it off after you store the color information. Use your finger or other object with a color different from the background to touch the square virtually. Note what happens with the yellow circle in the center:

When your finger touches the square (hotspot), the yellow circle becomes bigger:

Making an air drum

To create a drum, we need to have sound. It is a new topic. *Chapter 7, Audio Programming*, will have a more detailed introduction to audio in Pure Data. In this example, we use a very basic feature of playing a sound file interactively. Before we start, we have to collect a few sound samples. We use a few free audio clips from the public domain, such as `http://freesound.org`. They will produce the sound of a kick drum, snare drum, and tom-tom. We also need to take a look at the sampling rate of the sound files. Analog sound is converted into discrete samples during digitization. Sampling rate is the number of sample units in a second. Ours is 44 kHz, which is a common standard. The sampling rate has to match the preference settings in Pure Data, otherwise they may be distorted. You can use the **Get Info** or **Properties** options to check the audio file information:

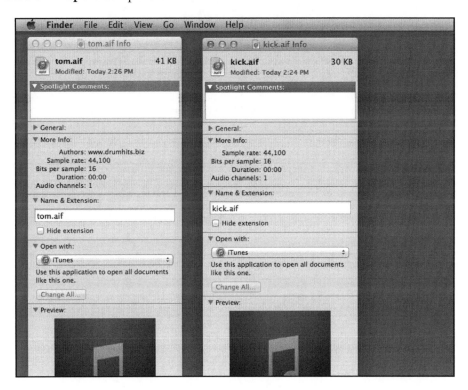

For the Pure Data audio information, go to **Preferences | Audio Settings...**:

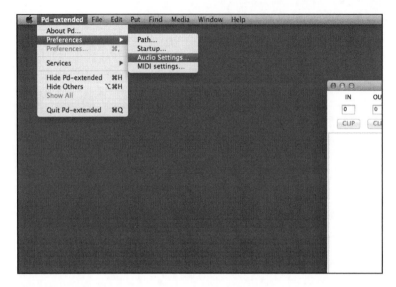

Within the **Audio Settings...** option, you can specify the sample rate (44 kHz) — the audio output device for this exercise:

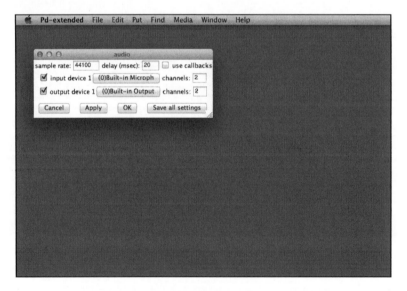

Remember to turn on audio processing by checking the **compute audio** box from the console window. By default, it is off. You will not hear anything if this box is unchecked:

Assuming that we have three audio clips, snare.aif, tom.aif, and kick.aif in the same folder with the other Pure Data patches, we try out our first audio program with the Audio001.pd patch. The object is readsf~. Pay attention to the tilde character after the keyword readsf. All audio-related objects in Pure Data have ~ as suffix. This object reads in an external sound file and plays it back through the audio interface, which is the digital-to-analog converter, dac~:

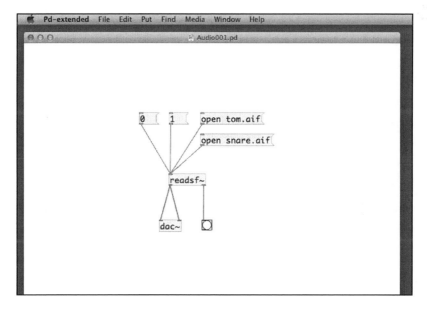

First, click on the open message to load the respective sound file. Then, click on the 1 message to start playing the sound. To stop the playback of the sound, click on the 0 message. Once the sound finishes, there will be an end-of-file message sent to the bang box. The left-hand outlet of the readsf~ object is the audio output. Note that the connection lines are thicker than the normal connection. The same audio signal is sent to the left-hand and right-hand channels of the dac~ object for playback through the audio interface. We can combine the two clicks into one by using a trigger object:

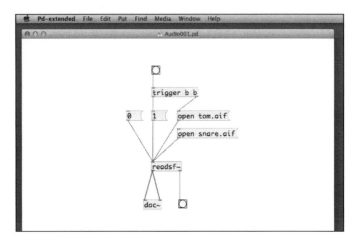

The trigger object first sends a bang message to the open tom.aif message. It then sends another bang to the 1 message. Receiving the open and 1 messages, the readsf~ object will playback the sound file. So much for audio processing here; we go back to the color-tracking patch Color006.pd to integrate with the audio part:

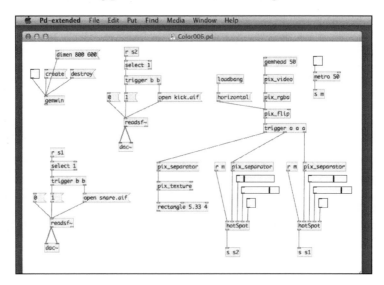

In this patch, we use the `hotSpot.pd` abstraction. Each of them controls a separate sound file. By putting the two squares on the left-hand and right-hand sides of the screen, you can use your two hands to play an air drum. We can further simplify the patch by combining the two `readsf~` objects into one, with two separate bangs for the two sound files:

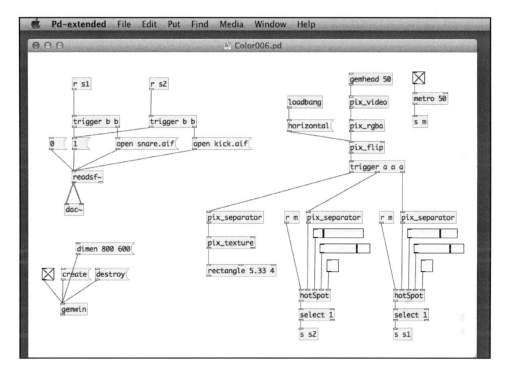

Summary

This completes a quick introduction to motion detection using Pure Data and the GEM library. We learned how to detect the presence of a subject in front of a static background. By comparing two consecutive frames, we identified movement in front of the webcam. Using the position given by the GEM library, we used graphical shape to follow the movement of a subject. By comparing the color information of a specific pixel, we could detect precise movement in a specific pixel in the video image. With this information, we could implement interactive hotspots that exist in virtual space. In the next chapter, we will enhance the graphical display by using particles system.

6

Animation with Particle System

In the previous chapters, we animated only a few objects. If we have to animate a large number of graphical objects in a patch individually, it will require a lot of effort. In the GEM library, the particle system enables us to streamline the process. If we want to animate a large group of similar shapes with similar movements, we can take advantage of the particle system to do the job.

When we model everyday life objects, we use primitive shapes, such as sphere, cone, and cube to construct more sophisticated forms. It can be easy to use this approach to model a chair, a car, or even a human figure. It can be very difficult if we want to model natural phenomena such as fire, fountain, or smoke. Those phenomena do not have very precise geometrical forms and yet we have fuzzy descriptions about their physical appearance and behaviors over time. Particle system is the modeling method to describe and generate those fuzzy forms. This chapter will include the following topics on particle system:

- Understanding a particle system
- Creating a basic particle system
- Applying forces to the particle system
- Interacting with the mouse
- Rendering particles with images
- Combining particle system with motion tracking

Understanding a particle system

In 1983, William T. Reeves from Lucasfilm Ltd published a paper: *Particle Systems – A Technique for Modeling a Class of Fuzzy Objects*. It described the fire simulation effects applied in the film *Star Trek II: The Wrath of Khan*. Modeling clouds, smoke, and fire is difficult, they do not have rigid primitive surface elements that define their boundaries. They only have a fuzzy volume of particles. Their forms also change over time. Their shapes and forms are recognizable but not accurately predictable.

To model a piece of fire, for example, with particle system, we have the following questions:

- How new particles are generated. Is it by birth?
- What types of visual and physical properties the new particles have?
- How existing particles disappear over time. Is it by death?
- How do the visual and physical properties of the existing particles change over time?
- How can we render the group of particles in each frame?

By answering these questions, we can define a particle system. In 1990, Karl Sims also published a paper: *Particle Animation and Rendering Using Data Parallel Computation*. Together with the animation work – *Particle Dreams*, he demonstrated the use of particle systems to simulate phenomena such as explosions, tornado, fire, and waterfalls.

To work with a particle system animation in Pure Data and GEM, we have to do the following:

- Identify the source of the particles
- Specify the initial position and velocity of each new particle
- Compute the updated position, color, and size of each particle in the latest frame
- Apply external forces that affect each particle in the system
- Remove old particles from the system
- Render the particles in the display system

Creating a basic particle system

In the Pure Data GEM library, the objects related with particle system come with a prefix part_, a short form for particle. The part_head object initializes a particle system. The part_source object creates a source of particles. The part_velocity object specifies the initial velocity and direction for each new particle. The part_killold object removes particles that exceed a predefined age. The part_draw object renders each particle in the GEM window as shown in the following screenshot:

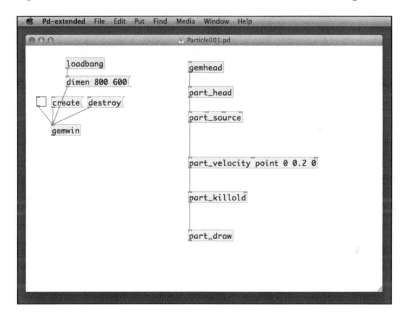

The only parameters are for the part_velocity object. This object defines the initial velocity for each particle in the system. In the example, Particle001.pd, it defines the velocity as a point with the parameters 0, 0.2, 0. It indicates that velocity has only Y direction value. For X and Z the values are zero. All particles in this case will move upward (positive value for Y direction). The three numbers correspond to the X, Y, and Z components of the initial velocity.

You can see from the following GEM window that all particles are moving upward:

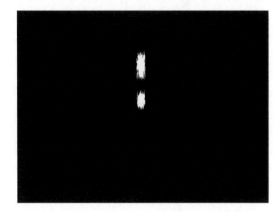

You can also change the visual appearance of the particles in the part_draw object. Similar to other primitive shapes, it accepts the draw line and draw point message. and you can easily observe the difference. The default one is draw line as shown in the following screenshot:

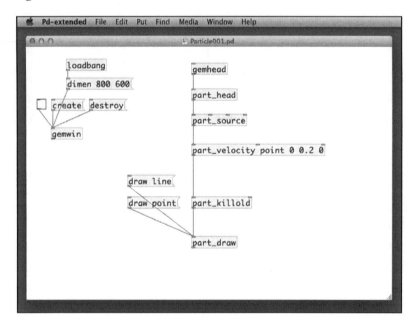

The following screenshot shows how the particles are displayed with the draw point message:

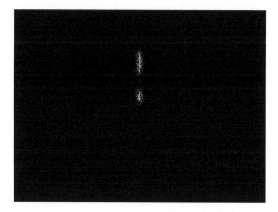

For each of the particle system related object, we can modify the parameters to see what may happen. In the part_head object, we can have a speed $1 message to alter the emission speed with a number box as shown in the following screenshot:

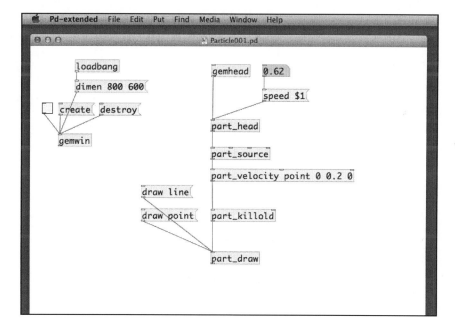

The `part_source` object controls how many particles to generate in each frame. We can put a number box to alter it as shown in the following screenshot:

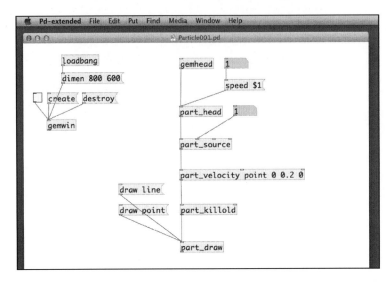

For the parameters for `part_velocity`, it is a bit complicated. The second inlet is the configuration domain. It can be a point, a sphere, a line, and so on. In our examples, it will be mostly a sphere, which is more intuitive. A sphere differs from a point by having a measurement of its radius. It generates a more scattering pattern of particles. The third inlet is the parameter to describe the initial velocity. A point has X, Y, and Z components. A sphere has X, Y, and Z components and a fourth one for the radius as shown in the following screenshot:

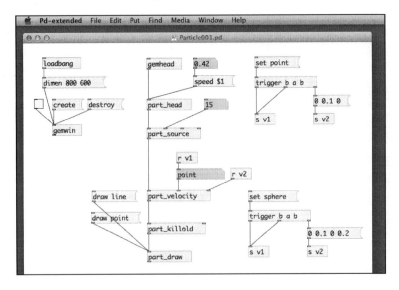

The patch has a new command. The second inlet of `part_velocity` is an empty symbol. To change the value of a symbol, we can either type the keyword, such as `point` or `sphere` into the symbol or use a `set` message to change the symbol value. If you want to change the velocity dynamically, you can modify the parameters in the list of numbers connecting to the `s v2` object that will send the velocity information to the third inlet of `part_velocity` as shown in the following screenshot:

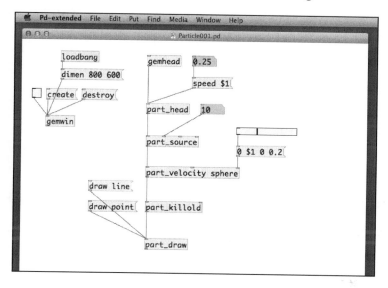

The horizontal slider has a range between 0 and 1. It sends out the number to the message with a parameter `$1`, which is the Y direction velocity component. The last object `part_killold` also comes with a number parameter. It is the age of each particle being measured in frames. Particle older than the age will disappear from the system. It controls how quickly or slowly the system removes the old particles. The larger the number, the longer the particles will stay.

Refer to the following screenshot:

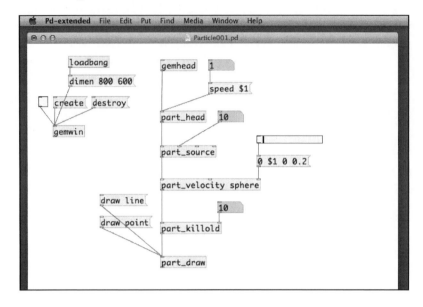

In the next version, `Particle002.pd`, we change the color of the particles, by using the `part_color` object. It can accept two colors. The particles will be either one of the colors. Refer to the following screenshot:

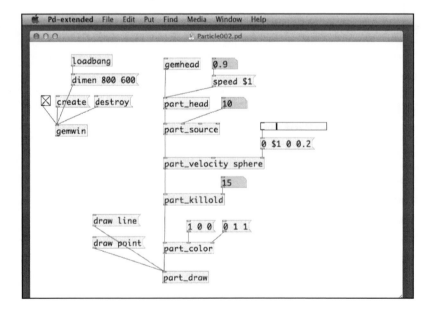

Another object `part_targetcolor` can also change particles' color. Each particle changes from its original color (white, by default) to the color specified in the `part_targetcolor` object. The number in the right inlet controls how fast the change is, as shown in the following screenshot:

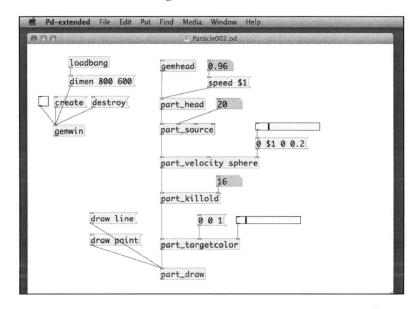

Applying forces to the particles system

The particles in the system come and go on their own. In fact, we can alter the ways that particles travel across the window. In this section, we introduce different ways to apply forces to the particles so that they can travel in different manners. The first object is `part_damp`. It is a damping force that changes the speed of each particle.

Have a look at the `Particle003.pd` patch in the following screenshot:

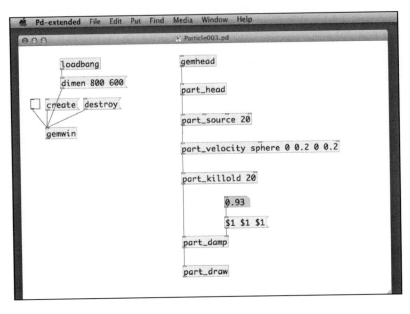

The `part_damp` object takes three numbers representing X, Y, and Z directions of the force. Values larger than 1 speed up the particles, while values smaller than 1 slow them down. It is pretty straightforward. The second object is `part_gravity`. It simulates the attraction of gravity. The next patch `Particle004.pd` demonstrates its usage as shown in the following screenshot:

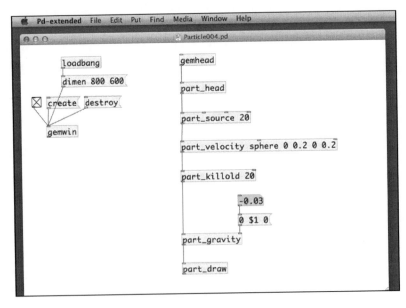

The object `part_gravity` also comes with three numeric parameters in its right inlet. To simulate the gravity, we usually only specify the Y direction with a small negative number. It denotes a downward attraction force in the Y direction. You can experiment with other values and directions. The display will look like a fountain:

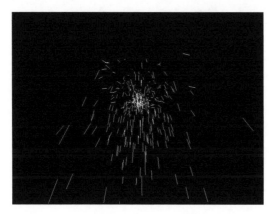

The next object `part_orbitpoint` is more interesting. It also simulates the attraction forces among celestial bodies. The object defines a single point in the three-dimensional space that attracts particles towards it. The patch `Particle005.pd` shows how it works, as shown in the following screenshot:

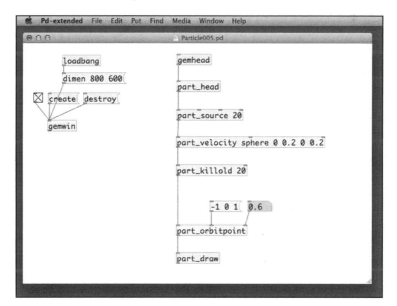

The second inlet defines the point in space. The right inlet defines the attraction force. The `part_orbitpoint` object attracts the particles toward it. The particles, however, do not just move in a straight line as shown in the following screenshot:

It can produce complex orbital paths that revolve around the point of attraction defined in the second inlet.

Interacting with the mouse

Now we can use the mouse to play around with the particles. The two objects, `part_source` and `part_orbitpoint` contain the specification of a point in three-dimensional space. For `part_source`, it specifies the location where particles are emitted. For `part_orbitpoint`, it indicates a point where other particles are attracted. For the mouse position, we use the `gemmouse` object. Remember that it will give us two numbers, X and Y positions in a normalized scale between 0 and 1 as shown in the following screenshot:

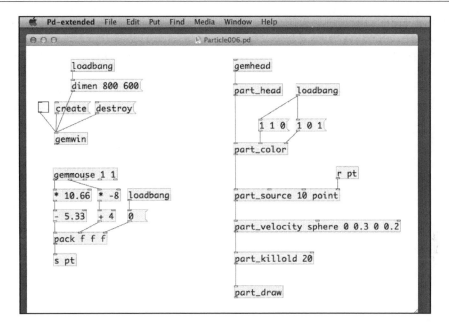

We are using the dimension of 800 x 600 pixels. The GEM window measurement for the screen is around 10.66 x 8.0. The Y direction is reversed between the mouse measurement and the GEM graphics measurement. The computation after the `gemmouse` object takes care of the unit conversion. The `pack` object combines the three numbers into a list of positions in three-dimensional space for the `part_source` object, as shown in the following screenshot:

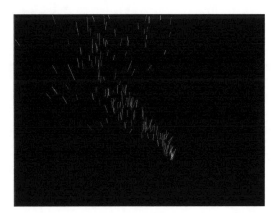

You may find that all the particles are moving upward in this patch. It would be nice if the particles could move in different directions depending on how you move your mouse. In the next patch `Particle007.pd`, we'll change the direction of the particles by moving the mouse. This logic makes use of a technique we learnt in *Chapter 5, Motion Detection*. In order to know the direction where the mouse goes, we compute the difference between the mouse positions in the current frame and the last frame as shown in the following screenshot:

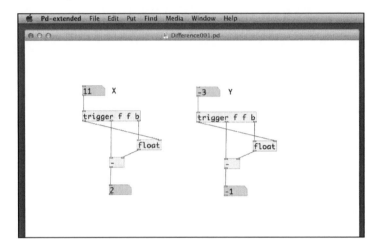

This patch segment computes the changes of two numbers X and Y, across each frame. You can click-drag the input numbers. The output number boxes indicate the difference between the values in the current frame and those in the last frame. We can combine this with the gemmouse object to track the change of positions across two frames as shown in the following screenshot:

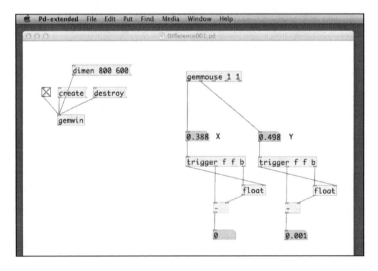

We can also convert the normalized range of the mouse position into the GEM window measurement unit before computing the position changes. The following version handles this as shown in the screenshot:

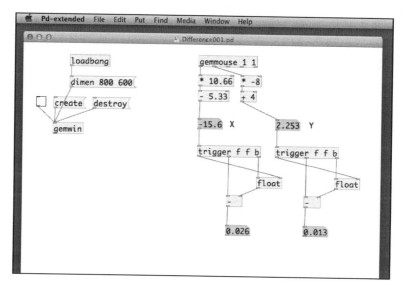

Now we are ready to combine this with the particle system patch. The two numbers from the position changes can fit into the values for the part_velocity object as shown in the following screenshot:

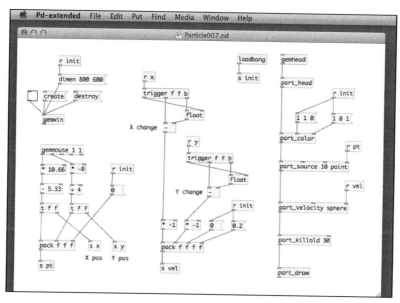

The right inlet for `part_velocity` takes a list of four numbers. We use the change in X positions for the X velocity component, Y positions change for the Y velocity component, zero for Z component, and a constant 0.2 for the radius. The `pack` object combines them into a list. Note that we have to reverse the emission direction and the mouse movement direction by a multiplication object, as shown in the following screenshot:

You will notice that the faster you move your mouse, the faster the emission rate of the particle system is. So far we have not used the mouse button. Try to think of a way to engage the users with the mouse button as shown in the following screenshot:

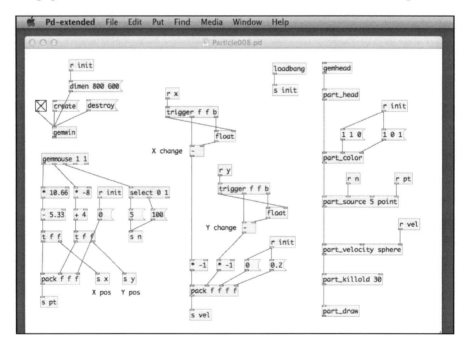

The patch `Particle008.pd` detects the left mouse button with a `select` object. When we press the button, it sends a bigger number (100) to the `part_source` object. It resumes to the number 5 when we release the button. The user can now assume the control of the particle emission rate as shown in the following screenshot:

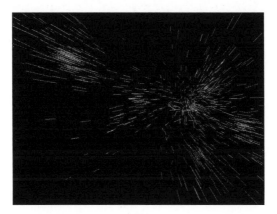

We now proceed to the `part_orbitpoint` object with the patch `Particle009.pd`. Using a similar approach, we convert the `gemmouse` position to a point in the GEM window three-dimensional space and use it as the location in `part_orbitpoint`, as shown in the following screenshot:

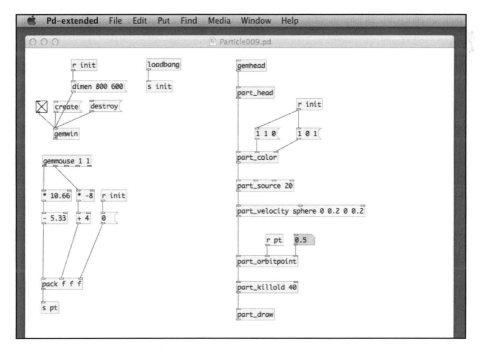

All particles come from the center of the screen and revolve toward the mouse pointer. The orbital paths change dynamically as you move the mouse around, as shown in the following screenshot:

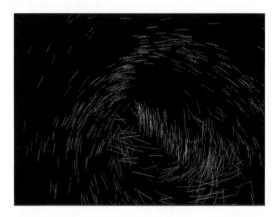

If we do not want the particles to always emit from the center, we can try to use the mouse button again. In the new patch, Particle010.pd, we intend to use the mouse click to register the particle point source. New particles are emitted from that point to move toward the new mouse position after the user releases the button, and the mouse moves as shown in the following screenshot:

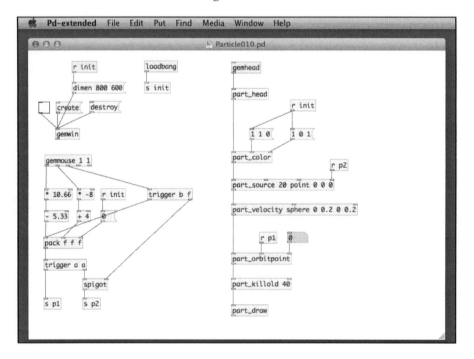

Rendering particles with images

Our examples use either lines or points to render the particle system. In the GEM library, we can have other choices. With the use of the part_render object, we can use other graphical shapes we have learnt to render the particles. In the next patch, Particle011.pd, we start with a 2D square as shown in the following screenshot:

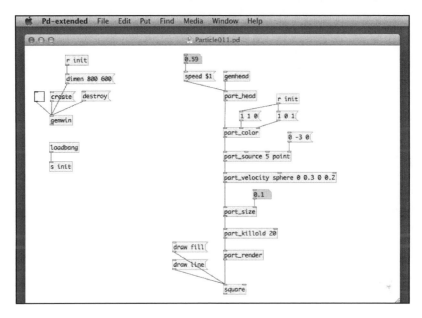

We put the square object below the part_render object. All particles from the patch become square shapes. We also have a new object part_size to modify the size of each particle. The patch uses the speed message in the part_head object to control the speed of emission. The following screenshot is what you expect to see with the draw line message enabled:

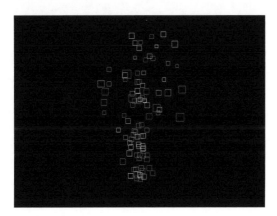

We can use a 3D shape, such as the `sphere` object with lighting on. The following is an example of the same and the resulting image in the GEM window:

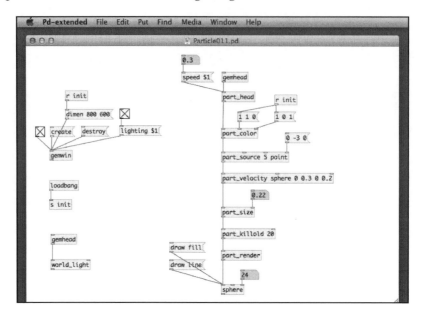

The resulting image of the particles in spheres is as follows:

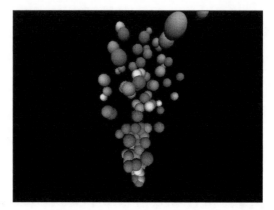

We can replace the particles by text messages. Using the `text2d` or `text3d` objects, the particles can be any text messages supplied to the objects, as shown in the following screenshot:

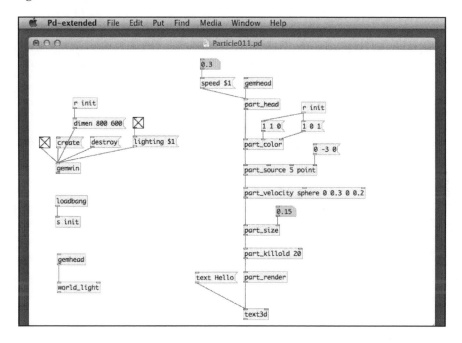

The following is the resulting image of using the text `Hello` as particles:

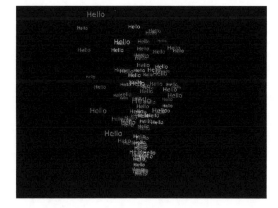

For the next version in `Particle012.pd`, we use the `pix_image, pix_texture` together with the `square` objects to render each particle with an external image. The logic is the same as what we did in *Chapter 3, Image Processing*. The following screenshot illustrates the same:

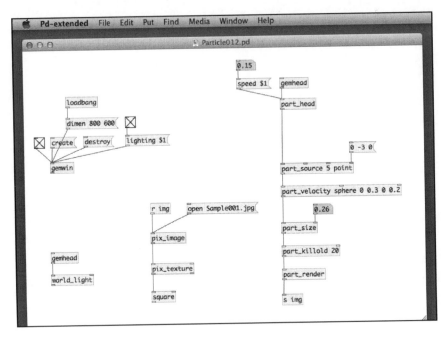

The following is the resulting image using a sample image with white background:

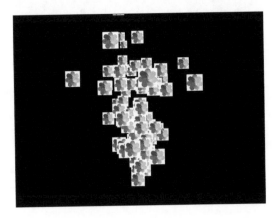

Of course, if we use an image with an alpha channel, we can remove the background by using the alpha channel as a mask. In the next display, we use a PNG image file with a transparent background as shown in the following screenshot:

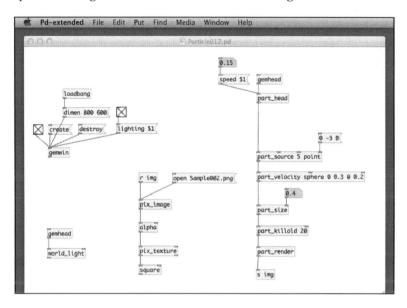

Remember to use the `alpha` object to enable alpha blending of the image. It is a very versatile technique to create custom graphics for the particle system, as shown in the following screenshot:

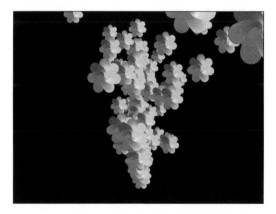

Another useful object for particle rendering is part_info. The object lists out every particle's information in terms of its position, color, velocity, size, and age. In the GEM library examples, there is one using the part_info object. We modify it to create a piece of motion graphics work. Firstly, we extract the position information of each particle, in this patch, Particle013.pd as shown in the following screenshot:

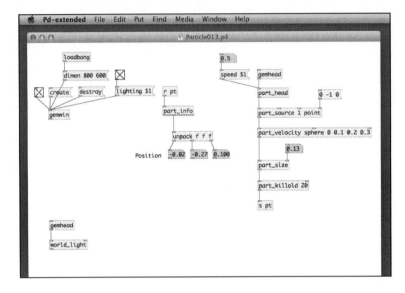

The three numbers next to the label Position move continuously corresponding to the position of the particles emitted from the source. The next step is to use a graphical shape to move according to those positions, as shown in the following screenshot:

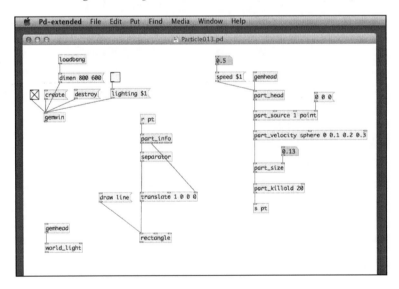

We use the `draw line` message for the `rectangle` object in order to reveal the overlapping squares. Note also the use of the `separator` object to display every single particle individually, as shown in the following screenshot:

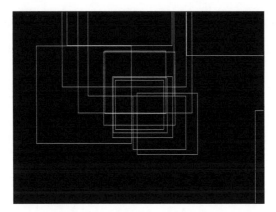

The next step is to add the size information for display with the `scale` object. We pass the size information directly from the `part_info` to the `scale` object with a scaling factor of 1, as shown in the following screenshot:

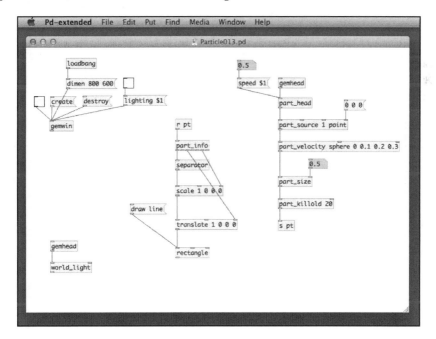

In the next version, we extract the velocity information from the part_info object. It is also a list of X, Y, and Z components of the velocity. We use the unpack object to extract it into the three number boxes, as shown in the following screenshot:

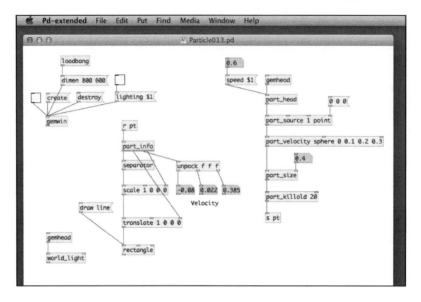

The visual display does not have anything to play with the velocity. We transform the velocity components into the rotation information for the rectangle object. Before passing it to the rotateXYZ object, we have to multiply each component by 360 degrees as shown in the following screenshot:

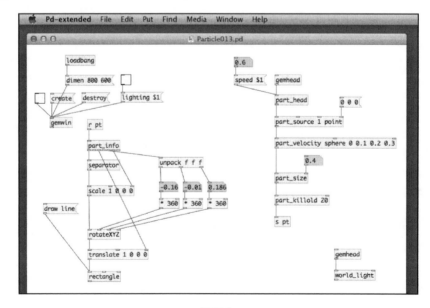

The resulting image can be an interesting animation of flying squares as shown in the following screenshot:

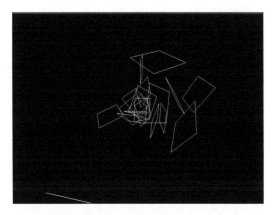

We can switch back to use draw fill and lighting to check out the effect. To make it more interesting, we can add texture mapping to rectangle with a pix_texture object. The texture source can be the live webcam video image from pix_video, as shown in the following screenshot:

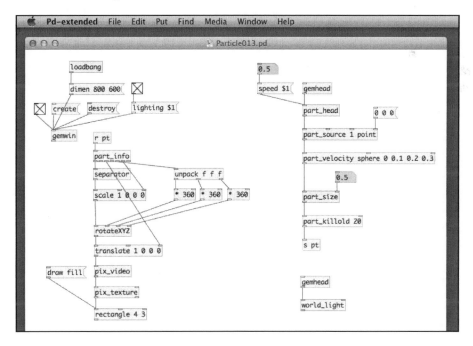

Instead of using `pix_video`, you can also use `pix_image` or `pix_film` for still images or digital videos. It can produce common motion graphics effects as shown in the following screenshot:

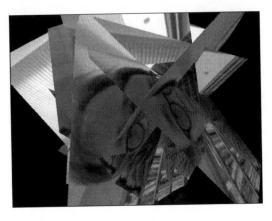

The following patch, `Particle014.pd`, takes advantage of the other two outputs from the `part_info` object. The first one is the second outlet. It is a number representing the identification number of each particle. The second one is the last outlet. It is the age of the particle. The patch will display the particle ID in the three-dimensional space. It creates the perspective illusion by using the age to rotate the text along the X-axis as shown in the following screenshot:

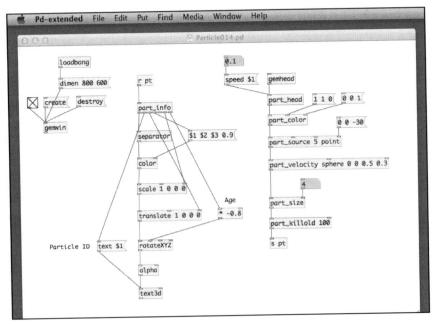

The effect is similar to that used in a number of movie title sequences, as shown in the following screenshot:

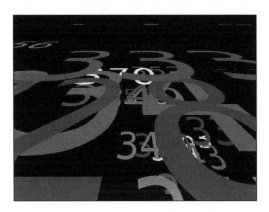

Combining particle system with motion-tracking

In the previous chapter, we have experimented with the motion-tracking technique by using a graphical shape to follow the user. Earlier in this chapter, we have tested how to control the particle system with the mouse. We can combine the two methods to use the user's body movement to control the particle system. Let's revisit the motion-tracking patch as shown in the following screenshot:

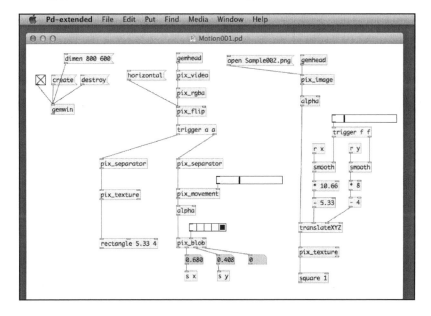

The pix_blob object sends the movement position to the translateXYZ object for the square to display the pixel image as texture. To combine particle system with motion tracking, it is pretty straightforward. Send the X and Y positions of movement to the X and Y positions of the part_source object. In this case, the user's body movement will trigger emission of the particles. In the following patch, Motion001.pd, the movement center will generate particles as spheres. We use a pack object to pack the X and Y positions together with a 0 as Z value for the part_source, as shown in the following screenshot:

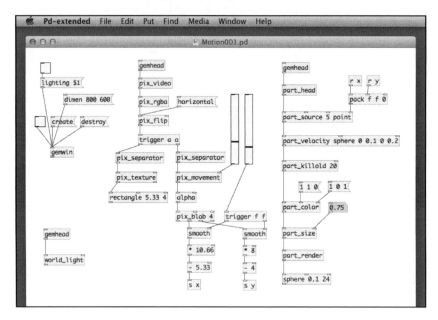

As expected from the previous patch, the particles will be emitted from where your body moves as shown in the following screenshot:

It is very easy to change the sphere object into text2d or text3d to create the particles as an animated text, as shown in the following screenshot:

Other than using the part_source, the next object will be the part_orbitpoint. The patch, Motion002.pd will send the X and Y positions to the point information in the part_orbitpoint object, as shown in the following screenshot:

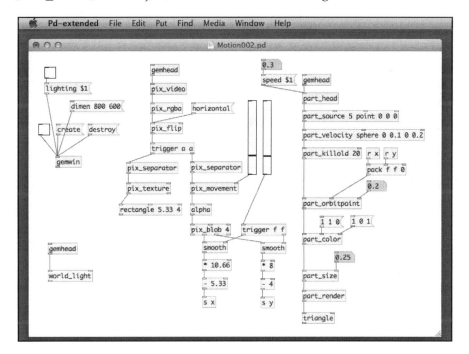

In this version, the particles move toward the movement center. The user's body functions as an attraction point that draws the particles together. You may need to adjust the `speed` message for `part_head` to slow down the particles' motion. The third inlet for `part_orbitpoint` may also need fine tuning to have an optimal attraction force, as shown in the following screenshot:

We can also use the `curve` object instead of `triangle` or `square` to work with particles. In the next example, `Motion003.pd`, it uses a number of vertical lines to chase around the movement center, as shown in the following screenshot:

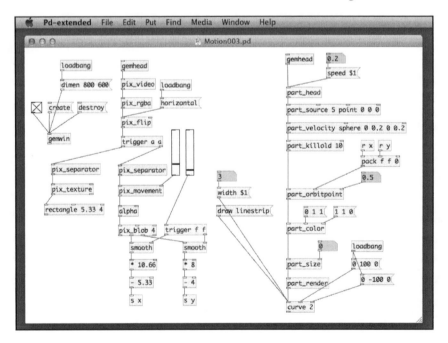

We have learnt how to use the `curve` object to draw a straight line in *Chapter 2, Computer Graphics with the GEM Library*. It needs a parameter 2 to specify two points. The lines are extremely long as they start from Y = 100 to Y = -100, in order for them to cover the whole GEM window vertically, as shown in the following screenshot:

Before we conclude this chapter, Let's have a look at a more complicated example. It can be a challenge how much you understand the use of a particle system in the GEM library. The patch is `Motion004.pd` as shown in the following screenshot:

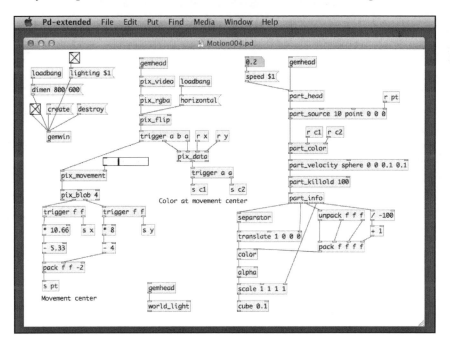

It does not have any new objects in the patch. The bottom-left part of the patch is the motion-tracking component we have covered in the previous chapter. We use the movement center as the point source for the `part_source` object. The `part_data` component extracts the color of the pixel in the movement center and sends it to `part_color` object to colorize the particles. The patch also uses the particle age to modify the particle's alpha component in its color. Pay attention to what we have done in the `color` object under the `part_info`. When the particles come closer to our eyes, they become more transparent, as shown in the following screenshot:

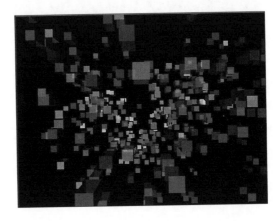

Summary

We completed an introduction of the particle system in the GEM library. In this chapter, we learnt how to render a particle system in different ways, such as simple graphical shapes, text, 3D objects, and custom images. By using the computer mouse, we created a painterly experience with the interactive control of a particle system and with the motion-tracking technique we used our own bodies to interact with a particle system for a more playful experience. When we work on audio programming in the next chapter, we will see how to integrate the audio information in multimedia projects.

7
Audio Programming

We have briefly encountered the use of audio programming in *Chapter 5, Motion Detection*, when we created the color-tracking air drum. In this chapter, we are going to have more extensive coverage of the sound basics in Pure Data.

The topics we are going to cover on audio programming are:

- Preparing for audio processing
- Using existing sound files
- Generating audio with waves
- Working with MIDI
- Obtaining audio input for interaction

Preparing for audio processing

We have covered the procedures to prepare for audio input and output in Pure Data in *Chapter 5, Motion Detection*. Let us revisit the key points. We have to check the **compute audio** box in the upper-right corner of the console window:

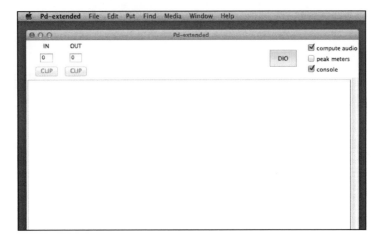

The next step is to prepare the audio settings in the **Preference** panel. Choose **Pd-extended | Preference | Audio Settings** from the menu bar. Select the input and output devices, such as **Built-in Microphone** and **Built-in Output**, and the default sample rate to **44100**. When transferring analog audio signal to digital, the sample rate controls how frequently the system takes samples of the audio signal. **44100** is the commonly used standard for audio files and processing. The measurement is in Hertz. It affects the fidelity and the file size of the audio information. Refer to the following screenshot:

Rather than clicking on the **compute audio** box in the console window, we can also include this action in the patch window. We can use a toggle and a message to enable/disable the digital signal processing function in Pure Data. Here is how you can do it:

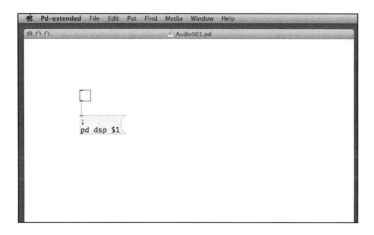

The semicolon message will direct the message to Pure Data itself with the value dsp 1 if you turn on the toggle box or dsp 0 if you turn it off. We shall use this option to switch on/off the audio processing from the patch window.

Using existing sound files

In the air drum exercise of *Chapter 5, Motion Detection*, we learned how to playback an external sound file. The Audio001.pd patch shown in the following screenshot shows how we can do so:

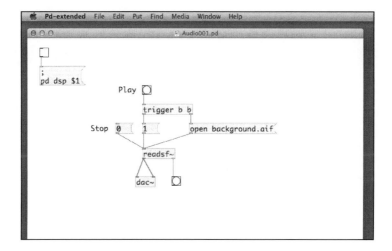

Remember that all audio-related objects come with the ~ character suffix. The object `readsf~` reads an external sound file through the `open` message. The message `1` starts the playback. The message `0` stops it. Its left-hand outlet is the audio signal going to the digital-to-analog converter, the `dac~` object. The `dac~` object will actually play the audio signal through the computer's audio interface. The right-hand outlet of `readsf~` is a bang message that will be triggered once the playback reaches the end of the sound file. Note that the line connecting audio outlet and inlet is thicker than normal data connection.

If you click on the `Play` button a few times before the first sound file ends, the patch will initiate a new playback every time you click. It may cause trouble in your design. To solve the problem, we can disable the `Play` button when the current sound file is still playing. We use a `spigot` object for this purpose:

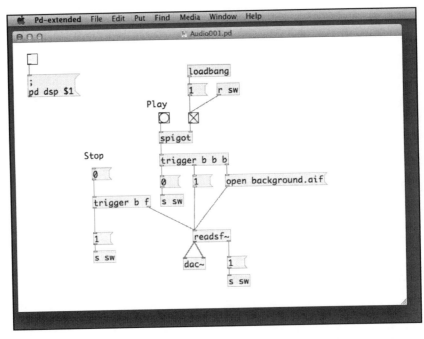

Another way to play a sound file is to load the audio data into the patch and then playback later. Firstly, we have to define an area to store the audio data. We use the **Array** object for this purpose. The arrays in Pure Data are similar to arrays in other programming languages. You can think of it as a cabinet of drawers. Each drawer is a storage location for a number. You access each drawer by its index, a number starting from `0`.

To begin with this new patch, `Audio002.pd`, we define an array item named `snare` for the snare drum sound. We choose **Put | Array** from the main menu bar:

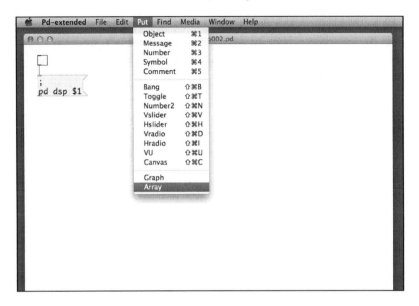

Type in the name `snare` for the array item and keep the rest as default:

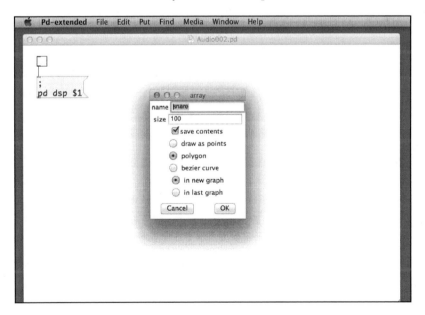

After we click on **OK**, we will have a graph with the label **snare** in the patch window. In the center of the graph (a line chart), there is a horizontal line indicating the value 0:

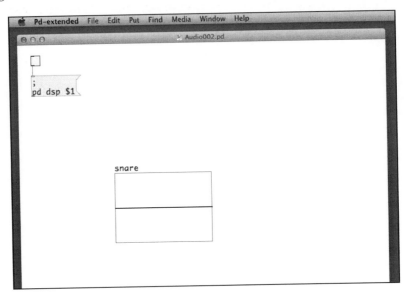

Next, we are going to load the snare drum sound file, snare.aif, that we used in *Chapter 5, Motion Detection*, into the snare array. The object is soundfiler:

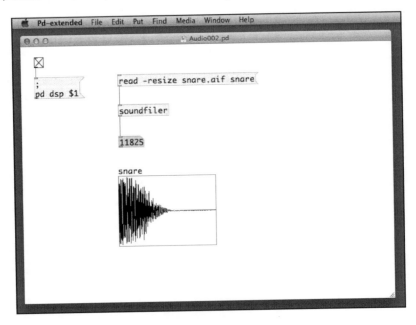

The `soundfiler` object has the message `read -resize snare.aif snare` to load the external `snare.aif` sound file into the array named `snare`. The `-resize` parameter is to resize the array size to hold all the sample data from the sound file. The number box below the `soundfiler` object indicates the number of samples loaded. The graph under the label `snare` shows the waveform of the sound sample.

The next step is to playback the sound sample from the computer storage. We use the `tabplay~` object:

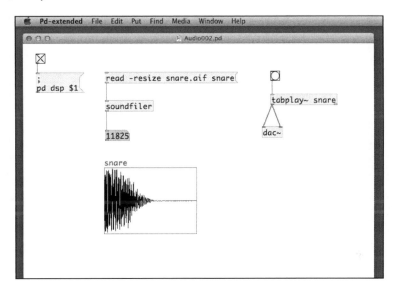

The object `tabplay~` plays an audio sample stored in an array. The name `snare` follows the `tabplay~` object that is the name of the array, which we have just loaded from the sound file. A bang message triggers the playback through the `dac~` object to the sound interface. Of course, we can put multiple sound samples into the patch to create a drum set.

Here is how we can have two sound samples together:

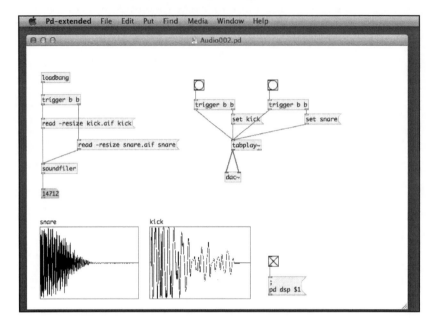

The `loadbang` object on the left-hand side of the patch loads the two sound samples into the arrays, `snare` and `kick`. For the `tabplay~` object, it has two sets of input signals: the first one for the kick drum and the second one for the snare drum. Within each set, the `trigger` object first sends a bang message to the `set` message to designate the array name, and then another bang message to `tabplay~` for the playback. You just need to click on each bang box to playback the corresponding drum sound. For usability, it will be much better if we make use of the keyboard to control the playback. Let's have a look at this version in `Audio003.pd`:

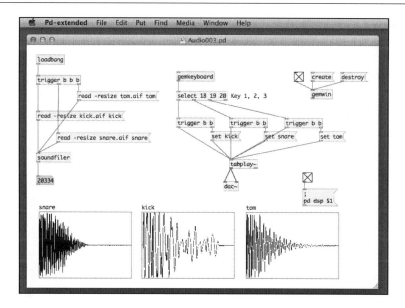

Remember what we have done in *Chapter 4*, *Interactivity*, about the use of keyboard for interactivity. We use the gemkeyboard object to detect which key the user is pressing. With the key code, we use the select object to find out which sound sample we should send the trigger message to.

We can also automate the playback by using another array item. In the following screenshot of the patch, Array001.pd, we explore in general how an array works:

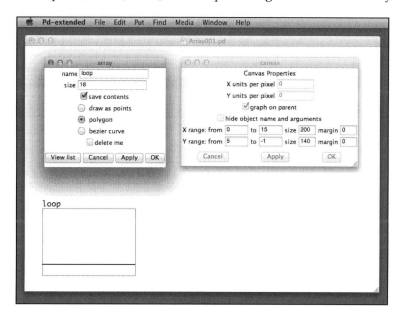

We define an array named `loop`. Its size is `16`. We also change the range of the Y value to a range from `-1` to `5`. In the beginning, all values in the array are zero. We can either manually key in the values or use a patch to input. To input the values to the array, we first right-click on the graph to choose the **Properties** option:

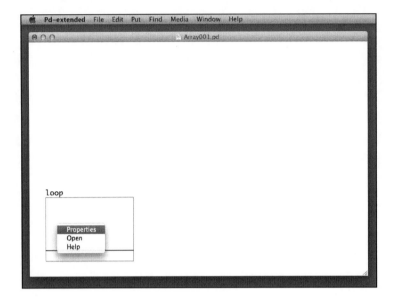

From the **array** panel, click the **View list** button:

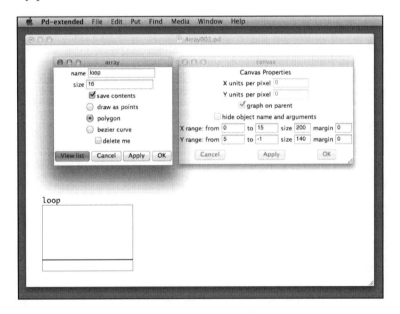

The **loop (list view)** panel has 16 rows of **0**. Each row is an entry in the array. The first number with the bracket is the index. The second number next to it is the value:

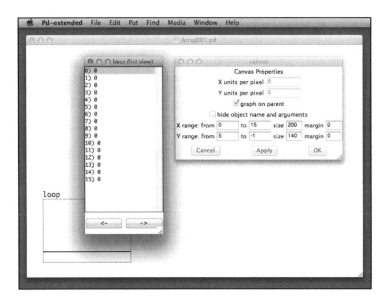

If you want to modify any entry, double-click on that row and type the new number. Press *enter* or *return* when you finish:

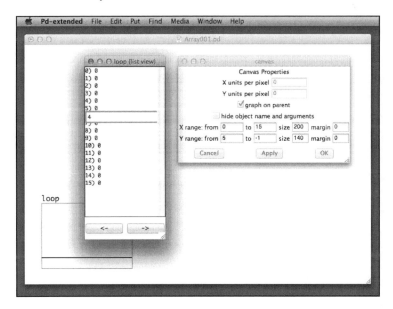

After you press *enter* or *return* to confirm, the graph in the patch window will show the new value in the line chart:

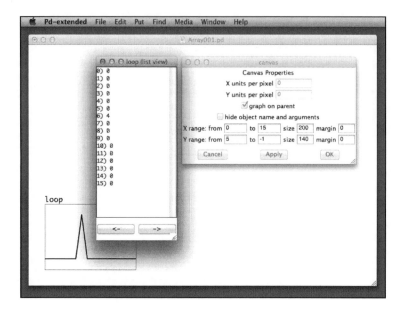

The second way to modify the array content is by using the `tabwrite` object. To retrieve the current content of the array, we use the `tabread` object. Both the `tabread` and `tabwrite` objects need to specify the array named `loop` in our case:

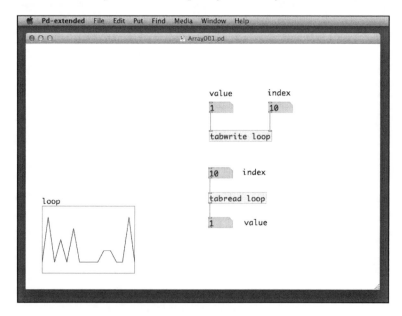

To store a value with the `tabwrite` object, we need to specify both the new value (left-hand inlet) and the index (right-hand inlet). First, input the index value, that is, which row in the array to update. Remember that the index starts from `0`, not `1`. Second, enter the new value in the left-hand inlet to update the array entry. To retrieve the latest value from the array, simply enter the index value in the inlet. The entry value will be ready in the outlet.

We can also have a third way to update an array. Right-click on the graph in the patch window and select **Open**. You can then interactively draw on the graph to alter the values. Nevertheless, it may not be very precise by drawing.

The next step is to automate the retrieval process. We use the `metro` object for the automation and the `counter` object to go through every single entry in the array. Here is how it works:

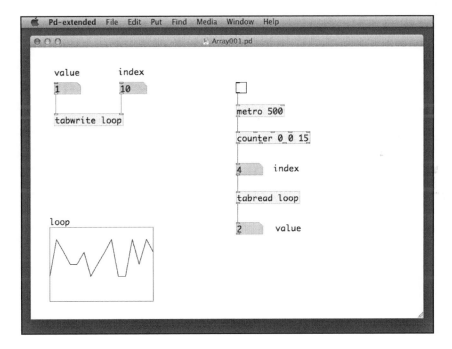

We go back to our `Audio003.pd` patch. If we have one more array loop, how can we automate the drum playback session? The array loop can only contains four numbers in its entries: 1, 2, 3, or 0. Number 1 starts the kick drum, number 2 the snare drum, and number 3 the tom-tom. Number 0 will have nothing, that is, a rest. When we loop through the array with `metro` and `counter`, it is like a drum sequencer:

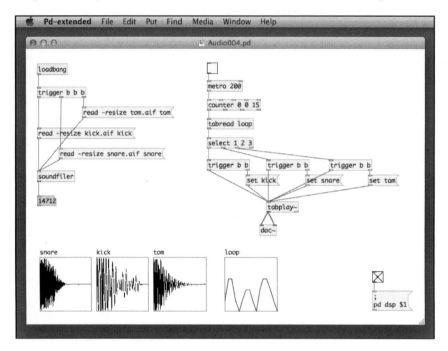

The way we input the sequence to the array loop is unnatural. As we understand how the `tabwrite` object can alter the array in real time, we can use it to input the drum sequence on the fly. The next version, `Audio005.pd`, will use a horizontal radio button group to input the drum signal, that is, a number from 0 to 3 when the metro object loops through the array loop. We can have a real-time response similar to those drum machines:

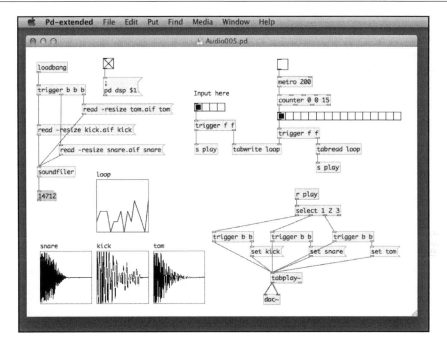

We also use a longer horizontal radio button group as a visual feedback of the current beat in the sequence. We click on the shorter radio button group under the label `Input here` in real time when the current drum sequence is being played. Note also that we have to play the selected drum sample right after the clicks on the buttons for immediate audio feedback.

Generating audio with waves

The last section mainly uses prerecorded sound for playback. We can generate original sound from Pure Data itself. We hear sound from our computers because the speakers transmit sound waves through the air. In Pure Data, we can create a sound wave with audio objects. The digital sound wave will play through the digital-to-analog converter and become the analog vibration of the speaker membranes.

In Pure Data, we create simple waveforms, such as sine wave and sawtooth wave. We shall see the waveform displays in the following patches. When we hear a piece of sound, we identify three properties: the first one is the loudness or amplitude, the second one is the pitch or frequency, and the third one is the quality or timbre. The first two properties are easy to understand. Acoustic musical instruments or our voice usually do not contain only one frequency. A note usually contains a number of different frequencies with different amplitude. They are the overtones. Usually, they are multiples of the primary frequency, the fundamental. Different musical instruments have different combinations of overtones. This is why we can identify different instruments by just hearing a few notes.

To start with, we create the patch Wave001.pd to generate a sine or cosine wave. Sine/cosine are mathematical functions in school trigonometry. The object we use is osc~. It is the cosine wave oscillator:

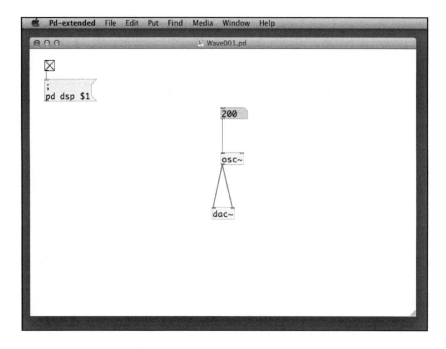

The number box inlet for osc~ is the frequency, that is, the number of oscillations per second. The unit is Hertz (Hz). The range of sound for the human ear is around 20 to 20,000 Hz. Make sure you turn on the toggle for the pd dsp message. Type a number, such as 200 in the number box to hear the sound. Change the number and hear the difference. In the following version, we visualize the waveform with an array object.

In the same patch, create an array named `wave` and default settings for the rest:

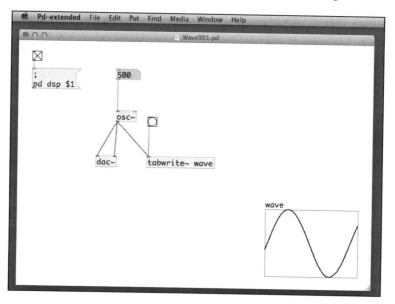

The new object `tabwrite~` reads as table write. It has the tilde suffix to indicate that it is for an audio signal. Its parameter wave corresponds to the array name we have just specified, and is shown in the graph in the bottom-right corner. The `tabwrite~` object also needs a bang input to send the oscillation signal to the array. Of course, we can automate the bang by using a `metro` object as shown in the following screenshot:

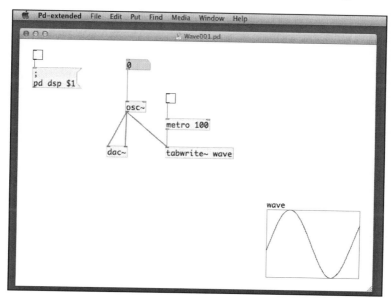

The second type of waveform Pure Data can generate is the sawtooth wave. The waveform of the saw tooth wave resembles a chain of sawtooth. The shape is sharp and has straight lines in triangular fashion. The next patch has a visual representation of the waveform. The object we use is phasor~. We can use the same patch layout and replace the osc~ object with phasor~. Take a look at the new patch, Wave002.pd:

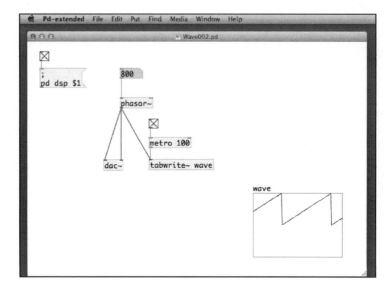

From the wave graph display, we will notice the visual difference between a sine/cosine wave and the sawtooth wave. We also see that the sine/cosine wave has both positive and negative values between -1 and 1, while the sawtooth wave has only positive values between 0 and 1.

The third type of waveform is the irregular signal that we call noise. In Pure Data, it is the noise~ object. To produce noise, we do not need to specify the frequency. We can try it out in the next patch, Wave003.pd:

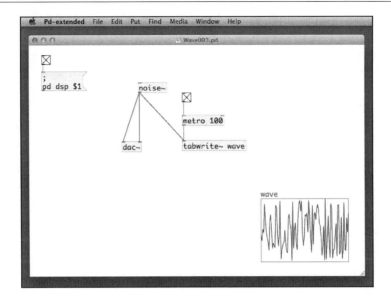

As shown in the graph display, the waveform is like a collection of random numbers. Pure Data also has another noise generator, the `pink~` object. The `noise~` object generates the white noise. The `pink~` object generates the pink noise. The technical difference is that white noise has equal energy per frequency and pink noise has equal energy per octave. The pink noise is less irritating. You will also notice the visual difference in the graph display. Here is the pink noise version:

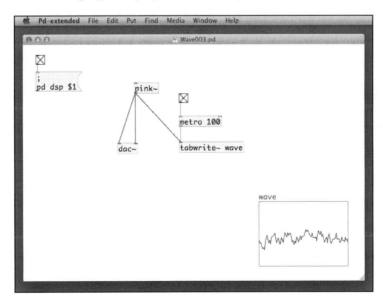

We use the number parameter in osc~ and phasor~ to specify the frequency, that is, the pitch of an audio signal. To change the amplitude (loudness), we use the multiplication operator, *~. Note that it is the regular multiplication operator with a tilde suffix. The next patch, Wave004.pd, shows how it works:

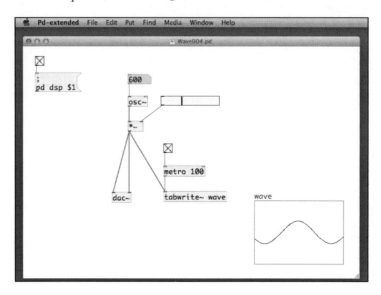

The multiplication operator has a number for its right-hand inlet. In the patch, we can use a horizontal slider with the range between 0 and 1. By moving the slider to the left-hand side or right-hand side, you can hear the change in the loudness of the sound. Pushing the slider to the right-hand margin will have the original sound volume. You will notice that the height of the graph also changes when you move the slider. The same technique can also be applied to the phasor~ and noise~ objects.

In the next Wave005.pd patch, we make use of the volume control with *~ to produce a short note, instead of a continuous sound:

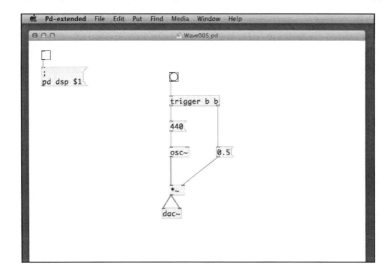

This is the one with continuous sound. You click on the bang object on the top. It branches out two signals: one to the 0.5 message for the volume control and another to the 440 message for the sound frequency.

 Note that 440 Hz is the A note in piano scale just above the middle C.

We need a new object to produce a short note. It is the delay object:

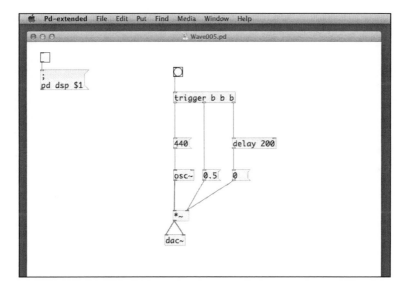

The delay object takes one parameter in a unit of milliseconds. The example will cause a delay in routing through the bang message by 200 milliseconds. The logic of the patch is: The bang box sends out three bang messages. The first one goes to the delay object and will be delayed by 200 milliseconds before it reaches the 0 message. The second bang message goes directly to the 0.5 message. The third bang message goes to the 440 message and then the osc~ object to generate the tone. After the tone is produced for 200 milliseconds, its volume will be turned down to 0.

We can use multiple frequencies to create an octave. We are going to use the horizontal radio button group to create this simple piano scale:

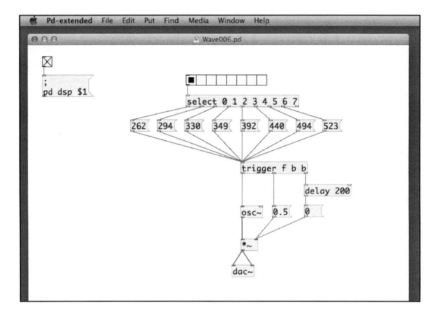

The sequence of numbers in the message boxes is the corresponding frequency in an octave.

You may notice that there may be minor glitches when you switch audio pitch or volume very quickly. It is because the Pure Data update periods for data and audio signal are different. When they are out of sync, it may result in minor disruptive sounds. When we go back to have a look at the general audio generation patch, we can further improve the quality by using more audio-related objects:

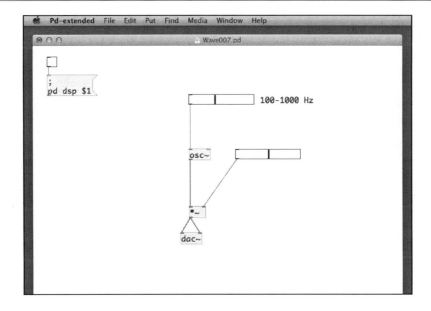

The osc~ and *~ objects can accept both numeric and audio signal inputs. In the previous example, you may notice the glitches when you move the sliders very quickly. To avoid these out-of-sync situations, we can convert the number into audio signal by using the sig~ object:

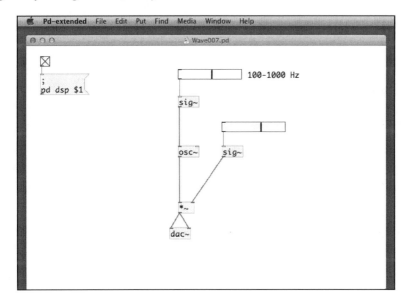

Both `sig~` objects convert the numeric values into audio signals to synchronize with other audio signals from the `osc~` and `*~` objects. To further enhance this patch, we can use another object `line~` to have a gradual change of the signals, rather than a sudden change:

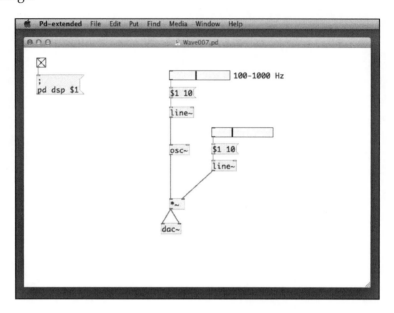

The `line~` object creates a sequence of signals, within a predefined period, changing from the original value to the new target value. Let's take the volume control slider as an example. If you push the slider from position `0.4` to `0.6`, it sends the new numeric value `0.6` to the message `$1 10`. The message substitutes `$1` with `0.6` and relays the message `0.6 10` to the `line~` object. As the former value for the `line~` object is `0.4`, it will create a gradual change of signals from `0.4` to `0.6` within the period of 10 milliseconds, as specified. It will essentially smoothen out the sound change, both for volume and frequency.

You can combine this with the piano scale example. In this patch, `Wave008.pd`, we create an instrument with more natural sound:

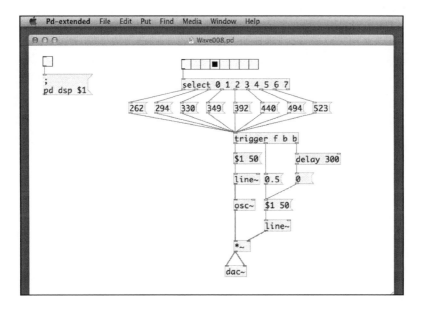

To be more expressive with the piano playing, it is always a good choice to make use of the computer keyboard rather than clicking on the radio buttons. We can just combine this with the `gemkeyboard` usage we learned in *Chapter 4, Interactivity*:

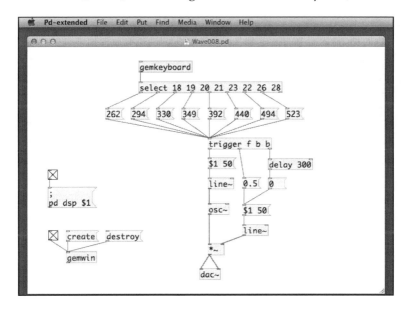

So far, we have used only one single oscillator, osc~ or phasor~ to generate the sound waves. If we have more oscillators, we can enrich the sound quality. In the following example, Wave009.pd, we include two osc~ objects and connect them together with another *~ object:

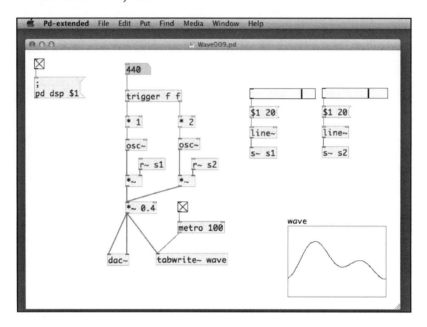

The number box sends out two signals through the trigger object. The left-hand outlet value will be the same as the original number. It is called the fundamental frequency. The right-hand outlet doubles the original number. It is called the second harmonic. The two horizontal sliders control the volume of the two osc~ objects. They are combined together through the third *~ object. Note also that we use the send and receive commands to connect the objects in a wireless way. The send and receive commands for audio signals are s~ and r~ respectively. We can have more harmonics of higher frequency. It creates the overtone that will be more similar to a natural instrument.

The other example, `Wave010.pd` will replace the amplitude of the original sound wave by another `osc~` oscillator. We will hear the resulting beat of the sound. Refer to the following screenshot:

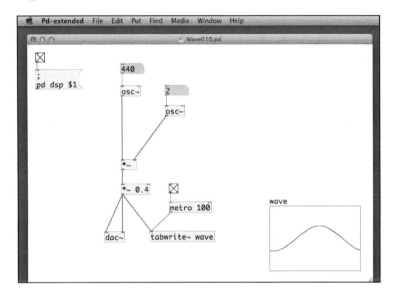

In this patch, the amplitude of the sound is actually another oscillation with a much lower frequency. We often call it as amplitude modulation. In the next example, `Wave011.pd`, we use another audio object `+~` to combine two oscillations:

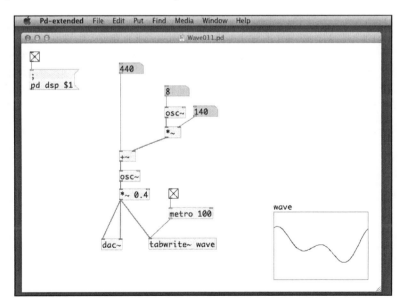

The original frequency, 440 Hz, in this case combines with another oscillating number returned by the first osc~ object on the right-hand side of the patch. The resulting number then drives another osc~ object to produce the final audio signal. We often call its approach as frequency modulation.

Working with MIDI

Musical Instrument Digital Interface (MIDI) can be found at http://www.midi.org. It is an international standard that enables various electronic musical instruments to communicate with each other. Pure Data has an extensive support of the MIDI operations. In this section, we look into simple use of MIDI signals in audio programming. We do not, however, assume readers will have external MIDI devices to work on with our examples. There are virtual synthesizers in various platforms where Pure Data is supported. We are going to use the virtual synthesizers to generate sound, instead of using external MIDI hardware. For the inputs, we'll just use the Pure Data number boxes to create the notes, instead of using a MIDI keyboard.

For Windows, built-in **Microsoft GS Wavetable Synth** can handle the MIDI output. For Linux, we can install TiMidity++ through your package manager or from http://timidity.sourceforge.net. For Mac OSX, we need to install the SimpleSynth software tool from http://notahat.com/simplesynth/.

Here is the configuration process for the SimpleSynth in Mac OSX. First of all, locate the Audio MIDI Setup program in the /Applications/Utilities folder. Double-click to run the setup process:

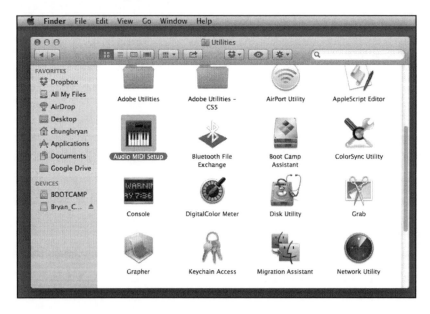

From the menu bar, choose **Window | Show MIDI Window**. Double-click on the
IAC Driver icon:

Check the box **Device is online** for the IAC Driver.

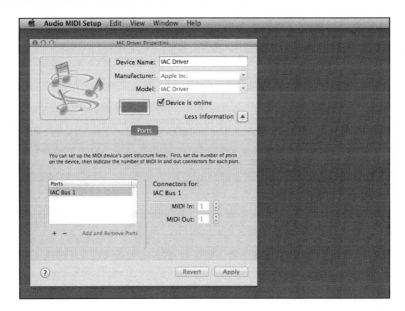

Quit the `Audio MIDI Setup` program. Then locate the `SimpleSynth` program inside the `Applications` folder. Double-click to run this program. It will show the following window:

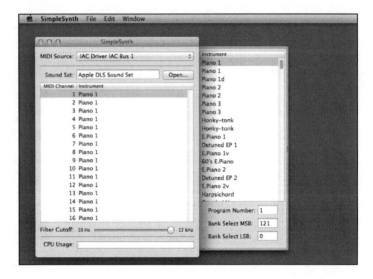

In the **MIDI Source** option, choose the **IAC Driver Bus 1** option from the pull-down menu. The left-hand side of the window shows the MIDI channels. The right-hand side of the window shows various musical instrument names. You can click on the instrument and note the corresponding program number changes in the bottom part of the panel. You do not need to close the `SimpleSynth` program, so just proceed to start the pd-extended software as usual:

In the Pure Data main menu, we choose **Preferences | MIDI settings**. For the option **output device 1**, we choose **IAC Driver Bus 1**. Finally, we click on **OK** to confirm and leave the MIDI settings panel:

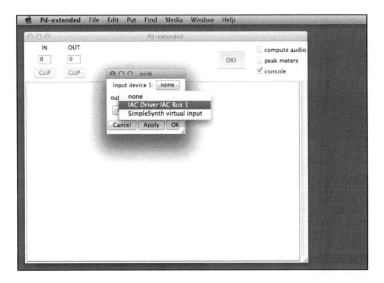

In Windows operating systems, we can choose **Microsoft GS Wavetable Synth** for the **Output device 1** option:

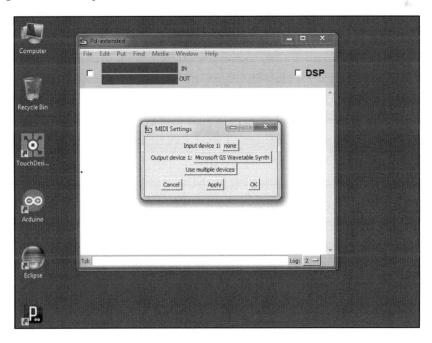

For Linux system, you can use QjackCtl (http://qjackctl.sourceforge.net) to connect the Pure Data MIDI output to the TiMidity MIDI input. From the Pure Data main menu, choose **Media | ALSA MIDI**:

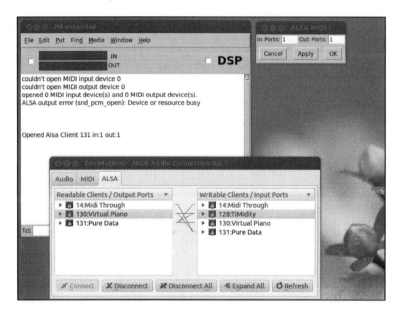

Now we are ready to prepare our first MIDI patch as `Midi001.pd`. We are going to use two MIDI objects, `makenote` and `noteout`:

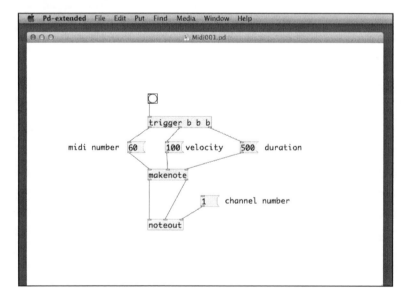

When you click on the bang box, you will hear the piano sound of a middle C note. The first object makenote will produce a MIDI note for a period of time. It takes three inlets. The left-hand one is the note number. The number 60 here is the middle C. MIDI uses numbers to represent the chromatic scale; the larger the number, the higher the pitch. The middle inlet is the velocity. You can consider it as the loudness of the note. The last inlet is the duration in milliseconds. Actually, the makenote object first generates a note-on signal and schedules a note-off signal after the duration expires. Usually, the MIDI note number and velocity number are within the range of 0 and 127.

The second object noteout transmits the note signal to the MIDI interface and plays the sound. Its first and second inlets take the MIDI note number and velocity number. The last inlet is the channel number that corresponds to the channel number in the SimpleSynth software.

In the next example, Midi002.pd, we introduce one more MIDI object, pgmout:

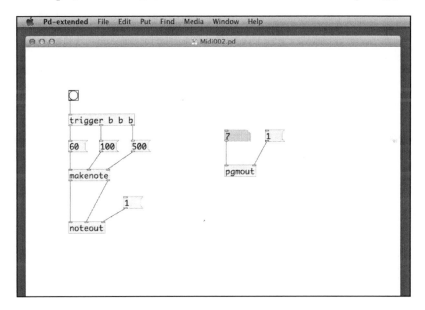

The program out object, pgmout, takes two inlets: the first one is the program number and the second one is the channel number. For the channel number, it will be the same number you used in the noteout object. For the program number, you should consider, in this case, a number that represents a different musical instrument. For example, in our patch, we use a number 7. If you go back to the SimpleSynth window and check out the instrument list, it will be the Harpsichord. You can try out different musical instruments with different program numbers.

By using these MIDI objects, we can create a piece of composition. In the next example, `Midi003.pd`, we will compose a piece using pure randomness:

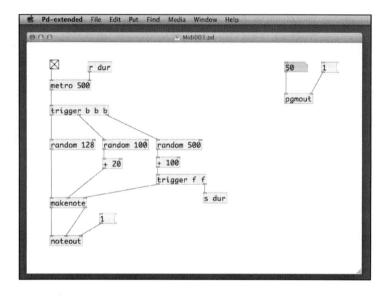

The patch has three `random` objects. The first `random 128` object will generate the MIDI note number representing the pitch. The second `random 100` object will produce the loudness of that note. We use an additional object in order to avoid a loudness value that is too small. The last `random 500` object will create the duration for that note. We also use another object to make sure the note will last at least 100 milliseconds. Note that the duration value will be sent back to the `metro` object to allow for a random interval for each note.

You can duplicate the whole patch and have two MIDI channels for playback. The next example, `Midi004.pd`, will have two channels and two different instruments. Again, they are all random notes. It can sound very much like a contemporary composition:

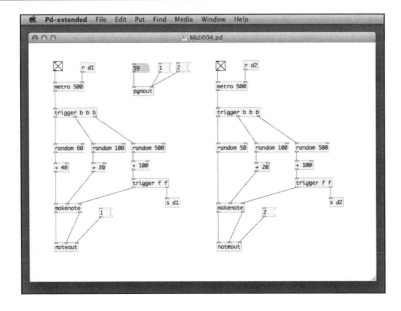

Note that we have made some modifications. The group on the left-hand side will generate a higher pitch by adding the random number with 40. The group on the right-hand side will produce the bass notes that are less than 50. For the best results, you can choose the bass instrument for the channel 2.

If you do not want to use the standard MIDI sound library, you can use the custom waveform that we created earlier in this section, with MIDI control. The new object `mtof~` will perform the conversion:

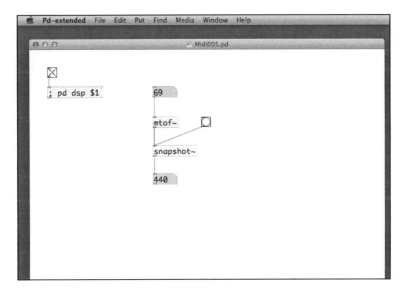

The object mtof~ stands for MIDI to frequency. It converts a MIDI note number to its corresponding audio frequency. In this example, the note number 69 is the A note with the frequency 440 Hz. The object snapshot~ converts audio signal into a number. It needs a bang message to sample the data. With this frequency data, we can send it to an oscillator such as osc~ or phasor~ to produce the audio as before:

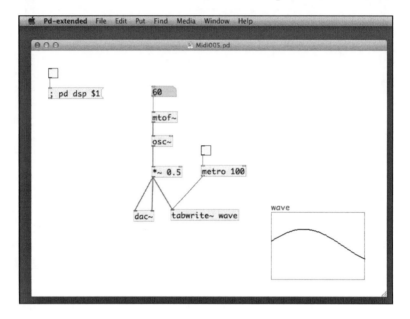

The Midi005.pd patch is very straightforward. The output from mtof~ is directly sent to the osc~ object to generate the sound wave. The rest is the same as before. So much for the MIDI part, we now move to the audio input in the next section.

Obtaining audio input for interaction

Pure Data can retrieve sound input data from your microphone. Before we start, we need to choose the proper sound input device from **Preferences** | **Audio Settings**. If you have multiple sound input devices, choose the one you would like to use. It will usually be the microphone input:

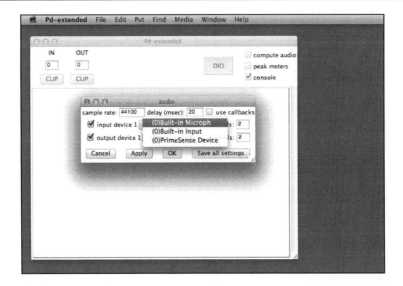

Once we select the input device, the next step is to capture the audio input data. The object is just the opposite of dac~ that we have used in previous sections. It will be the adc~, analog-to-digital converter:

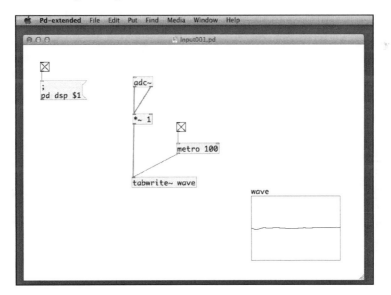

The adc~ object, by default, produces two outlets for stereo channels. We route them to the same inlet of a *~ object. The graph named wave will display the waveform of the microphone input signal. For interactive use of the microphone input, we often need to convert the sound volume into a number so that we can test it against a threshold.

For example, we can test the sound volume if it is louder than a limit or not. If it is louder, we can trigger an effect, such as playback of a digital video. To obtain the sound volume, we use the env~ object:

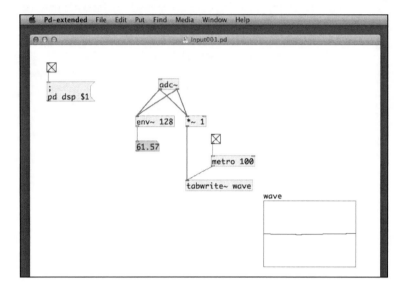

The env~ object returns the amplitude of the audio signal. The unit is decibels, normalized to 100. The number 128 is the window size of the analysis. It defines the number of samples the env~ object uses to compute the average amplitude. You can observe the value in the number box. Louder sound will produce a larger number. In the following patch, Input002.pd, we use a comparison object to test the volume and to control a graphical display:

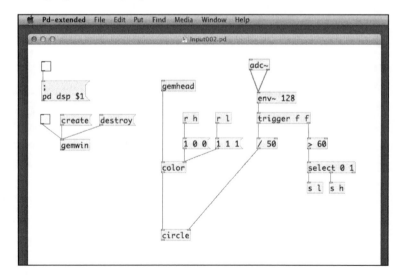

The logic is simple. The loudness data is sent to two objects. The first one is a division object that divides the number by 50, so that it can be used for the size of the circle object. The second one goes to a comparison object > 60. If the number is larger than 60, it changes the color of the `circle` to red, otherwise it will be white.

To conclude this section, let's introduce another audio object, `fiddle~`. It is a very complex object and yet we just make use of the simple functions. It will be based on the audio samples and detect the frequency and amplitude of sound in real time:

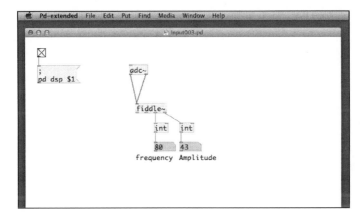

The third outlet is the frequency in MIDI note number unit. The fourth outlet is the amplitude. We also use two `int` objects to convert the numbers into integers. In this patch, `Input004.pd`, we use the frequency to produce a MIDI note with the corresponding amplitude sent to a `makenote` object. We also refer to the former random note example to generate the music:

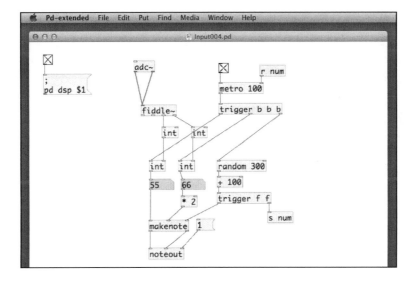

The `fiddle~` object sends out the frequency and amplitude of the audio signal. The first pair of `int` objects convert the decimal numbers into integers. The second pair of `int` objects temporarily store the numbers in the variables and wait for the bang message to route them out. The bang messages come from the `metro` object. We use the `metro` object to slow down the speed of generating the MIDI notes. If we just connect the `fiddle~` outputs to the `makenote` object, it will be too speedy to sound like a real piece of music. The `metro` object with its random intervals will slow down the tempo. You can play around with different values in the random object. This patch will try to pick up the audio information from the microphone. It then tries to reproduce the sound by using the MIDI notes from a musical instrument. Of course, the process may not be too accurate and there are also delays in the reproduction. Nevertheless, it demonstrates a generative approach to produce music where the original sound functions as a feedback to generate the subsequent notes.

Summary

In this chapter, we have learned to work with audio programming in the Pure Data environment. We understand how to playback an existing sound file and visualize its waveform. With the use of different oscillators, we can synthesize our own custom sounds. By using the software MIDI synthesizer, we can produce a sequence of musical notes within Pure Data. And finally, we can use a microphone as an interactive device to detect changes in sound volume in order to trigger visual feedback. In the next chapter, we investigate how to connect Pure Data with other external hardware devices.

8
Interface with the Outside World

Pure Data provides a number of objects to connect with other computers and peripheral hardware. In this chapter, we explore the possibilities to connect two computers through a local area network. With a smart phone, we can connect it to a computer running a Pure Data application and use the phone as an interaction device. By using a micro-controller board – the Arduino, we can integrate a Pure Data application with custom electronics, such as light sensor and LED light display. It provides developers with a wide range of tools to build custom interfaces that go beyond the conventional mouse, keyboard, and webcam. In this chapter we will cover the following topics:

- Communicating through the Internet
- Controlling the visual display of another computer
- Using Open Sound Control with mobile devices
- Interfacing with custom hardware with Arduino

Communicating through the Internet

We can send and receive data between two Pure Data applications in different computers provided that they are connected in a network. Before we can start the communication, we have to know the addresses of the two computers. The address that Pure Data uses is the IP address that we often come across the Internet. Once your computer is connected to the network, either through the wired Ethernet or the wireless Wi-Fi, we can obtain the IP address by the following methods.

In Mac OSX, we use the **Network Utility** inside the /Applications/Utilities folder. After we double-click on it to start the **Network Utility**, the front panel will show the IP Address of your computer. Alternately, we can also use the ifconfig command in the Terminal window of the Unix environment in OSX. Check for the active interface to note the IP Address. In Linux, you also use the ifconfig command in the terminal window to display the IP Address as shown in the following screenshot:

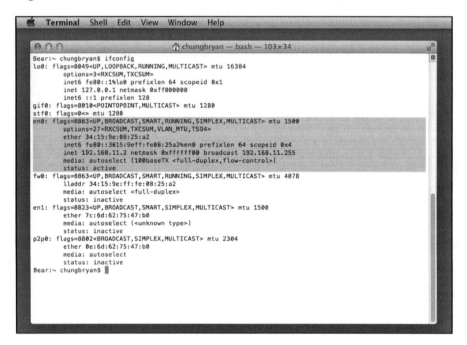

In Windows environment, we can click on the network icon in the notification bar to start the **Open Network and Sharing Center**. Within the **Network and Sharing Center**, choose the type of network connection you have, **Local Area Connection** or **Wireless Network Connection**. In our case, we have the local area network connection. Clicking on its link will take us to the next panel. Click on the **Details...** button to retrieve the detailed network information.

It will show you the IP Address as follows:

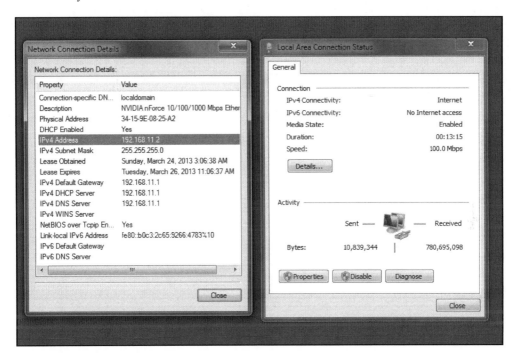

If you do not have two computers for the exercises, you can just use one. In this case, the address name `localhost` will indicate the same computer that you are using.

The Pure Data objects for network communication are `netsend` and `netreceive`. If you are familiar with the Internet technology, Pure Data uses the same TCP/IP communication protocol. Pure Data can use both **TCP (Transmission Control Protocol)** and **UDP (User Datagram Protocol)**. TCP provides a more reliable and orderly communication between software programs in a network with a prior established session. UDP provides an efficient and yet unreliable communication between software programs in a network without a prior established session.

Making the connection

In our first example, we are going to use TCP connection within the same Pure Data patch, Net001.pd for testing, as shown in the following screenshot:

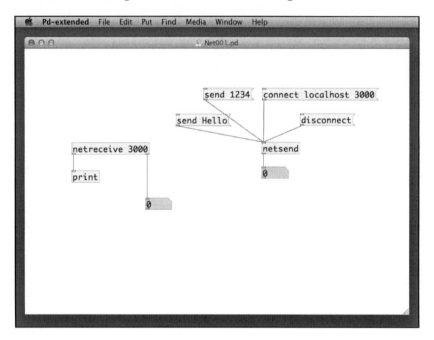

In this example, both the netsend and netreceive objects are in the same patch. The netreceive object is simple. For TCP connection, it needs just one parameter, its port number, 3000. Since a computer with one IP address can run multiple applications at the same time, we use a port number to identify which application that we would like to talk to. For example, a computer running a web server will normally use the port number 80 for communicating with the client's browser. Port numbers less than 1024 are dedicated to existing Internet applications. For individual usage, we are going to use port numbers larger than 1024.

The object netreceive 3000 will open a communication channel – a port, identified by the number 3000, and be ready to receive incoming connections. To complete the connection, the netsend object with a connect message will do the job. The connect localhost 3000 will establish the TCP connection with itself (localhost) using the port number 3000. If you are connecting to other computer, replace the localhost keyword with the IP address of that computer. Once you make the connection by clicking on the connect localhost 3000 message, you can notice the two number boxes showing a value 1. It is the number of current connection.

We can have multiple incoming connections to the `netreceive 3000` object as shown in the following screenshot:

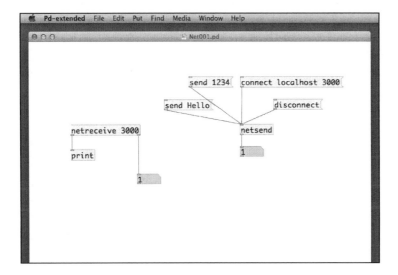

Sending messages

Once we establish the connection, we can send messages by clicking on the `send 1234` or the `send Hello` messages and you will notice the response from the console window displayed as follows:

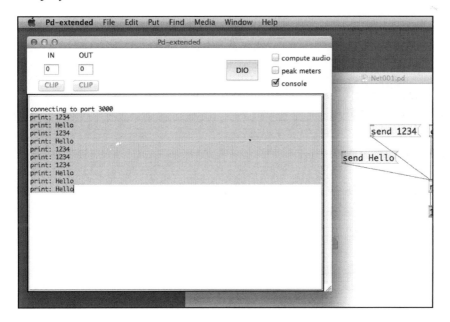

To end the connection, just click on the `disconnect` message. Now we revise the patch, `Net002.pd` to cater for sending and receiving numbers.

Sending numbers

The modification is straightforward. We replace the original send message with the `send $1` to receive the number box value. In the receiving end, we only need to replace the `print` object with a number box as shown in the following screenshot:

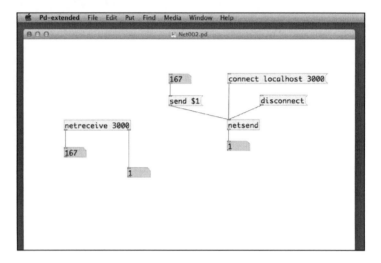

We can add one more number to send through the network. The next patch, `Net003.pd`, in the following screenshot will use the `pack` and `unpack` objects to send multiple numbers:

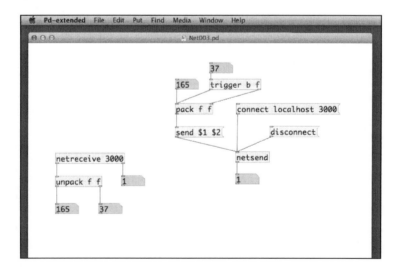

We have covered the usage of `pack` and `unpack` objects. Note the use of a `trigger` object to ensure it will send out the message even though the second number is in the cold inlet of the `pack` object. Sending a list of numbers through the network is a common technique, for example, the coordinates of a graphical shape with X, Y, and Z components.

Until now, we have only one patch that handles both the send and receive processes. The following two patches, `Net005.pd` and `Net006.pd` will demonstrate the communication can be across two separate Pure Data patches.

The patch, `Net005.pd`, contains the `netreceive` object. The patch, `Net006.pd`, contains the `netsend` object and the other messages. When both of the patches are in Run Mode, the number box value changes in the sending patch will affect the corresponding changes in the number box in the receiving patch in real time. The following screenshot is the content of the two patches we use:

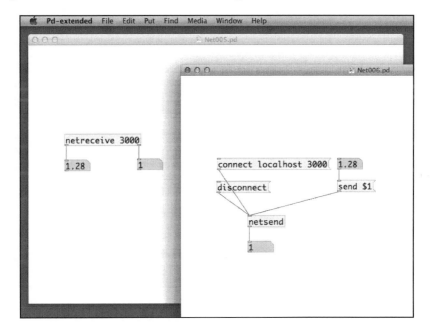

If you have two computers in the same network, you can try to put the sending patch in one computer, and the receiving patch in the other computer. Change the `connect localhost 3000` message to `connect nnn.nnn.nnn.nnn 3000`, where `nnn.nnn.nnn.nnn` is the IP address of the receiving computer. In this case, you can communicate between the two computers running Pure Data with the value in the number box.

The previous example demonstrated one-way communication between two computers. If you want to have two-way communication, we have to put the both netsend and netreceive objects in one single patch. In the first computer, we use the patch, Net005.pd. In the second computer, we use the patch, Net006. pd. Suppose the first computer has an IP address 192.168.1.10 and the second computer has an IP address 192.168.1.11. It is further explained as follows:

- Computer 1 has IP address 192.168.1.10, port 3000, patch Net005.pd
- Computer 2 has IP address 192.168.1.11, port 3001, patch Net006.pd

The patch, Net005.pd will be as as shown in the following screenshot:

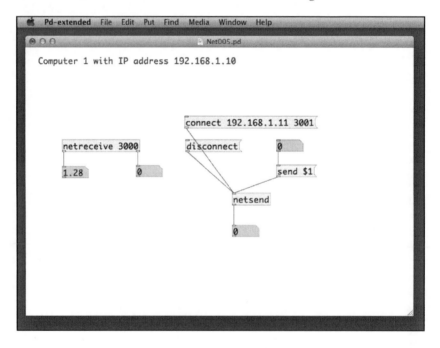

The patch, Net006.pd will be as shown in the following screenshot:

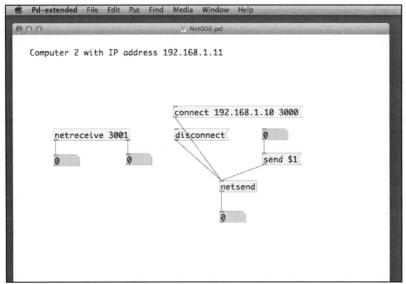

Computer 1 (192.168.1.10) listens to the port number 3000 for incoming connection. Computer 2 (192.168.1.11) listens to the port number 3001 for incoming connection. Computer 1 will connect to Computer 2 using the port number 3001. Computer 2 will connect to Computer 1 using the port number 3000.

Controlling the visual display of another computer

In the next example, we set up two patches, Net008.pd and Net009.pd. If you have two computers, you can execute the patches in separate computers. For demonstration, we open them on one single computer. In Net008.pd, we have the netsend object to send out the mouse position information to Net009.pd, using the gemmouse object. In Net009.pd, we decode the mouse position from the information obtained from the netreceive object, and display a square to follow the remote mouse position.

The following screenshot is `Net008.pd` for sending out the mouse position:

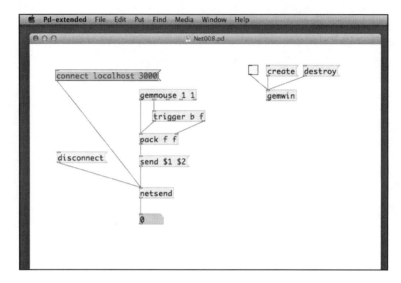

Since we are using one computer, we put the `connect localhost 3000` message for the `netsend` object. If you are using two computers, you need to use the `connect nnn.nnn.nnn.nnn 3000` message, where `nnn.nnn.nnn.nnn` is the IP address of the computer running the second patch, `Net009.pd`.

The following screenshot is `Net009.pd` for receiving the mouse position and displaying it with a square:

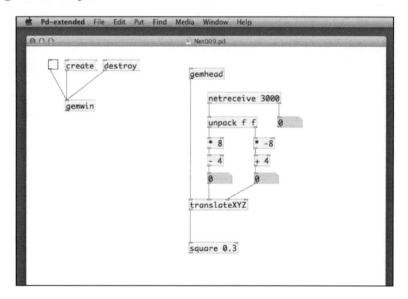

Before creating the GEM window in Net008.pd, you click on the connect message to establish the communication with Net009.pd. After that, create and render the GEM windows in both computers. If you are using one computer, only one GEM window will appear. When you move your mouse within the GEM window in Net008.pd, the white square in Net009.pd will move with the same path. In effect, you are controlling the mouse pointer of another computer within the Pure Data applications.

With the knowledge you gained in *Chapter 4*, *Interactivity*, you can extend the interaction by using the keyboard and mouse of one computer to interact with the media elements in another computer.

Using Open Sound Control with mobile devices

Open Sound Control (http://opensoundcontrol.org) is a communication standard among computers, audio synthesizers, and multimedia devices within a computer network. Pure Data supports the **Open Sound Control** (**OSC**) protocol through a library mrpeach packaged within the pd-extended software.

With the gaining popularity of multi-touch technology, it is common to use the versatile multi-touch devices to control the operation of the host software, in applications such as audio-visual performance, and multimedia display. Information exchange among the multi-touch devices use another protocol, TUIO (http://www.tuio.org), and the one that is based on the OSC. For example, we can use an iPhone to control the animation within a GEM window in a host computer running Pure Data. This is the method that we are going to explore.

The first thing is to download a free iPhone app that supports TUIO. One of the choices is the TUIOpad (http://code.google.com/p/tuiopad/) created by Mehmet Akten and Martin Kaltenbrunner. It is available at the iTunes store. The Android version is called TUIOdroid (http://code.google.com/p/tuiodroid) written by Tobias Schwirten and Martin Kaltenbrunner. It is available at the Android Market. In the next example, we'li use the iOS version for demonstration.

Connecting the TUIOpad to the host computer

To connect the TUIOpad with the Pure Data application, the iOS device has to have Wi-Fi connectivity to the same network with the host computer running Pure Data. We need to know the IP address of the host computer and a port number to receive the OSC data. The following screenshot shows a typical configuration setting for the TUIOpad:

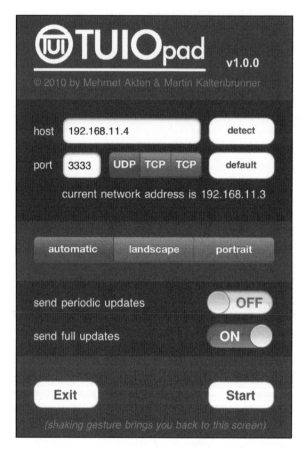

The host `192.168.11.4` is the IP address of the host computer running the Pure Data patch. The port `3333` is communication port number. We choose UDP for the communication protocol. In the host computer, we use this patch, `OSC001.pd` to receive the OSC data sent from the iPhone as shown in the following screenshot:

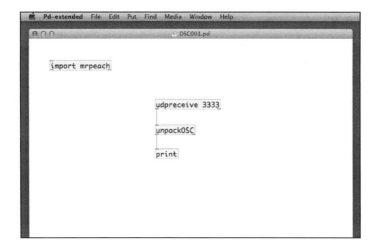

The `import` object loads the `mrpeach` package that manages the OSC communication protocol. The `udpreceive 3333` object specifies the patch will receive UDP data through the port number 3333. The `unpackOSC` object will unpack the incoming data into readable formats for the `print` object to display in the console window. Once both sides are ready, we click on the **Start** button from the TUIOpad. A blank screen appears where you can use your fingers to draw on the display.

When you start tapping and drawing on the iPhone screen, you will notice the OSC data stream in the console window. The following screenshot is a sample of the messages in the console window:

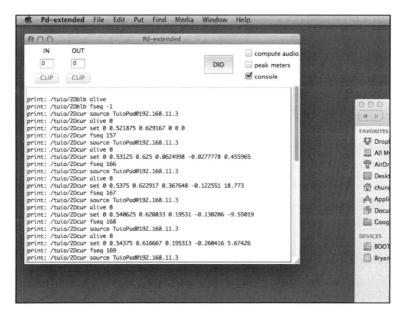

Decoding the OSC messages

The next step will be the decoding of the OSC messages. The following is a typical listing of the OSC messages from the TUIOpad. It starts with a first prefix /tuio and the second prefix /2Dcur:

```
/tuio/2Dcur source TuioPad@158.182.188.142
/tuio/2Dcur alive 2 3
/tuio/2Dcur set 2 0.41875 0.76875 0 0 0
/tuio/2Dcur set 3 0.3 0.304167 0 0 0
/tuio/2Dcur fseq 7717
/tuio/2Dcur source TuioPad@158.182.188.142
/tuio/2Dcur alive 2 3
/tuio/2Dcur set 2 0.3875 0.7625 -0.315657 -0.0631316 3.25159
/tuio/2Dcur set 3 0.35 0.297917 0.50505 -0.0631313 5.14122
/tuio/2Dcur fseq 7723
```

We'll use the routeOSC object to select the types of messages we are interested in. The routeOSC object is the OSC version of the original route object in Pure Data. It scans through the incoming message from the inlet, looks for the OSC keywords specified as parameters in the routeOSC object, and distribute the message streams to the different outlets according to which keywords they belong to.

A regular route object performs similarly. The route object usually has a number of keywords as arguments. It scans through the incoming message from its inlet; identifies those keywords in the message, and routes that message to different outlets according to the keyword that prefixed it.

The first routeOSC object selects the all the TUIO messages with prefix keyword /tuio. The second routeOSC object selects the messages for 2D cursor with prefix keyword /2Dcur. Of those messages about 2D cursor, we use the regular route object to filter the set messages that define the cursor positions. The route set object will locate the set keyword in the message and route the remaining information after the set keyword to the first outlet as shown in the following screenshot:

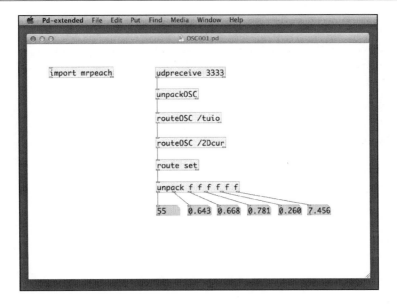

The output in the `set cursor` message is a list of six numbers. The first one is the cursor id. Every time you touch the screen, it is assigned with a new cursor id. The second and third number boxes are the X and Y positions of the cursor, with a normalized range between 0 and 1. The fourth and fifth number boxes are the X and Y velocity values. The last number is the acceleration value. Since the iPhone screen is a multi-touch interface, it can return multiple cursor points. For simplicity, the following example will use only one cursor point for demonstration. We are going to create a GEM window with a piece of text following your interaction on the iPhone screen. Once we acquire the X and Y positions of the cursor, we can easily send them to a `translateXYZ` object in the GEM environment.

The patch sends the cursor ID to the `text2d` object for display. The normalized X and Y positions are mapped to the -4 and 4 range of the X and Y axes in the GEM window.

The following screenshot is the `OSC002.pd` patch:

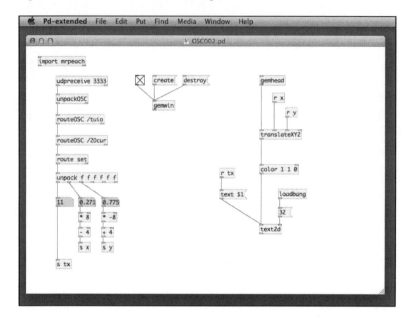

The GEM window output together with the TUIOpad screen will look like the following screenshot:

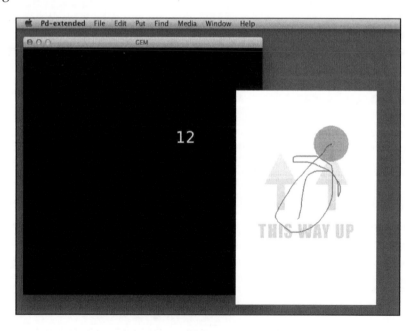

Once we have the X and Y positions of the touch point in the GEM window, we can treat the cursor as the mouse, or the motion tracking position that we learned in previous chapters. Our smartphone or tablet can now function as a control device for interactivity in the host computer.

Tracking multiple points

If we want to incorporate more touch points in the interaction, the patch can become very complex. The patch, OSC003.pd will try to track two touch points as shown in the following screenshot:

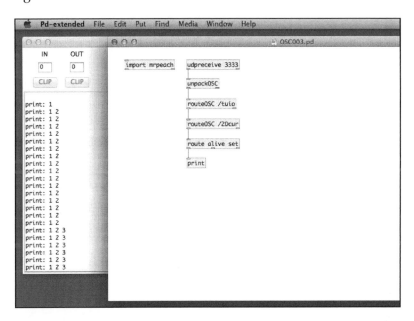

The alive message contains a list of cursor IDs that are active in the multi-touch screen. We see from the console window that we can have multiple touch points in one single alive message. In the next step, we use the list object to determine the number of touch points. A list data structure in Pure Data is a variable length message of a sequence of items, usually of the same type. The list object manipulates the data structure with the following functions:

- **list append / list prepend**: These functions concatenate two lists together either at the end or at the front respectively
- **list split**: This function splits a list into two
- **list trim**: This function trims the list selector off the original list
- **list length**: This function returns the number of items in a list

A `list` object without any arguments is a container, which is like a variable of a list.

The `list length` object in the previous image has a list as input and outputs the number of elements in the list through its outlet. We come across the use of list in the studies of the `pack` and `unpack` objects. Once we know the number in the list, that is the number of touch points, we can split the list into the two number boxes as shown in the following screenshot:

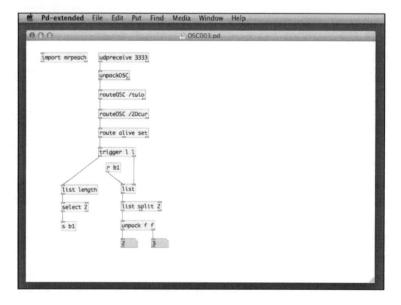

The new command is the object `list split 2`. We first temporarily store the `alive` message list into a `list` object. Once we determined the length of the list is two, through the `select 2` object, we send a `bang` message to the hot inlet of the `list` object to output the list to `list split 2`. It will split the `list` and output the first two elements from the first outlet and the rest of the list to the second outlet. We then use an `unpack` object to separate the list into two numbers, representing the cursor ID of the two touch points.

When we obtain the two IDs of the touch points, we can search the `set` message for the X and Y positions of the two touch points. Again, it will be quite complex. We'll use the `list` object again as shown in the following screenshot:

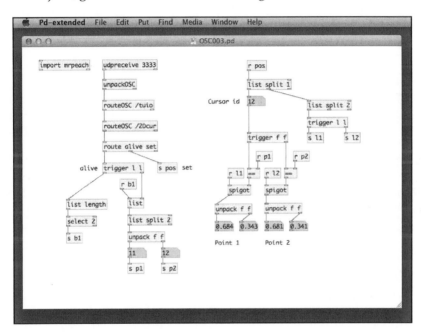

In the `route alive set` object, it sends out the `set` message list for each touch point. We first use the `list split 1` object to extract the first item from the list, and which is the cursor id. It is then compared with the two cursor ids stored from the alive message, by using the comparison operator `==`. From the second outlet of the `list split 1` object, another `list split 2` object will extract the X and Y positions of the touch point. If the cursor ID from the `set` message matches with any one of the cursor ID stored from the `alive` message, it will turn on the `spigot` object to pass X and Y positions to the `unpack` object, and finally deposited into the two number boxes. Since we just maintain two touch points from the `alive` message, we use four number boxes to store the X and Y positions for the two points.

Drawing the graphics

To complete this patch, we add the graphics display with the GEM library. The patch window is now quite full. If we want to introduce more objects, we can consider using sub-patch. For example, we can put all the GEM graphics display into a sub-patch named show-graphics. To create a sub-patch, we put an empty object on the patch window and name it pd show-graphics. An empty patch window pops up where you can put your additional objects and messages. Here is the sub-patch show-graphics shown in the following screenshot:

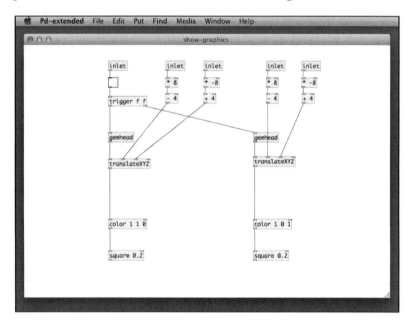

The sub-patch has two gemhead objects that draw two small squares with different color. We also define five inlets. The first one is a toggle that enables/disables the display of the two squares. When we have exactly two touch points on the screen, we enable the display in GEM window. The other four inlets are the X and Y positions of the two points. We use them to translate the position of the squares. For the main patch, OSC004.pd, we modify it slightly to send the corresponding information to the sub-patch's inlets as shown in the following screenshot:

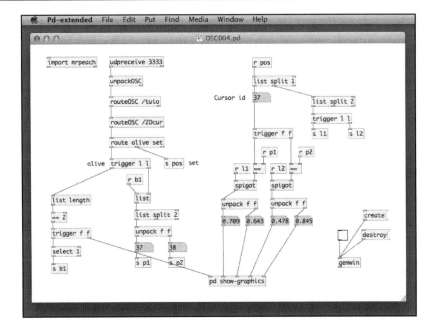

After comparing the length of the list in the `alive` message, we send the result to the first inlet of the sub-patch. The other four inlets are for the X and Y positions of the two touch points. We also include the `gemwin` setup in the patch. Now, when you connect your TUIOpad from iPhone, and use two fingers to touch on the screen, the GEM window will have two squares following the movement of your two fingers.

We have just done the communication between a mobile device and the Pure Data application in a host computer. In the next section, we try to use Pure Data to control an external micro-controller board.

Interfacing with custom hardware through Arduino

When we design the interface for an interactive artwork or product, we may need to use physical objects for the interaction design, such as a touch sensitive paper, a weight sensing chair, or a motor-controlled device. In this case, we have to look for a computing device that can interface with those custom hardware. A micro-controller will serve the purpose. A micro-controller is a small computer that mainly takes care of external inputs and outputs with custom electronics. Arduino (http://www.arduino.cc) is a popular choice in the creative communities, due to its simplicity and online support.

Before we start, you have to get an Arduino board with a number of accessories from its official store at `http://store.arduino.cc/ww/index.php` or other worldwide distributors. Besides the Arduino micro-controller, we also need a few LED lights, resistors, on-off switches, connection wires, servomotors, and photo-resistors. The following figure is of an Arduino board with a breadboard:

The breadboard on the left-hand side is for easy connection of the wires. We do not need to solder the connection permanently. For prototyping, we can just use the connection wires to build the circuit on the breadboard. If you buy the Arduino kits, you may have the following parts supplied with the kits. Otherwise, you may need to buy the parts in local electronics stores. The resistors we use in the examples are of 330 Ohm and 10K Ohm are as shown in the following figure:

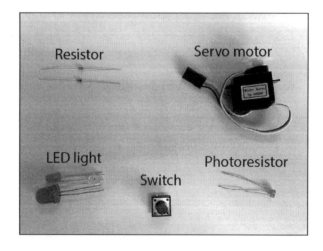

There are more electronic parts in the kits. For our examples, we use just a few of them to demonstrate the following functionalities of Arduino:

- Digital output
- Servomotor control
- Digital input
- Analog input

The next step is to download the Arduino software. It is available at `http://arduino.cc/en/Main/Software`. Choose your platform; download the corresponding software and install it in your computer. Follow the installation instructions for your specific platform. If you have older Arduino board, that is other than the UNO, you may also need to install the driver for serial communication from `http://www.ftdichip.com/Drivers/VCP.htm`. The Arduino website has clear installation instructions.

Once the software and driver are ready, you can connect the Arduino to your computer with a USB cable. After the driver is installed, we start the Arduino application as shown in the following screenshot:

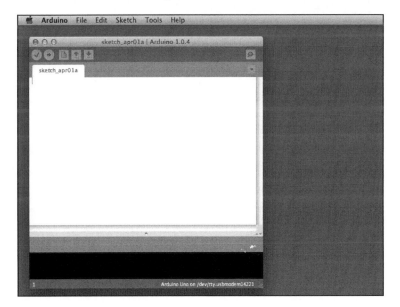

The previous image is the default window for an empty program in Arduino. We have to check the Arduino board type and the connection before we can start using the board. To select the proper type for the Arduino board, we navigate to **Tools | Board**. In our example, we have an Arduino UNO, so choose **Aduino Uno** as shown in the following screenshot:

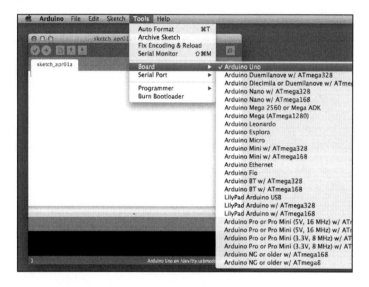

The next option is the serial connection. Your computer and the Arduino board will communicate through the USB cable in serial, that is one message at a time. To specify it, choose **Serial Port** from the **Tools** menu as shown in the following screenshot:

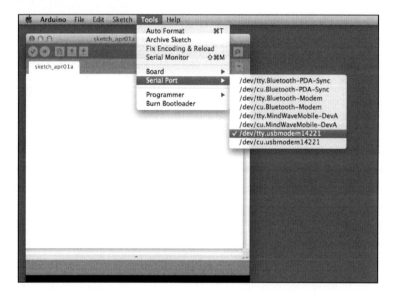

In Linux and Mac OSX, the serial port appears as **/dev/tty...** In Windows, the serial port is like, COM1, COM2, and so on. If you do not have other serial devices, your Arduino will usually be the only one you can choose from the **Serial Port** panel. Once we have selected the board type and serial port, we can start to use the Arduino board. In this book, we do not learn to write custom programs for the Arduino board. Instead, we are going to use the standard programs that belong to the firmata standard. **Firmata** (http://firmata.org/wiki/Main_Page) is a standard protocol for micro-controller to communicate with the host computer. In Arduino, we can open one of the standard firmata programs and load it to the Arduino board by navigating to **File | Examples | Firmata | StandardFirmata** as shown in the following screenshot:

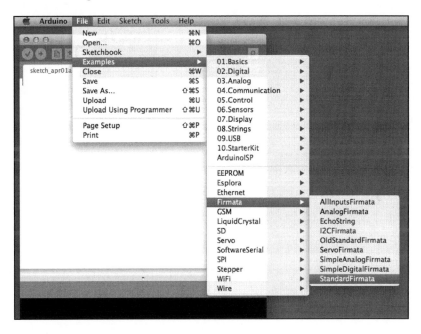

Then navigate to **File | Upload** to upload the program to your Arduino board. Or you can also click on the **Upload** button for the same purpose as shown in the following screenshot:

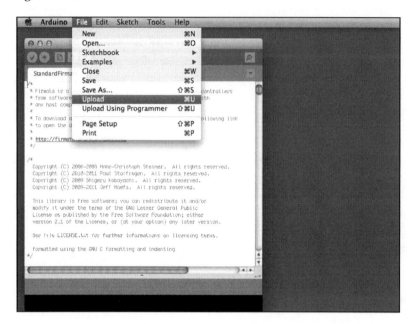

The program will respond with a successful message **Done uploading**. A failure is usually due to wrong board type or serial port selections. Now, the program is residing in the Arduino's memory. Even if you disconnect the USB cable, the program will still be there. The next step will be in the Pure Data. We are going to use the Pduino library, http://at.or.at/hans/pd/objects.html from Hans-Christoph Steiner. Download the Pduino-0.5.zip file. Unzip it. Copy the files arduino.pd and arduino-help.pd into the folder where you keep your Pure Data patches for the coming exercises.

In this book, we do not cover the details of electronics and the schematic diagrams. Readers can use the reference in the Arduino website. In the following examples, we may refer to some standard examples in the Arduino website. Readers are advised to read them when appropriate. As we are using Pduino for Pure Data, it is not necessary to copy the Arduino codes in the websites. You only need to reference the hardware connection procedures.

Digital output

The first example is to use Pure Data to turn on and off an LED light in the Arduino board. We connect one LED light to the digital pin 13 of the Arduino board, in series with a 330 Ohm resistor. You can also reference the hardware connection diagram on the Arduino website at `http://arduino.cc/en/Tutorial/Blink`. The actual connection will be as seen in the following screenshot:

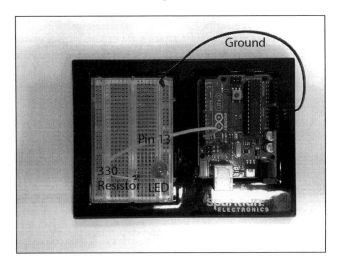

With the `arduino.pd` in your folder, we create a new patch, `Micro001.pd`. The main component in the patch will be the Arduino abstraction. Before we control the LED light, we learn how to communicate with the Arduino board first as shown in the following screenshot:

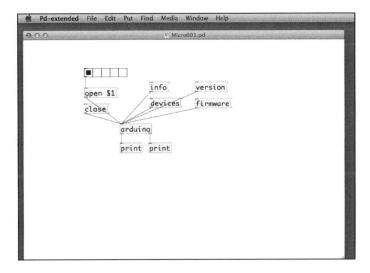

First of all, we use the `devices` message to list out all the available serial port devices in our computer. From the console window, note the index of the proper serial port device for your Arduino board as shown in the following screenshot:

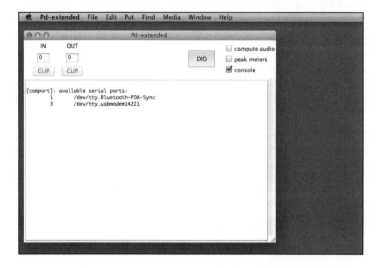

In our case, we use the number 3, `/dev/tty.usbmodem4221`. We have to click on the number 3 radio button above the `open $1` message. Remember that the button value start from 0, not 1. Once the port is opened, you can click on other messages to check information of your Arduino board and the connection. To finish, click on the `close` message.

Then we include other details for the LED light control in the new patch, `Micro002.pd` as shown in the following screenshot:

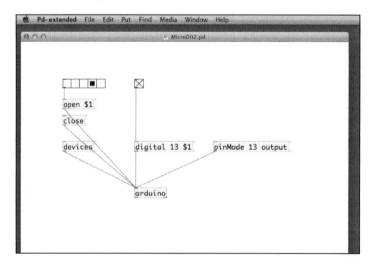

The `pinMode 13 output` message tells the patch that pin 13 will be used for output. To begin, we click the corresponding radio button for the serial port device, in our case, the number 3. Then we click on the `pinMode 13 output` message. The `digital 13 $1` message will take care of the actual switching on and off of the pin 13. We can turn on and off the toggle and check with status of the LED light in the Arduino board. Turning on/off the toggle will also turn on/off the LED light respectively. To finish, click on the `close` message.

As an exercise, try to connect a `metro` object to flash the LED light automatically. If you remember what we have learnt in the color tracking examples, it would be wonderful that you can extend the virtual hotspot to trigger a real LED display.

Servomotor control

The second example is to use a Pure Data slider to control the direction of a servomotor in the Arduino board. Servomotor is a type of electric motor that changes and maintains a direction. The Arduino website has the detailed connection diagram and explanation at `http://arduino.cc/en/Tutorial/Sweep`. A typical servomotor has three wires. The red one goes to the supply voltage, 5V in our case. Other servomotor may use 6V instead. You need to check the specification before wiring it. The black wire goes to the ground input. The white one goes to the pwm pin, 9 in our case. The actual connection is as shown in the following screenshot:

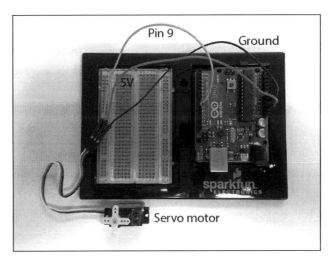

Similarly we have to inform the Arduino abstraction that the pin will be used for servomotor control as shown in the following screenshot:

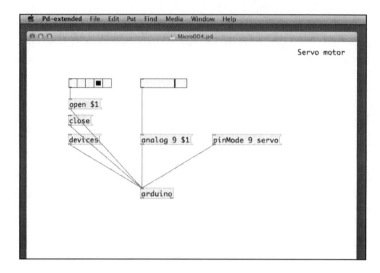

Again, with this patch, `Micro004.pd`, select the proper serial port device and click on the `pinMode 9 servo` message. The `analog 9 $1` message will inform the Arduino that the data value will be for analog output. The horizontal slider range is between 0 and 1. Moving the slider will change the direction of the servomotor. The range of the motor rotation is usually a bit less than 180 degree. You can also note that the motor will hold at a position even though you stop moving the slider.

Remember what we have done with the motion tracking examples. If we use the X position of the tracked position and send it to the servomotor direction control, we can implement a physical object that can always point to you wherever you move in front of the webcam.

Digital input

The third example is to use an on/off switch from the Arduino board to control a toggle in Pure Data. The switch is like a push button. It turns on when you push it down. It turns off when you release your finger. A similar reference can be found in the Arduino website at `http://arduino.cc/en/Tutorial/DigitalReadSerial`. You can ignore the serial part and the Arduino codes. Let's first connect the 5V power supply to one leg of the switch, while the other leg of the switch will connect first to a 10K resistor and finally to the ground. In the second leg of the switch, we also connect it to the digital pin 2 of the Arduino board. The following figure gives the connection in detail:

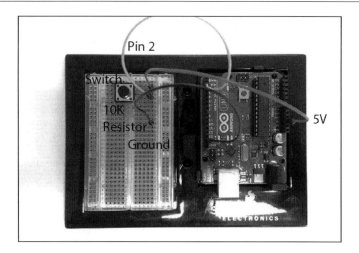

Similarly, we need to inform the Arduino abstraction that the digital pin 2 is for input. The following screenshot shows the patch, `Micro005.pd`, for digital input:

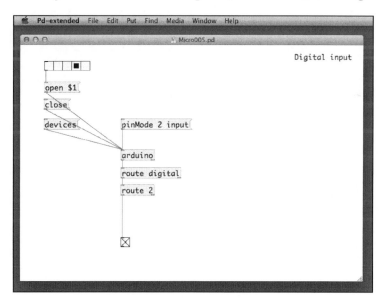

Click on the `pinMode 2 input` message to let the Arduino board know that the pin 2 is for input. Note that digital pins in the Arduino can be configured as either input or output, with the `pinMode` message. Now, you can turn to the Arduino board and press the on/off switch. Pressing the switch will turn on the toggle. Releasing it will turn it off. It is the opposite direction of digital output. Note the use of the two `route` objects. The first one will pick up the digital input message. The second one picks up only those for the pin 2.

Referring to our previous VJ equipment, we use the keyboard to control the video effects selection. With this patch, we can actually build our own buttons for such devices.

Analog input

The fourth example is to use a photo-resistor (light sensor) from the Arduino board to control a slider in Pure Data. It is similar to the previous example for digital input, except that we use a photo-resistor, instead of a switch. A photo-resistor is a resistor that changes its resistance value according to the lighting condition. With its light sensitive property, we can use it as a light sensor. A similar example can be found in the Arduino playground website at `http://playground.arduino.cc/Learning/PhotoResistor`. We connect the 5V power supply to a 10K resistor. The other end of the 10K resistor will connect to the first leg of the photo-resistor. The second leg of the photo-resistor will go to the ground. The analog pin 0 from the Arduino board will connect to the first leg of the photo-resistor. The following is a figure of the wiring:

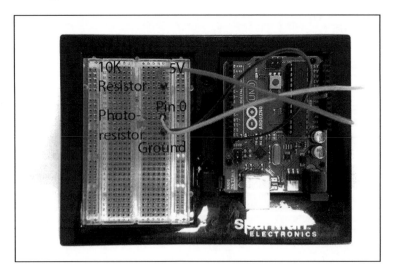

The analog input example, Micro006.pd is a bit different from the previous one. We can turn on and off the detection of an analog pin of the Arduino as shown in the following screenshot:

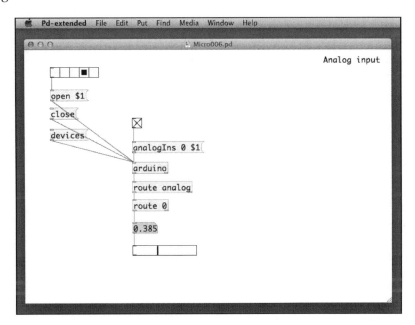

After we choose the serial port device, we turn on the toggle for the detection of the analog pin 0, by the analogIns 0 $1 message. A number between 0 and 1 will be returned from the Arduino abstraction. It is the normalized voltage detected by the analog pin 0. In our case, it will be a measurement of the resistance value of the photo-resistor. You can try to cover and reveal the photo-resistor to observe the changes in value of the slider. It may not cover the whole 0 to 1 range. The value indicates how much light is shed on the photo-resistor. We can use it as a proximity sensor or non-contact touch sensor. Imagine we can use the light intensity to change the frequency of the audio signal. It will be like a pitch bend device with just your hands waving in the air.

Summary

We have gone through a long and complex chapter. In this chapter we tried to extend the use of Pure Data beyond a desktop computer. We made use of the Ethernet or Wi-Fi network to connect two computers for information exchange. A mobile device, such as a smartphone or a tablet computer can communicate with a Pure Data application through the OSC protocol. We can take advantage of the multi-touch screen to control applications in the host computer. Finally, we introduce the use of micro-controller, a small piece of computer interfacing with sensors, motor, and LED light. With the Arduino platform, we can extend a Pure Data application to control LED light display and motor rotation. It also enables Pure Data to use physical switch and light sensor as input devices. We have covered more or less all the essential elements in Pure Data for multimedia programming. In the next chapter, we'll have a short conclusion of what we have learnt and also the explanation on how we can use other libraries that the pd-extended package does not include, for more advanced applications.

9
Extending Pure Data

We have learned basic concepts and techniques for multimedia programming with Pure Data in the previous chapters. It covers the major tasks that interactive media artists/designers may encounter in their creative practices. Before we conclude the book, we present a number of external libraries that are not included in the standard pd-extended package. The libraries are common in the interactive media communities that greatly enhance the capabilities of Pure Data. We'll cover the topics on:

- Integrating with OpenCV
- Working with the Microsoft Kinect camera

To work on with the OpenCV examples, you need a webcam for your computer. For the Kinect examples, you need to have the Microsoft Xbox Kinect camera (http://www.xbox.com/en-US/kinect) together with the A/C power adapter.

> Please also note that the libraries we are going to use only come with the handy pre-built versions for the Mac OSX platform. In order to work in the latest operating systems and Pure Data, the Windows and Linux versions have to be built from source, and which is beyond the scope of this book. As a result, the following sections cover only the Mac OSX platform.

Integrating with OpenCV

OpenCV, Open Source Computer Vision, http://opencv.org, is an established free library for computer vision applications on various platforms. Typical computer vision applications are visual pattern recognition, face detection, motion tracking, and so on. The original OpenCV has interfaces for programming languages such as C++, C, Python, and Java. Pure Data also has an external library that interfaces with OpenCV to include a subset of the functions. The version that integrates with GEM is pix_opencv. The original project page for pix_opencv is at http://hangar.org/wikis/lab/doku.php?id=start:puredata_opencv.

For the Mac OSX environment, you can have a precompiled version at `http://puredata.info/downloads/opencv/releases/0.2`. It includes the necessary dependencies, such as the OpenCV framework. After you unzip the downloaded file, it includes the following three items:

1. `OpenCV-Private-Framework-1.2.dmg`

2. `pix_opencv` folder

3. `puredata_opencv.pdf`

The `OpenCV-Private-Framework-1.2.dmg` file is the disk image for the OpenCV framework. You can mount the disk image and extract the framework as `OpenCV.framework`. The `pix_opencv` folder contains everything we need to run the OpenCV library in Pure Data. The `puredata_opencv.pdf` file is the documentation of the library. To install the library, we need to put them into the `~/Library folder`, and which is the personal folder for each user account in the Mac OSX system. Normally, the folder is invisible. To locate it, you have to hold down the *Option* key and click on **Go** from the main menu bar.

Within the `~/Library folder`, locate the `Frameworks` folder and place the `OpenCV.framework` folder into it. If the `Frameworks` folder is not available, create a new one.

Within the `~/Library folder`, locate the `Pd` folder. If it does not exist, create it. Copy the `pix_opencv` folder into it.

The OpenCV library works with the GEM library at Version 0.93.3. The pd-extended program we have been using does not meet the minimum requirement. By the time of writing this chapter, the latest pd-extended program has already upgraded to 0.43.4 that can fulfill the GEM library requirement. In order to work with the OpenCV library, we have to upgrade our pd-extended installation to the latest 0.43.4. The steps are the same as what we have mentioned in the *Preface*.

Now we are ready for our first patch with the OpenCV library, OpenCV001.pd. Here it is the patch with the pix_opencv_threshold object.

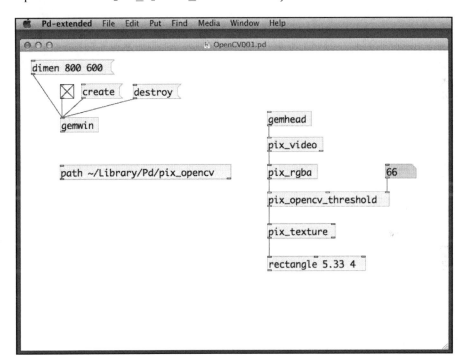

Before we can use the pix_opencv functions, we use the path object to inform Pure Data that it has to search the folder ~/Library/Pd/pix_opencv for the library files. The pix_opencv_threshold object is like a threshold filter in image processing. The number box in the right inlet defines the threshold value that turns the pixels black.

The next example, OpenCV002.pd is the famous face detection program in OpenCV. The object is pix_opencv_haarcascade. It requires a parameter file that is the trained data for recognition of various facial features. In the pix_opencv folder, there is a subfolder haarcascades that contains all the available parameter files for face and body recognition. In the following patch, we are going to use an openpanel object to select the appropriate parameter file for face detection.

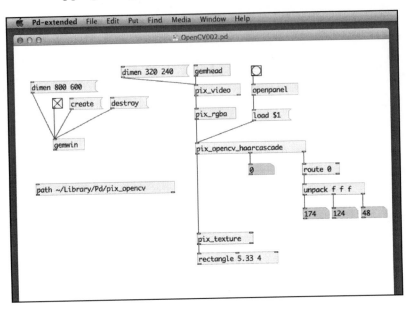

To run the patch, we click on the **bang** object and choose the parameter file for the face detection program. Again, within the file choosing panel, type slash /, to invoke the data entry box, and type in ~/Library/Pd/pix_opencv/haarcascades, that is the folder containing all the trained parameter files.

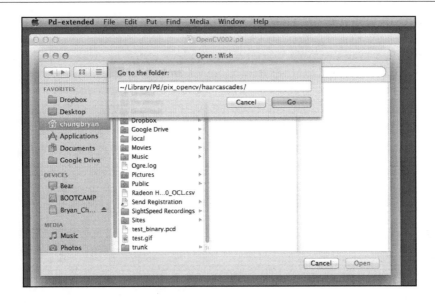

Choose one of those files for frontal face, such as `haarcascade_frontalface_alt.xml`. Go back to your patch window and start the GEM window and rendering process as usual. The GEM window display will be as what follows.

The GEM window will show a circle to indicate a face. The number inside the circle is the index for the face detected. If you have more faces in the scene, the numbers count from 0, 1, 2, and so on. In your application, you may want to have your own graphics to follow the face. In that case, you can make use of the second and third outlets from the `pix_opencv_haarcascade` object.

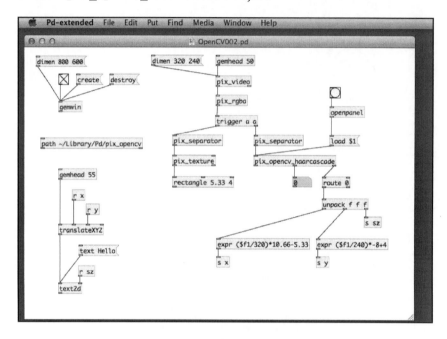

In the preceding patch, the second outlet from the `pix_opencv_haarcascade` object is the total number of faces detected. The third outlet is a list of all faces information in a format of `id x-position y-position radius`. We use a `route` object to extract only the first face data with the ID 0. Of course, you can extract more faces data by specifying more numbers after the `route` object. After the `route` object, we use a `unpack` object to split into three numbers. The first one is the X position of the face. The second one is the Y position. The last one is the radius of the face detected. The unit of measurement is pixel. Since we use the default video size with the message `dimen 320 240`, the X and Y positions of the face are measured against this dimension. The two `expr` objects convert the 320 x 240 range into the 10.66 x 8 range for the GEM window size. Note that the Y direction is reversed between the two measurements. These scaled position values are sent to the `translateXYZ` object to alter the position of a piece of text—**Hello**. For the radius value, we send it directly to the point size value of the `text2d` object. It can roughly match with each other. The result display in GEM window is like the following screenshot:

There are a lot more examples in the OpenCV library. Interested readers can follow the help file for each object to try out the effects. We do not intend to cover all the functions here.

Working with the Kinect camera

The Microsoft **Kinect** camera is a consumer 3D depth-sensing device. The use of a 3D camera will greatly enhance the effectiveness of body tracking. The official Microsoft SDK runs only in the Windows environment. There are, however, a few open source alternatives, that support multiple platforms, such as Mac OSX and Linux. They are as follows:

- The **OpenKinect** software, `http://openkinect.org/wiki/Main_Page`
- The **OpenNI** software, `http://www.openni.org/`

For Pure Data, Matthias Kronlachner, `http://www.matthiaskronlachner.com`, has developed a number of external libraries that support both OpenKinect and OpenNI. The `pix_freenect` object supports the use of OpenKinect driver—`libfreenect`. The `pix_openni` object supports the use of the OpenNI driver. A Kinect camera will give you two images, one normal RGB color image and one depth image. The depth image will provide you the depth information of each pixel in the color image. The `pix_freenect` object will give you both the RGB color image and the depth image as normal GEM pixel data. In addition, the `pix_openni` object can give you body information about the positions of the skeleton, such as head, neck, hip, arm, leg, and so on.

The pd-extended version we are going to use is 43.4. Before we can use the Pure Data libraries, we have to install both the OpenKinect driver—`libfreenect` and the OpenNI software. The installation process demands a little working knowledge of the Unix environment in Mac OSX. We'll go back to the command line environment by using the `Terminal` application. To invoke the `Terminal` application, go to the folder `/Applications/Utilities`. Double-click on the **Terminal** icon to start the command line window.

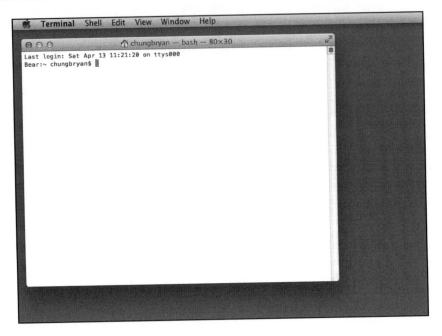

Installation of libfreenect

The OpenKinect website has detailed instructions for the installation of `libfreenect`. If you do not want to do it yourself, you can use the **Homebrew** installation method. Homebrew is a friendly way to install software packages in the Mac OSX environment. The Homebrew software is available at `http://mxcl.github.io/homebrew/`. Firstly, you need to have a password for your account. The Homebrew installation process will ask for your Mac OSX user password later. To install Homebrew, just type the following in the **Terminal** window:

```
ruby -e "$(curl -fsSL https://raw.github.com/mxcl/homebrew/go)"
```

Starting from Mac OSX 10.4 Tiger, the operating system pre-installed the Ruby programming language. You can just run the preceding command line in the **Terminal** window. Other Ruby distributions can also be found at `http://rubyosx.rubyforge.org/`.

It is simple. The preceding command will install the Homebrew software in your computer. Follow the steps to continue the `libfreenect` driver installation:

1. Type `brew update` to update all the software package formulae.

2. Type `brew info libfreenect` to check the information of this package.

3. Type `brew install libfreenect` to install the package.

4. Plug in your Kinect power supply and the USB cable to your computer.

5. Type `glview` in the **Terminal** window to verify.

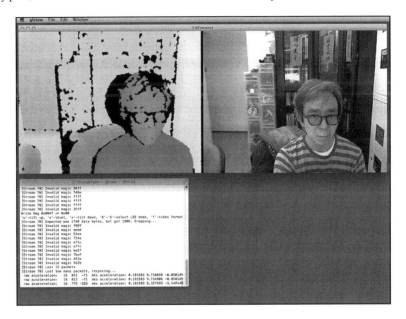

The preceding screenshot is a typical display of the `glview` program. The left windowpane is the depth image. The right windowpane is the normal RGB color image. It will be the indication of a successful installation of the `libfreenect` driver.

In the next step, we install the Pure Data external library for the `libfreenect` driver. The location is at `https://github.com/kronihias/pix_freenect`. Click on the **ZIP** icon to download the package. Unzip the file `pix_freenect-master.zip` you have just downloaded. It will create a folder `pix_freenect-master`. Open the folder and have a look of the content. It contains a folder named `build` and a Pure Data help patch `pix_freenect-help.pd`. We have to copy these into our Pure Data external library folder, located at `~/Library/Pd/`, similar to what we have done with the OpenCV library. We then double-click on the `build` folder to check out its content. The `build` folder contains four files. Three of them are as follows:

- `libfreenect.0.1.2.dylib`
- `libusb-1.0.0.dylib`
- `pix_freenect.pd_darwin`

These are the essential components for the library. We are going to copy them together with the help file, `pix_freenect-help.pd`, into the folder at `~/Library/Pd/pix_freenect/`. Remember what we have done to create the external library folder for OpenCV. We have to click on the **Go | Library** from the **Finder** menu bar with the *Option* key pressed down. Double-click the `Pd` folder inside `Library`. Create a new folder named `pix_freenect`. Copy the following four files into this folder, like what shown in the following screenshot.

- `libfreenect.0.1.2.dylib`
- `libusb-1.0.0.dylib`
- `pix_freenect-help.pd`
- `pix_freenect.pd_darwin`

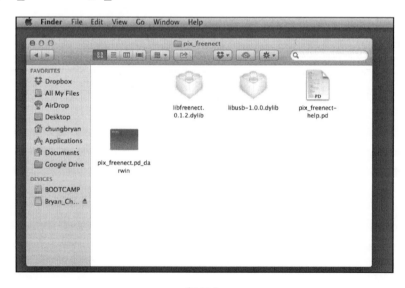

Now we complete the lengthy installation process and will be ready to proceed with the testing. Here is our first patch with Kinect, `Freenect001.pd`.

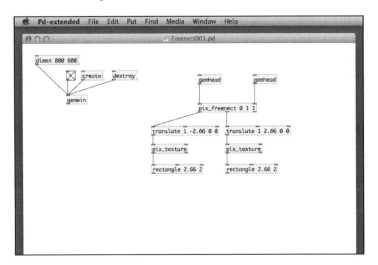

The new object is `pix_freenect`. It has three parameters. The first one `0` is the first Kinect. It can support up to two Kinect cameras. The second parameter `1` is the indicator to turn on the RGB color image. The third parameter `1` is the indicator to turn on the depth image. The object has two inlets, one for each image stream. We use a `gemhead` object to connect to each. The `pix_freenect` object has three outlets. The first and second are the GEM pixel images. We use the `translate` objects to align them in the left and right halves of the screen. The right outlet is for status message. It contains information about the tilt sensor data and the tilt angle of the motor. The result display in the GEM window is as follows:

It may not make a lot of sense by just showing the RGB and depth images. To use the depth image, we may need to extract the depth data for each pixel in the RGB image. The next patch, Freenect002.pd, will use the pix_data object we learned before to achieve this purpose.

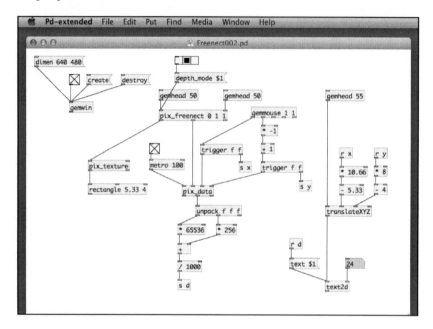

The preceding patch makes use of a pix_data object to extract the RGB information from a pixel image. In this patch, we use the mouse to navigate around the color image; the number moving along the mouse pointer is the depth information for that pixel, measured in the unit of a meter. The red and green components of the depth image make up the depth data. The unpack object and the following calculation extract the depth data from each pixel. The result GEM window display will be as what follows:

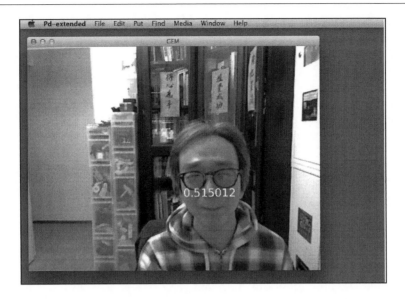

So much for the `pix_freenect` object, in the next section, we move to a more high level external library for the Kinect camera, the `pix_openni` object. It can detect the presence of human body and is able to extract the skeleton data from the depth image.

Installation of OpenNI

At the time of writing, OpenNI has upgraded to Version 2. The Pure Data library, however, uses the Version 1. On the OpenNI website, you can still download the former version in the archive at `http://www.openni.org/openni-sdk/openni-sdk-history-2/`. Download the following two files, `OpenNI SDK v1.5.4.0` and `NITE v1.5.2.21`, for the Mac OSX platform. We do not need to download the `OpenNI-Compliant Sensor Driver v5.1.2.1`. Instead, we have to download the hacked OpenNI driver from other source at `https://github.com/avin2/SensorKinect`. Click on the **ZIP** icon to download the zipped files. All together, we have downloaded the following three files:

- `SensorKinect-unstable.zip`

- `OpenNI-Bin-Dev-MacOSX-v1.5.4.0.tar.zip`

- `NITE-Bin-MacOSX-v1.5.2.21.tar.zip`

Move all the files into a folder, say OpenNI inside your Documents folder. Unzip them within the folder.

We need to go inside the SensorKinect-unstable folder to find the Bin folder. Within the Bin folder, copy the zipped file SensorKinect093-Bin-MacOSX-v5.1.2.1.tar.bz2 to the outside OpenNI folder. Unzip it within the OpenNI folder. It will create the folder Sensor-Bin-MacOSX-v5.1.2.1. We are going to use the following three folders for the installation process:

- OpenNI-Bin-Dev-MacOSX-v1.5.4.0
- Sensor-Bin-MacOSX-v5.1.2.1
- NITE-Bin-Dev-MacOSX-v1.5.2.21

Next, we move to the **Terminal** program again to use the command line interface. When you open the **Terminal** program, it will go to your root folder. You can now proceed to the folder where you keep the OpenNI installation programs. Type from the terminal window the following change directory cd command.

```
cd Documents/OpenNI
```

Install the OpenNI SDK with the following commands:

```
cd OpenNI-Bin-Dev-MacOSX-v1.5.4.0
sudo ./install.sh
```

Type your password when you are prompted to enter the password, because we have used the sudo command to run the step in super user mode. Next, we proceed to install the Kinect sensor driver.

```
cd ..
cd Sensor-Bin-MacOSX-v5.1.2.1
sudo ./install.sh
```

Finally, we install the NITE package that provides the hand and skeleton tracking functions.

```
cd ..
cd NITE-Bin-Dev-MacOSX-v1.5.2.21
sudo ./install.sh
```

Now we finished the installation of the OpenNI software for Kinect in our computer. The next step is to install the Pure Data external library, pix_openni. Its download location is at https://github.com/kronihias/pix_openni. Click on the **ZIP** icon to start the download. Unzip the file to create the pix_openni-master folder.

Identify the following files in the folder that we are going to copy to the Pure Data external library folder.

- `filter.pd`
- `gem_selection.pd`
- `joint.pd`
- `pix_openni-help.pd`
- `vera.ttf`

We also need to double-click inside the `build` folder to copy another file:

- `pix_openni.pd_darwin`

These files need to be copied to the `~/Library/Pd/` folder for Pure Data to use the OpenNI software. We can again, press the *Option* key and click on the **Go | Library** from the main menu bar to open the `~/Library/` folder. Double-click on the `Pd` folder, and create the `pix_openni` folder inside it. Copy the six files just listed into the newly created `pix_openni` folder.

The installation process is now completed. We can proceed to test the external library, with this patch, `OpenNI001.pd`.

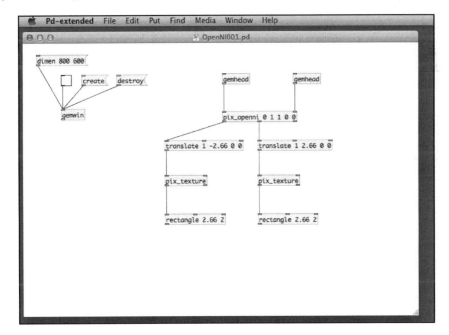

The preceding patch is similar to the one we use in the `pix_freenect` version. The object here is `pix_openni`. It requires five parameters, `0 1 1 0 0`. The first `0` identifies the first Kinect. It can support two Kinect cameras. The second parameter `1` turns on the RGB color image. The third parameter `1` turns on the depth image. The fourth parameter `0` turns off the skeleton tracking. The fifth parameter `0` turns off the hand tracking. We are going to turn on skeleton and hand tracking in later examples. The preceding patch, `OpenNI001.pd`, will show the color and depth displays similar with the one for `pix_freenect`.

Next, we move on with the new features in `pix_openni`. In the following patch, `OpenNI002.pd`, we experiment with the hand-tracking feature:

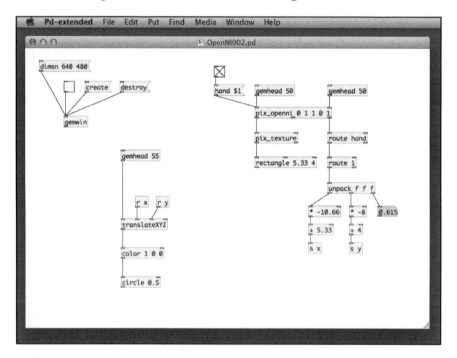

The right outlet of the `pix_openni` object sends out the status message. If we enable the hand-tracking by the `pix_openni` parameter or the `hand $1` message, the right outlet will send out the tracking result with a prefix of `hand` and the number `1`. The rest will the X, Y, and Z positions of the hand tracked. Here is what you can expect from the patch.

The last example we work on will be for human body tracking. In this patch, OpenNI004.pd, we enable skeleton tracking feature in OpenNI. In the same way we work with hand tracking, we use the right outlet of the pix_openni object to obtain the body information.

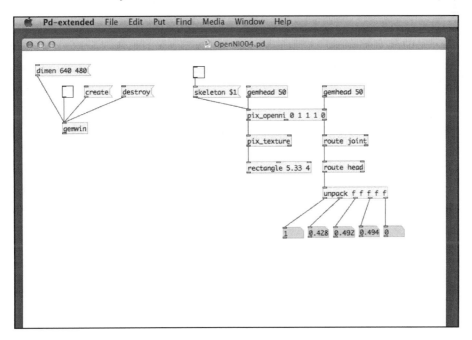

In the preceding patch, OpenNI004.pd, we specify the pix_openni object with the parameters 0 1 1 1 0. The fourth parameter turns on the skeleton tracking. We can also enable it by using the skeleton $1 message. The right outlet of pix_openni first goes to a route joint object to pass only the joint data of the skeleton. The second route object specifies the parameter head to pass only the position data for the head of the skeleton. The pix_openni object will produce the following 24 joint data:

- head, neck, and torso
- l_collar, l_shoulder, l_elbow, l_wrist, l_hand, l_fingertip, r_collar, r_shoulder, r_elbow, r_wrist, r_hand, and r_fingertip
- l_hip, l_knee, l_ankle, l_foot, r_hip, r_knee, r_ankle, and r_foot

Each piece of joint data contains five numbers: the first one is the user identification. The next three numbers are the X, Y, and Z positions of the joint. The fifth one is the confidence value. A value 0 for the confidence indicates it can be a duplicate and invalid. We should use the data with confidence value 1.

In the last patch of this chapter, OpenNI005.pd, we use the pix_openni object to track three joints: head, left elbow, and right elbow of the body. There are three gemhead and each with a white square to follow the movement of the joints. Here is the screenshot of the patch.

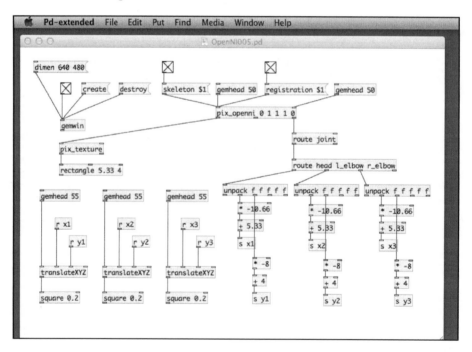

The second `route` object has parameters `head l_elbow r_elbow`. Each joint will send out the X and Y positions mapped in the range of GEM window coordinates. In order to have more accurate display, we enable the `registration $1` message in order to align the depth and RGB image from the Kinect camera. Here is a sample display from the GEM window.

Summary

Besides the features in the pd-extended package, we can further enhance the functionalities of Pure Data through the use of external libraries. In these sections, we learned how to install external libraries, with the examples of OpenCV and the Microsoft Kinect camera. The OpenCV library provides us with a lot of functions to work on computer vision applications that feature live object tracking. With the Kinect camera, we can obtain depth information from live video image. It can facilitate more flexible body part tracking for interactive applications.

We have worked on most multimedia programming tasks with Pure Data and the GEM library: starting from the basic data types and logics, 2D and 3D graphics, digital image, audio and video content, particles system graphics, interactivity with keyboard, mouse and motion tracking, network programming, interfacing with mobile devices, and electronic components and the depth-sensing camera. The skills and knowledge can prepare multimedia artists/designers for applications in interactive multimedia productions.

Communities and References

Pure Data is an open source software. There are online communities that provide development and support for the software. In the following sections, we would like to introduce the various communities, events, documentation that readers can obtain for further reference, and support.

Pure Data communities

The major communities are the official Pure Data website at `http://puredata.info` and the related website from the author Miller Puckette at `http://www-crca.ucsd.edu/~msp`. There are also a number of regional Pure Data information websites in different countries.

- Pure Data Japan at `http://puredatajapan.info/`
- Pure Data Taipei at `http://pdtaipei.blogspot.hk/`
- Pure Data at IEM, `http://pd.iem.at/`

Pure Data events

The International **Pure Data Convention (Pd-con)** has been around for a few years. The first one was in 2004. Besides the presentation of academic papers, there were performances, demonstrations, and exhibitions in the convention. The Pure Data website maintains the documentation for each of the conventions.

The Austrian association **Pd~graz**, `http://pd-graz.mur.at`, organized the First International Pure Data Convention in 2004. Documentation of the convention can be accessed at `http://puredata.info/community/conventions/convention04`.

In 2007, the 2nd International Pure Data Convention was held in Montreal, Canada. The information is available at `http://pure-data.artengine.ca/en/`.

In 2009, the 3rd International Pure Data Convention was in Sao Paulo, Brazil. In the Pure Data website, `http://puredata.info/community/conventions/convention09/`, you can find the complete documentation.

In 2011, the 4th International Pure Data Convention took place in Weimar, Germany. The documentation is now available at the website `http://www.uni-weimar.de/medien/wiki/PDCON:Start`.

Pure Data artists and organizations

There are a number of individual artists and institutions that either employ Pure Data as a major creative tool or contribute extra functionalities to the Pure Data communities. Here are a few of them for reference.

Reactable

Sergi Jordà, Günter Geiger, Martin Kaltenbrunner, and Marcos Alonso of the **Music Technology Group (MTG)** in the Universitat of Pompeu Fabra, Spain, designed and built the first Reactable, `http://mtg.upf.es/project/reactable`, with the audio engine created with Pure Data. It is a tangible musical instrument taking the form of a table. Users move around small pieces of rubber block—the puck, to generate electronic music. At the bottom of the puck is a piece of printed marker, called the **fiducial** marker. Here are samples of the fiducial markers.

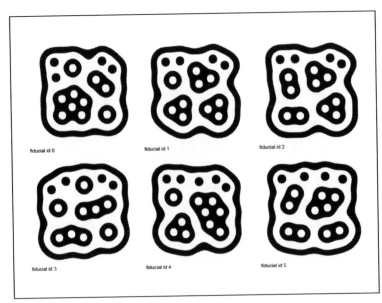

A camera underneath the table tracks the markers' position and orientation to generate the music. In the Pure Data GEM library, we have the object `pix_fiducialtrack` that performs a similar tracking function.

GOTO10

It is a collective of international artists and programmers, focusing on Free Libre Open Source Software—FLOSS, and digital arts. GOTO10, `http://goto10.org/`, aims to support and develop digital art projects and software tools for artistic creation with software programming.

Claude Heiland-Allen

Claude is a London media artist using free software, including Pure Data for artistic creation. His website is at `http://mathr.co.uk/blog`.

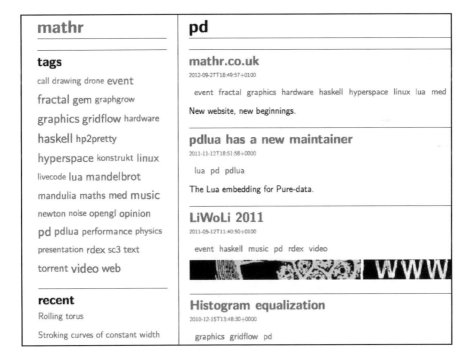

Jun Lee

Jun Lee is a London based Taiwanese sound and media artist who has been using Pure Data for exhibition, live performance, and education. His information related to the GOTO10 is available at `http://sonicvariable.goto10.org/`.

Hans-Christoph Steiner

Hans-Christoph Steiner has been developing interactive software and composing music. He is one of the primary developers of Pure Data. His works and information can be found at `http://at.or.at/hans`.

Piksel

Piksel, `http://piksel.no`, is an annual event in Norway for artists and software developers to meet, present, and develop artistic and software projects, with focus on open source free software.

Baran Gülesen

Baran Gülesen created software, music composition, and musical instruments for media arts installation, performance, and video. The website `http://barangulesen.com` documents the creative works and education material.

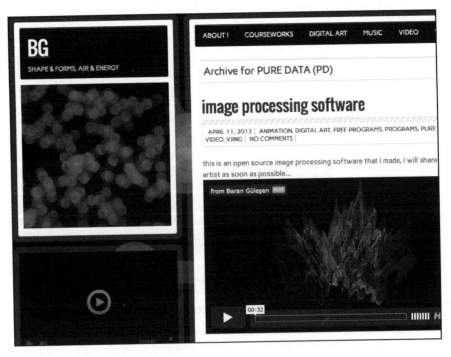

Andy Farnell

Andy Farnell is the author of the book, *Designing Sound*. The book is one of the few books on Pure Data. It is mainly written for sound designers and uses Pure Data as the main software tool to create the sound samples. The official website of the book is at `http://aspress.co.uk/ds/` and it comes with the sample Pure Data patches for reference. Andy Farnell's personal website is at `http://obiwannabe.co.uk/index.html`.

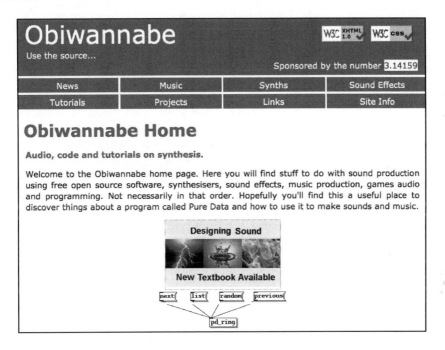

Ben Bogart

Ben Bogart created a number of artworks using his ideas of memory association machines and self-organizing systems, which had been presented in various Pure Data conventions. His website is `http://www.ekran.org`.

Matthias Kronlachner

In the last chapter, we used the Pure Data external libraries, such as, `pix_openni` and `pix_freenect`. Matthias Kronlachner was the author of them. Besides writing software, he works with sound programming and audio-visual performance, mainly with the use of Pure Data and GEM. His website is at `http://www.matthiaskronlachner.com`.

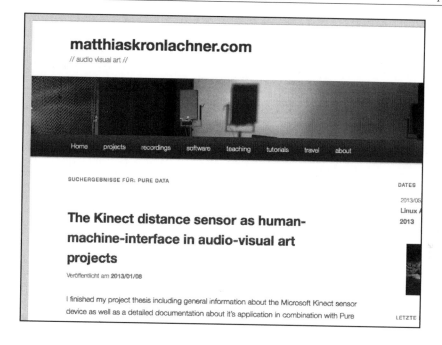

References

Kreidler, Johannes. *Loadbang – Programming Electronic Music in Pure Data.* Hofheim: Volke Verlag, 2009.

Pd-graz. *Bang.* Hofheim: Volke Verlag, 2006.

Farnell, Andy. *Designing Sound: Practical Synthetic Sound Design for Film, Games, and Interactive Media Using Dataflow.* London: Applied Scientific Press, 2008.

Puckette, Miller. *The Theory and Technique of Electronic Music.* Singapore: World Scientific Publishing Company, 2007.

Barkl, Michael. *Pure Data as a Meta-Compositional Instrument.* Germany: LAP Lambert Academic Publishing, 2009.

Matsumura, Sei. *Pd Recipe Book.* Tokyo: BNN, Inc., 2012.

Pure Data FLOSS online manual – http://flossmanuals.net/pure-data/.

Index

About Packt Publishing

Packt, pronounced 'packed', published its first book "*Mastering phpMyAdmin for Effective MySQL Management*" in April 2004 and subsequently continued to specialize in publishing highly focused books on specific technologies and solutions.

Our books and publications share the experiences of your fellow IT professionals in adapting and customizing today's systems, applications, and frameworks. Our solution based books give you the knowledge and power to customize the software and technologies you're using to get the job done. Packt books are more specific and less general than the IT books you have seen in the past. Our unique business model allows us to bring you more focused information, giving you more of what you need to know, and less of what you don't.

Packt is a modern, yet unique publishing company, which focuses on producing quality, cutting-edge books for communities of developers, administrators, and newbies alike. For more information, please visit our website: www.packtpub.com.

About Packt Open Source

In 2010, Packt launched two new brands, Packt Open Source and Packt Enterprise, in order to continue its focus on specialization. This book is part of the Packt Open Source brand, home to books published on software built around Open Source licences, and offering information to anybody from advanced developers to budding web designers. The Open Source brand also runs Packt's Open Source Royalty Scheme, by which Packt gives a royalty to each Open Source project about whose software a book is sold.

Writing for Packt

We welcome all inquiries from people who are interested in authoring. Book proposals should be sent to author@packtpub.com. If your book idea is still at an early stage and you would like to discuss it first before writing a formal book proposal, contact us; one of our commissioning editors will get in touch with you.

We're not just looking for published authors; if you have strong technical skills but no writing experience, our experienced editors can help you develop a writing career, or simply get some additional reward for your expertise.

Processing 2: Creative Programming Cookbook

ISBN: 978-1-84951-794-2   Paperback: 306 pages

Over 90 highly-effective recipes to unleash your creativity with interactive art, graphics, computer vision, 3D, and more

1. Explore the Processing language with a broad range of practical recipes for computational art and graphics

2. Wide coverage of topics including interactive art, computer vision, visualization, drawing in 3D, and much more with Processing

3. Create interactive art installations and learn to export your artwork for print, screen, Internet, and mobile devices

Mastering openFrameworks: Creative Coding Demystified

ISBN: 978-1-84951-804-8   Paperback: 300 pages

Boost your creativity and develop highly-interactive projects for art, 3D, graphics, computer vision and more, with this comprehensive tutorial

1. A step-by-step practical tutorial that explains openFrameworks through easy to understand examples

2. Makes use of next generation technologies and techniques in your projects involving OpenCV, Microsoft Kinect, and so on

3. Sample codes and detailed insights into the projects, all using object oriented programming

Please check **www.PacktPub.com** for information on our titles

Mastering OpenCV with Practical
Computer Vision Projects

Step-by-step tutorials to solve common real-world computer vision problems for desktop or mobile, from augmented reality and number plate recognition to face recognition and 3D head tracking

[PACKT] open source *

Mastering OpenCV with Practical Computer Vision Projects

ISBN: 978-1-84951-782-9   Paperback: 340 pages

Step-by-step tutorials to solve common real-world computer vision problems for desktop or mobile, from augmented reality and number plate recognition to face recognition and 3D head tracking

1. Allows anyone with basic OpenCV experience to rapidly obtain skills in many computer vision topics, for research or commercial use

2. Each chapter is a separate project covering a computer vision problem, written by a professional with proven experience on that topic

3. All projects include a step-by-step tutorial and full source-code, using the C++ interface of OpenCV

Quick answers to common problems

OpenCV 2 Computer Vision
Application Programming Cookbook

Over 50 recipes to master this library of programming functions for real-time computer vision

Robert Laganière   [ ] open source *

OpenCV 2 Computer Vision Application Programming Cookbook

ISBN: 978-1-84951-324-1   Paperback: 304 pages

Over 50 recipes to master this library of programming functions for real-time computer vision

1. Teaches you how to program computer vision applications in C++ using the different features of the OpenCV library

2. Demonstrates the important structures and functions of OpenCV in detail with complete working examples

3. Describes fundamental concepts in computer vision and image processing

Please check **www.PacktPub.com** for information on our titles

Printed in Great Britain
by Amazon.co.uk, Ltd.,
Marston Gate.